SALES AND LEASES OF GOODS

IN A NUTSHELL

(with brief discussion of letters of credit, documents of title, and the Uniform Computer Information Transactions Act)

FOURTH EDITION

By

FRED H. MILLER

Member of the Oklahoma Bar
Kenneth McAfee Chair in Law
and Centennial Professor
and George Lynn Cross Research Professor
University of Oklahoma

D0180730

THOMSON

™

WEST

Mat #15673184

West, a Thomson business, has created this publication to provide you with accurate and authoritative information concerning the subject matter covered. However, this publication was not necessarily prepared by persons licensed to practice law in a particular jurisdiction. West is not engaged in rendering legal or other professional advice, and this publication is not a substitute for the advice of an attorney. If you require legal or other expert advice, you should seek the services of a competent attorney or other professional.

Nutshell Series, In a Nutshell, the Nutshell Logo and West Group are trademarks registered in the U.S. Patent and Trademark Office.

COPYRIGHT © 1968 JOHN M. STOCKTON
COPYRIGHT © 1981, 1982 WEST PUBLISHING CO.
COPYRIGHT © 2003 By West, a Thomson business
        610 Opperman Drive
        P.O. Box 64526
        St. Paul, MN 55164–0526
        1–800–328–9352

Printed in the United States of America
ISBN 0–314–23214–1

TEXT IS PRINTED ON 10% POST CONSUMER RECYCLED PAPER

WEST'S LAW SCHOOL
ADVISORY BOARD

JESSE H. CHOPER
Professor of Law,
University of California, Berkeley

DAVID P. CURRIE
Professor of Law, University of Chicago

YALE KAMISAR
Professor of Law, University of Michigan
Professor of Law, University of San Diego

MARY KAY KANE
Chancellor, Dean and Distinguished Professor of Law,
University of California,
Hastings College of the Law

WAYNE R. LaFAVE
Professor of Law, University of Illinois

ARTHUR R. MILLER
Professor of Law, Harvard University

GRANT S. NELSON
Professor of Law, University of California, Los Angeles

JAMES J. WHITE
Professor of Law, University of Michigan

PREFACE

This is a revised edition of the Sales and Leases of Goods Nutshell, which was published in 1992. This edition updates the law on sales of goods under Uniform Commercial Code (UCC) Article 2, as amended, and on leases under Article 2A of the UCC, as amended. In addition, it briefly discusses software contracts and licenses of information under the Uniform Computer Information Transactions Act (UCITA) and other law (which may include UCC Article 2). It also incorporates the current text of UCC Articles 1, 5, 7, 8 and 9 in the discussion as relevant, but omits any discussion of Article 6, as it has been repealed in most states. There also is brief mention of the Uniform Electronic Transactions Act (UETA) and the Electronic Signatures in Global and National Commerce Act, 15 U.S.C. § 7001 et seq., as well as relevant other law, such as the Bankruptcy Code, 11 U.S.C. § 101 et seq., the Convention on Contracts for the International Sale of Goods (CISG), essentially applicable in the United States under Article 1 of the Convention if the parties to the contract have their business in different contracting states one of which is the United States unless, under Article 6, the parties have excluded the application of the Convention, and the Magnuson-Moss Warranty Act, 15

U.S.C. § 2301 et seq. and other consumer protection law.

As in earlier editions, many of the provisions of Articles 2 and 2A that are discussed are in substance set forth in the body of the text. This was done with some hesitation because of space limitations. However, inclusion of the text allows the reader to evaluate the discussion and analysis without the need to have a copy of the UCC constantly at hand.

Some provisions discussed include a modest amount of historical background. While this is done at the sacrifice of a more complete coverage of other sections, in some cases historical background is desirable to a thorough understanding of the concepts and rules discussed.

Much aid in the preparation of this edition was derived from the large number of decided cases. The many excellent law review articles, particularly the annual surveys published in The Business Lawyer during those years, also have been of great assistance. So too were various treatises.

Debts to others are numerous. The others include, in particular, John M. Stockton, the original author of this work, who generously allowed me to work with him and then bequeathed his and our joint work so I could carry it on in future editions, and research assistants, support persons who prepared the manuscript, the American Law Institute

(ALI) for permission to quote from *Restatements**
and the ALI and the National Conference of Commissioners on Uniform State Laws (NCCUSL) to
quote from the official comments and the Code.**

Professor Miller specifically acknowledges the assistance of Dawn Tomlins, the head of the University of Oklahoma College of Law Support Staff, and of
the support staff.

Ultimately, any errors are those of the author
alone. The discussion distinguishes between the
previous and amended or revised version of a UCC
Article by preceding the citation to the Article or a
section of an Article by the description "old" or "former" or "prior" or "revised," as appropriate; e.g., old
§ 1–103; revised § 1–103. If there is no particular
difference, the citation will be merely to the Article
or, in the case of a section, to the old section, which
may be followed by a citation to the revised section
in parentheses, as § 1–101 (1–101).

FRED H. MILLER

August, 2003

*

---

* Copyright by the American Law Institute. Reprinted with
the permission of the American Law Institute.

** Copyright by the American Law Institute and the National
Conference of Commissioners on Uniform State Laws. Reprinted
with the permission of the Permanent Editorial Board for the
Uniform Commercial Code.

OUTLINE

*

TABLE OF CASES

References are to Pages

XVII

TABLE OF CASES

*

TABLE OF REFERENCES TO UCC PROVISIONS AND COMMENTS

UNIFORM COMMERCIAL CODE

TABLE OF STATUTES

UNIFORM COMMERCIAL CODE

TABLE OF STATUTES

UNIFORM COMMERCIAL CODE

XLIII

TABLE OF STATUTES

UNIFORM COMMERCIAL CODE

TABLE OF STATUTES

UNIFORM COMMERCIAL CODE

TABLE OF STATUTES

UNIFORM COMMERCIAL CODE

UNIFORM COMMERCIAL CODE

UNIFORM COMMERCIAL CODE

UNIFORM COMMERCIAL CODE

UNIFORM COMMERCIAL CODE

UNIFORM COMMERCIAL CODE

TABLE OF STATUTES

UNIFORM COMMERCIAL CODE

UNIFORM COMMERCIAL CODE

TABLE OF STATUTES

UNIFORM COMMERCIAL CODE

TABLE OF STATUTES

UNIFORM COMMERCIAL CODE

LV

TABLE OF STATUTES

UNIFORM COMMERCIAL CODE

UNIFORM COMMERCIAL CODE

TABLE OF STATUTES

UNIFORM COMMERCIAL CODE

TABLE OF STATUTES

UNIFORM COMMERCIAL CODE

TABLE OF STATUTES

UNIFORM COMMERCIAL CODE

TABLE OF STATUTES

UNIFORM COMMERCIAL CODE

TABLE OF STATUTES

UNIFORM COMMERCIAL CODE

TABLE OF STATUTES

UNIFORM COMMERCIAL CODE

TABLE OF STATUTES

UNIFORM COMMERCIAL CODE

UNIFORM COMMERCIAL CODE

TABLE OF STATUTES

UNIFORM COMMERCIAL CODE

TABLE OF STATUTES

UNIFORM COMMERCIAL CODE

TABLE OF STATUTES

UNIFORM COMMERCIAL CODE

UNIFORM COMMERCIAL CODE

UNIFORM COMMERCIAL CODE

TABLE OF STATUTES

UNIFORM COMMERCIAL CODE

TABLE OF STATUTES

UNIFORM COMMERCIAL CODE

LXXII

UNIFORM COMMERCIAL CODE

UNIFORM COMMERCIAL CODE

TABLE OF STATUTES

UNIFORM COMMERCIAL CODE

UNIFORM COMMERCIAL CODE

UNIFORM COMMERCIAL CODE

TABLE OF STATUTES

UNIFORM COMMERCIAL CODE

TABLE OF STATUTES

UNIFORM COMMERCIAL CODE

TABLE OF STATUTES

UNIFORM COMMERCIAL CODE

UNIFORM COMMERCIAL CODE

TABLE OF STATUTES

UNIFORM COMMERCIAL CODE

UNIFORM COMMERCIAL CODE

UNIFORM COMMERCIAL CODE

TABLE OF STATUTES

UNIFORM COMMERCIAL CODE

TABLE OF STATUTES

UNIFORM COMMERCIAL CODE

TABLE OF STATUTES

UNIFORM COMMERCIAL CODE

TABLE OF STATUTES

UNIFORM COMMERCIAL CODE

TABLE OF STATUTES

UNIFORM COMMERCIAL CODE

SALES AND LEASES OF GOODS

IN A NUTSHELL

(with brief discussion of letters of credit, documents of title, and the Uniform Computer Information Transactions Act)

FOURTH EDITION

*

CHAPTER 1

SUBJECT MATTER AND SE-
LECTED IMPORTANT
DEFINITIONS

---

1. SCOPE AND APPLICABILITY OF ARTICLES 2 AND 2A

Conceptually, a sale or a lease transaction may involve goods, or land, or other forms of property, such as a sale of securities or promissory notes. The scope of Article 2, however, is limited to transactions in goods, and that of Article 2A to leases of goods, including fixtures (Article 2 deals with goods

1

related to real estate in Section 2–107). See also Fischer v. Zepa Consulting A.G. (2000) (where purchase was not just of right to sever standing timber but deeded right to all hardwood and softwood and right to enter premises to inspect, cut, and remove timber, transaction was transfer of interest in land). Money in which the price or rent is to be paid, investment securities and choses in action are not goods. Sections 2–103(1)(k) and 2A–103(1)(n).

Section 2–102 states that Article 2 is applicable to transactions in goods. "Transaction" is a broader term than "sale," and could include leases (but see Article 2A), bailments (see, e.g., Section 2–403(3)), consignments (but see Sections 9–102(a)(20) and 9–109(a)(4)) and gifts. Given Article 2A and Section 9–109(a)(4), their more particular provisions apply to leases and consignments; bailments remain for the most part under the common law. Article 2 has been applied to a distributorship agreement. Watkins & Son Pet Supplies v. The Iams Co. (2001). A right of first refusal is not a contract for the sale of goods, however, as it does not ripen into an option contract until the right is triggered. Sel–Lab Marketing, Inc. v. Dial Corp. (2002). In any event, most sections in Article 2 are limited in application either explicitly or implicitly, to contracts for the sale of goods. See, e.g., Sections 2–204, 2–314, 2–402, 2–703. Nonetheless, the reach of Article 2 still is very broad; it has been applied, for example, to transactions as diverse as the sale of electricity (see Cincinnati Gas & Electric Co. v. Goebel (1988), but see Mattoon & Others v. City of Pittsfield (2002) (supplying water to city not an Article 2 activity but more of a service)), and foreign currency (see Saboundjian v. Bank Audi (USA) (1990), but now see Section 2–103(1)(i) and (k)). Article 2 even has been applied where the person in possession of goods has not yet purchased them but intends to purchase, such as the case of the supermarket shopper. See Giant Food, Inc. v. Washington Coca–Cola Bottling Co. (1975).

Section 2A–102 states Article 2A applies to any transaction that creates a lease, and Section 2A–103(1)(p) defines a lease as a transfer of the right to possession and use of goods for a period in return for consideration. Thus, loans of goods, such as a tool borrowed by a neighbor, and some bailments, as in the case of checking one's coat with a restaurant coatroom, are not covered while, on the other hand, an automobile lease clearly is.

The concept of "goods" also is a limitation. A further discussion of what constitutes goods is postponed until later in this chapter.

If a sale or lease involves parties in different countries or states, Articles 2 or 2A, as enacted by a jurisdiction whose law has been selected by the agreement of the parties, generally is applicable to substantive as opposed to procedural issues (forum law governs procedural issues—see Wilson v. Hammer Holdings, Ind. (1988)), except as otherwise provided for a transaction where one of the parties is a consumer, and with limited other exceptions (see Sections 1–201(2)(k) and 1–301), or unless the

Convention on Contracts for the International Sale of Goods (CISG) is applicable. CISG has been ratified by and entered into force in a number of states, including the United States. See CISG Articles 1 through 6, which apply CISG where, among other cases, the parties to the contract have places of business in different states which are contracting states to the Convention. The provisions of CISG are different in many respects from those of Article 2 (see Honnold, The New Uniform Law for International Sales and the UCC: A Comparison, 18 Int'l Law. 21 (1984)). Thus recognizing the applicability of CISG is important.

Absent agreement, the rights and obligations of the parties under the sale or lease are determined by the law of the jurisdiction that is selected by the application of conflicts of laws principles. Section 1–301(d) and see, under prior law, Island Creek Coal Co. v. Lake Shore, Inc. (1986) (agreement) and Cherry Creek Dodge, Inc. v. Carter (1987) (no agreement). In consumer transactions, however, choice of law or forum agreements (clauses) also may be subject to further limitations. See Section 2A–106, 1974 Uniform Consumer Credit Code Section 1.201, and Colonial Leasing Co. v. McIlroy (1988) (choice of forum possibly unfair and unreasonable).

Article 2 and Article 2A, of course, as state law, do not apply to determine the rights of the United States in a sale or a lease, but the court may adopt the Uniform Commercial Code (UCC) rule as the federal common law rule. See In re Murdock Machine & Engineering Co. (1980) and United States v. Wegematic Corp. (1966). Nor as state law can they control the relationship with federal law. That can only be done at the federal level by Congress (for example, see § 111 of the Magnuson–Moss Warranty Act, 15 U.S.C. § 2311), by appropriate regulation (see, e.g., Federal Trade Commission Regulation for Door to Door Sales, 16 C.F.R. § 429.2), or by decision (see, e.g., Haas v. Daimler Chrysler Corp. (2000)) (automobile manufacturer's warranty limitation requiring that second purchaser pay fee to transfer the remaining warranty did not violate the Magnuson–Moss Warranty Act) (or the UCC).

The issues raised in the application of Articles 2 and 2A to electronic data interchange (EDI), by which a sale or a lease may be accomplished and which may involve the exchange of business information (including purchase orders, invoices and the like) electronically rather than by means of paper, illustrate the reason why commercial law must change as commercial practices change. The 2003 amendments to Articles 2 and 2A adapt these Articles to electronic commerce. For example, they change the writing requirements of Sections 2–201 and 2A–201 (the statutes of frauds for these laws), which generally require a signed writing, to instead allowing a signed record. A "record" means information that is inscribed on a tangible medium, such as writing on paper, or information that is stored in an electronic or other medium and is retrievable in perceivable form, such as in a computer. Sections 2–

103(1)(m) and 2A–103(1)(cc). See also "signed" at Sections 2–103(1)(p) and 2A–103(1)(dd) and Sections 2–111–2–213 and 2A–222–2A–224 (recognition of electronic contracts and signatures, attribution, and electronic communication). Old Article 2 contained no less than some 19 references to a "writing" or "written" notices or agreements, which before these requirements were overridden by either the Uniform Electronic Transactions Act (UETA), as state law, or the Electronic Signatures in Global and National Commerce Act (E-sign), as federal law, were handled to a degree on the basis of model trading partner agreements, which attempt to contract around writing requirements in accordance with Section 1–302, which allows the parties by agreement to vary the effect of UCC provisions. See The Commercial Use of Electronic Data Interchange—A Report, 45 Bus. Law. 1645 (1990).

Scope issues occupied a significant portion of the attention in the drafting of the 2003 amendments Article 2 and the corresponding amendments to Article 2A. A study of non-uniform amendments to Article 2 conducted by the Subcommittee on General Provisions, Sales and Documents of Title of the Uniform Commercial Code Committee of the Business Law Section of the American Bar Association identified specific areas where the volume of non-uniform amendments to Article 2 raised questions as to the appropriateness of its coverage. For example, the medical profession and particularly blood transfusions and human organ transplants are covered by non-uniform statutes in forty-six states (thirty-three had independent statutes, thirteen had non-uniform amendments to the Code—see, e.g., 63 Okl.Stat.Ann. § 2151), and consumer issues spawned both non-uniform amendments and separate legislation. The 2003 amendments to Articles 2 and 2A follow the study, and provide appropriate rules defining the relationship with these other state laws. In Article 2, Section 2–108 subjects transactions subject to Article 2 to a certificate of title statute; consumer laws; and statutes relating to agricultural products, blood, blood products, and human tissues or parts, works of art, distribution agreements and franchises, misbranding or adulteration of food or drugs, and dealers in particular products such as automobiles and hearing aids. In the event of conflict, except for the rights of a buyer in ordinary course of business in relation to Section 2–403(2), the other law controls. The Article 2A list is shorter due to the fact less variety of goods is leased, and only deals with a certificate of title law and consumer law. See Sections 2A–104 and 2A–105.

Many other scope or relational issues (some of which are discussed later in this chapter) exist beyond this, such as what is the appropriate law to govern service contracts and services provided in relation to sales and leases, and for contracts for computer software and the transfer of other property of both a tangible and intangible variety whether by sale, lease or license. The 2003 amendments to Article 2 exclude the subject matter of "foreign exchange transactions" (essentially a transaction in which a specified quantity of foreign money or a unit of account is delivered through funds transfer, book entry or the like, as opposed to physical delivery of the currency–Sections 2–103(1)(i) and (l)), because the practice is not consistent with Article 2 requirements, and Official Comment 7 to Section 2–314 (and Official Comment 2 to Section 2A–212) speaks to an aspect of the relationship between the implied warranty of merchantability and the tort law of products liability, and harmonizes the concepts of what is a defective product in tort law with the UCC concept of merchantability, where there is personal injury or property damage. To some extent the problems raised may be alleviated if a court applies Article 2 or Article 2A by analogy. Some invitation to do so exists in Article 2 (see Official Comment 4 to Section 2–313) and in Article 2A (Official Comment to Section 2A–102), and courts have not been reluctant on the whole to accept the invitation. See Printers II, Inc. v. Professionals Publishing, Inc. (1985) (contract to publish a magazine a service contract but Section 2–305 on open price applied by analogy). As discussed later, this approach may be inappropriate in certain contexts.

2. CONTRACT FOR SALE AND SALE DEFINED; LEASE AGREEMENT, LEASE CONTRACT AND LEASE DEFINED

Despite the lack of a definition of "transaction" in Article 2, it is clear that Article 2 covers both a present sale and a contract for the sale of goods. "A 'sale' consists in the passing of title from the seller

(Section 2–103(1)(*o*)) to the buyer (Section 2–103(1)(a)) for a price." Section 2–106(1). In some instances, this occurs with the making of the contract, in which case the transaction is called a "present sale." Section 2–106(1). A contract for sale includes both a present sale and a contract to sell at a future time. Section 2–106(1). A contract to sell is a transaction in which the seller agrees to transfer title to the buyer at some future time for a price. This latter transaction becomes a "sale" as soon as title to the goods passes to the buyer. Under Article 2, the price is due upon tender by the seller unless credit has been negotiated. Section 2–507(1).

A contract for sale represents the legal obligation which results from the agreement of the parties. Section 1–201(b)(12). The parties' agreement is their bargain in fact as found in their language or from other circumstances including course of dealing (Section 1–303(b)), usage of trade (Section 1–303(c)), or course of performance (Section 3–303(a)). Section 1–201(b)(3). Thus, the contract for sale can be less than the parties' agreement if procured by fraud, or more due to, for example, implied warranties imposed in law. See, as illustrative examples under prior law, Provident Tradesmens Bank & Trust Co. v. Pemberton (1961) (course of dealing) and Posttapes Associates v. Eastman Kodak Co. (1978) (usage of trade). A further discussion appears in Chapter 4.

The same duality exists between a lease contract (Section 2A–103(1)(r)) and a lease agreement (Section 2A–103(1)(q)). Of course, a lease does not involve the passage of title but rather is a transfer of the right to possession and use of goods for a term in return for consideration. Section 2A–103(1)(p). Thus, in every lease the lessor retains a "residual interest." Section 2A–103(1)(w). The concepts of sale and lease are mutually exclusive; a sale, including a sale on approval (Section 2–326(1)(a)) or a sale or return (Section 2–326(1)(b)), is not a lease. Unless the context clearly indicates otherwise, a lease includes a sublease. Section 2A–103(1)(q).

One of the most heavily litigated issues under the UCC is whether an agreement that is denominated a lease instead grants a security interest. If so, it is governed by Article 9, and not by Article 2A. Sections 2A–103(1)(p) and 1–203.

Former Section 1–201(37), before it was amended in conjunction with the promulgation of Article 2A, was not very helpful on this issue; it stated that the result depended upon the facts of each case and the only guidance provided was that an agreement that upon compliance with the terms of the lease the lessee would or could become the owner of the property for no or a nominal consideration was conclusive of security interest status. Thus, a lease allowing the lessee to purchase for $1 at lease end is a security interest, as the lessee substantively occupies the same status as a buyer who will pay off the security interest with the last payment and then own the goods. The point is the lessor has no meaningful residual interest, which is the hallmark of a true lease. But see In re Charles (Morris v. U.S. Bancorp Leasing & Financial) (2002), decided under a provision common in the states, although not a uniform provision, that provides "an agreement involving the leasing of a motor vehicle or trailer does not create a sale or security interest solely because the agreement provides for an increase or decrease adjustment in the rental price of the motor vehicle or trailer based upon the amount realized upon the sale or other disposition ... following the termination of the lease" (terminal rent adjustment clause or TRAC lease). The court ruled against the bankruptcy trustee's contention that this arrangement qualified the lease as a disguised sale because the debtors could have acquired the goods pursuant to the TRAC clause at the end of the lease for nominal consideration.

Section 1–201(37) was revised when Article 2A was promulgated to codify the better case law gloss on the meager former provision. The 2001 amendments to UCC Article 1 carried this approach on. Thus an option in the lessee to become the owner of the goods for no or a nominal consideration upon compliance with the lease agreement, if the consideration the lessee is to pay the lessor for the lease is an obligation for the term of the lease and not subject to termination by the lessee, still makes the transaction one in which a security interest is created. Section 1–203(b)(4). In addition, Section 1–203(b) also provides that a transaction creates a security interest if the original term of the "lease" is equal to or greater than the remaining economic life of the goods; if the "lessee" is bound to renew for the remaining economic life of the goods or is bound to become their owner; or if the "lessee" has an option to renew for the remaining economic life of the goods for no or a nominal consideration. Section 1–203(b)(1), (2) and (3). In each case the lessor has no meaningful residual. The comment cites cases applying these principles. In addition, the Official Comment to the definition of "lease" in Section 2A–103 provides the following illustration: assume a copying machine costing $1000 with an estimated useful life of three years. First, suppose a one month lease for $100. This clearly is a lease. Next, suppose a lease for 36 months. This clearly is a secured transaction even if there is no option to purchase.

Section 1–203(b) also clarifies that for a lease to be a secured transaction the consideration the lessee is to pay the lessor for the lease must be an obligation for the term of the lease not subject to termination by the lessee. Thus, the fact a lessee actually leases a machine with a useful life of 36 months for 36 months does not make the lease a secured transaction if the lessee could terminate the lease from month to month. In re Royer's Bakery, Inc. (1963) is overruled.

Section 1–203(c)(1) through (6) also repudiate various factors some courts have used to determine security status which, when viewed individually, are not an appropriate measure. Included are: the fact the present value of the consideration the lessee is to pay is substantially equal to or is greater than the fair market value of the goods at the time the lease is entered into—the "full payout" lease; the fact the lessee assumes the risk of loss or agrees to pay taxes, insurance, filing, recording or registration fees, or service or maintenance costs—the "net" lease; the fact the lessee has an option to renew the lease or to become owner of the goods— contrast with Section 1–203(b)(2)-(4); the fact the lessee has an option to renew the lease for a fixed rent that is equal to or greater than the reasonably predictable fair market rent for the use of the goods for the term of the renewal at the time the option is to be performed (as determined under Section 1– 203(d)(1) with reference to the facts and circumstances at the time the transaction is entered into); and the fact the lessee has an option to become the owner of the goods for a fixed price that is equal to or greater than the reasonably predictable fair market value of the goods (under Section 1–203(d)(2) determined with reference to the facts and circumstances at the time the transaction is entered into) at the time the option is to be performed. A transaction is not a secured transaction merely because one of the above facts exists.

As the Official Comment 2 to Section 1–203 notes, there is a set of purchase options whose fixed price is less than fair market value but more than nominal. As defined in Section 1–203(d) and (e), consideration is *not* nominal if, when the option to become owner is granted, the price is stated to be the fair market value of the goods determined at the time the option is to be performed, but *is* nominal if it is less than the lessee's reasonably predictable cost of performing under the lease agreement if the option is not exercised. In these cases, lease or security status must be determined on the facts of each case. Some courts have postulated that an option price of less than a percentage of original cost is nominal, but this is an imprecise standard; the better standard is to measure the price against the value of the goods when the option is to be exercised, with that value being that reasonably predicted when the lease was entered into. In this context the courts have held that a price of 20% or less is nominal. The line probably is somewhat higher—more than the lessee's reasonably predictable cost of performing under the lease if the option is not exercised but a figure that still leaves the lessee no sensible alternative to exercising the option. See, e.g., In re Marhoefer Packing Co. (1982) (option price of almost $10,000, which amounted to 50% of fair market value, is not nominal).

3. GOODS DEFINED; MIXED SALES AND LEASES OF GOODS AND SERVICES; COMPUTER INFORMATION TRANSACTIONS

The scope of Articles 2 and 2A is defined in part by the term "goods." In general, "goods" refers to tangible personal property, but the precise meaning of the term varies among UCC articles. Article 2 of the UCC defines "goods" in the following words in Section 2–103(1)(k):

"Goods" means all things that are movable at the time of identification to a contract for sale.

The term includes future goods, specially manufactured goods, the unborn young of animals, growing crops, and other identified things attached to realty as described in Section 2–107. The term does not include information, the money in which the price is to be paid, investment securities under Article 8 the subject matter of foreign exchange transactions (see supra), or choses in action.

The definition in Article 2A at Section 2A–103(1)(n) is slightly different, primarily in being more precise with respect to fixtures and omitting property not of a type that is leased.

Special problems existed under pre-UCC law regarding property that is a part of or that is attached to realty. Pre–UCC case law relating to sales commonly treated crops that are planted yearly and regularly cultivated, such as wheat, corn, tomatoes, and potatoes, as goods, although there were cases to the contrary. Some courts treated growing crops such as orchard fruit, hops, and timothy seed as goods even though they are not planted annually and may not be regularly cultivated. Under Article 2 growing crops are goods; as to Article 2A, the point is moot as growing crops are not rented. Also under pre-UCC sales law, confusion existed regarding standing wild timber and grass, unmined minerals, and buildings. It was generally agreed that these types of property were not goods so long as they remained attached to the land, but became goods as soon as they were severed or removed. The chief difficulty lay in those situations in which a contract for sale was made while the property was attached to the land; courts differed as to whether the contract was one for the sale of goods. Under Article 2, the contract is for goods if the seller is to sever or remove minerals or a structure; for timber; the contract is for a sale even if the buyer is to cut and remove. Sections 2–107(1) and 2–107(2); contrast Fischer v. Zepa Consulting A.G. (2000). Thus assume the property contracted to be sold while still related to the realty is minerals or a structure. The sale is of goods only if the seller is to sever. If the buyer will sever, the sale is treated as one of an interest in real estate. Even if the seller is to sever, a present sale of the "goods" is impossible because there are none; only a contract to sell is possible. In order to protect persons who deal with the land, their rights are superior to those of the buyer unless the buyer records the contract. Section 2–107(2). Under Article 2A, minerals cannot be leased as goods before extraction, and a lease of a structure is subject to real estate law unless the structure is a fixture. Section 2A–103(1)(n). Article 2A, like Article 9, does not determine when goods are fixtures. Section 2A–309(1)(a) and (2).

The problem of whether a transaction of sale involving "fixtures" is one involving goods was especially troublesome under pre-UCC law. One difficulty is that the word "fixtures" has been given so many different meanings. Usually the term refers to goods which have become physically attached to but not incorporated into the land or, in a few states, to include goods, even though not attached, that have a use associated with the land. Thus, bricks are not fixtures, but a furnace is. Whether the goods have become fixtures as between the parties to a sale is largely a question of the intent of the parties. The relationship of the parties, the type of transaction involved, and the degree of fixation and ability to remove without material harm have been important factors in determining intention. Under Article 2, a sale of a fixture in place but apart from the land, such as an air conditioning unit, is a sale of goods if the fixture is capable of severance without material harm. It does not matter whether the subject matter is to be severed by the buyer or by the seller even though it forms part of the realty at the time of contracting, and the parties can by identification effect a present sale before severance. Section 2–107(2). Under Article 2 the term "fixtures" is not used. Instead, whether property of this kind is goods or real property for the purposes of Article 2 depends on whether it can be severed without material harm to the realty. Of course, that determination essentially is the test for whether property is or is not a fixture under both Article 2A and Article 9. See Sections 9–334(a), 9–604, and 2A–309(1)(a) and (8).

Under Article 2A, the lease of a fixture is covered and the rights of the parties and third parties are governed under Section 2A–309 as a lease includes a lease of fixtures. Section 2A–103(1)(n) and (p).

While the court's opinion in In re Park Corrugated Box Corp. (1966), deals with the problem of priority to the fixtures as collateral, which is dealt with in Article 9, the fact situation is helpful in illustrating how a court might determine what is a fixture under Articles 2 and 2A. In the case, a machine approximately 125 inches by 8 feet long and weighing 45,000 pounds was anchored by two or three big screws on each side to the floor of a plant and connected to a 200 volt electric line. It could be removed by unbolting the screws, disconnecting the electric line, jacking it up, putting it on rollers, and taking it out. In fact, it had been moved two or three times to other sections of the plant by plant employees. The court indicated in its opinion that the machine could be removed without material harm to the realty. Thus a court should hold on the same facts that a contract to sell the machine while it is bolted to the floor, whether the seller or buyer is to remove it, is a contract to sell goods, not realty, and that a lease of such a machine to be bolted to the floor is a lease under Article 2A.

Virtually every sale and lease involves not only goods but services, such as dealer preparation on a car or the installation of a furnace, carpeting or an air conditioner. There has been considerable litigation as to whether a transaction involving a sale or lease and the rendition of services is one for the sale or lease of goods or the rendition of services. Some of the earliest cases involved blood transfusions during operations; if the transaction was for services the courts applied a negligence standard rather than the absolute liability standard of warranty when the blood produced hepatitis or a like medical condition. See, e.g., Lagalo v. Allied Corp. (1998)

(jury finding of negligence but not breach of warranty not inconsistent). Today these cases often are subject to special statute. See Section 2–108(1)(c)(ii). When they are controlled by the UCC, most courts use a "predominate purpose" test to characterize the transaction, and find a sale of services. However, some courts focus on the actual problem, and apply Article 2 since a sale of the blood alone is a sale of goods. See Perlmutter v. Beth David Hospital (1954). This has been called a "gravamen of the action" test. This issue also may arise in a sale of goods and other property, and in a lease.

The UCC does deal explicitly with some areas in this context. A contract for specially manufactured goods is one for goods, not services. Section 2–103(1)(k). The Article 2A rule does not differ. Section 2A–103(1)(n). For the purpose of the implied warranty of merchantability (see Chapter 9), "the serving for value of food or drink to be consumed either on the premises or elsewhere is a sale." See Section 2–314(a). Of course, food is not leased so Section 2A–212 does not contain similar language.

Another problem often characterized as involving goods versus services, but which more accurately involves goods versus computer information, and which is not dealt with explicitly in Articles 2 or 2A for the most part, involves computer software contracts, which mainly are licenses, not sales, and normally should be recognized as such and not recharacterized. Compare Adobe Systems, Inc. v. Stargate Software Inc. (2002) (agreement only conferred a license and was not a sale) with Softman Products Co., LLC v. Adobe Systems, Inc. (2001) (transaction that involved single payment giving person unlimited period of possession is a sale). However, since Article 2 and Article 2A apply to a "transaction" in goods, it must also be recognized that many cases involve information and not goods, and even when the software is embedded in a disc, the true value is in the information, much the same as in the case of a book. That goods are not involved certainly is true, for example, for information downloaded from the internet. See Multi–Tech Systems, Inc. v. Floreat, Inc. (2002) and Specht v. Netscape (2002) (decided under former law); now see Sections 2–103(1)(k) and 2A–103(1)(n) (excluding information from goods); compare UCC Section 9–102(a)(44) and (75) (excluding software from goods). While courts have indicated information on a disc may be considered goods (see the Multi–Tech case, above), this analysis, as noted, is not entirely sound; the disc is goods but the value is the information, and the medium is largely irrelevant. See Official Comment to Section 2–103 definition of "goods" (an architect's provision of plans on a computer disk is not a transaction in goods); compare UCC Section 9–102(a)(44) ("goods") do not include a computer program embedded in goods that consist solely of the medium in which the program is embedded. See also Section 2A–103(1)(p) (a lease does not include a license of information). Thus, the difficult problems involve "mixed transactions" involving goods that are more than a medium and the provision of information; transactions involving so-called "smart goods," where a computer program or programs are contained in and sold or leased as a part of goods.

Today, courts often handle these situations by using the predominant purpose test. To illustrate, in Micro–Managers, Inc. v. Gregory (1988), the court used a predominant purpose analysis and concluded the transaction was a sale of services when $55,000 of the $59,000 price for a software design and development agreement was for labor charges. Of course such a finding need not mean the buyer is without relief. See Broyles v. Brown Engineering Co. (1963) (warranty of good results in service contract to develop engineering plans for drainage of tract). In Data Processing Services, Inc. v. L.H. Smith Oil Corp. (1986), the court found the seller was engaged primarily to design, develop and implement an electronic data processing system and accordingly held the transaction was one for services with any resulting floppy disk, hard disk, punch card or magnetic tape only being goods incidental to the transaction. The court also stated that those who hold themselves out to the world as possessing skill and qualifications impliedly represent they possess the skill and will exhibit the diligence ordinarily possessed by well informed members of the trade or profession. The seller was found to have breached this obligation. Other courts, recognizing that the UCC technically does not govern software licenses, nonetheless determine that the familiar provisions of Article 2, which were the inspiration for the Uniform Computer Information Transactions Act (UCITA), better fulfill the expectation of the parties to such agreements that some law will govern them than would the common law. I. Lan Systems, Inc. v. Netscout Service Level Corp. (2002).

These approaches can, however, possibly lead to undesirable results by applying inappropriate law to the goods involved, or the services involved. See Rhone–Poulenc Agro, S.A. v. DeKalb Genetics Corp. (2002) (the bona fide purchaser rule of the UCC should not apply to the licensing of intellectual property) and Specht v. Netscape Communications Corp. (2002) (a body of law based on images of the sale of manufactured goods ill fits licenses and other transactions in computer information). Thus while both UCC Article 9 and the Uniform Computer Information Transactions Act draw more concrete lines (UCC Section 9–102(a)(44), addressing computer programs embedded in goods; UCITA Section 103(b)(1), which states in a transaction involving computer information and goods, UCITA applies to the part of the transaction involving computer information, informational rights in it, and creation or modification of it, unless a copy of a computer program is contained in and sold or leased as part of the goods, in which case UCITA applies to the copy and computer program only if the goods are a computer or computer peripheral or giving the acquiring party access to or use of the program is ordinarily a material purpose in the type of transaction), UCC Article 2, in its Official Comment to the definition of "goods" in Section 2–103 states:

[T]he sale of "smart goods" such as an automobile is a transaction in goods fully within this article even though the automobile contains many computer programs. * * * When a transaction includes both the sale of goods and the transfer of rights in information, it is up to the courts to determine whether the transaction is entirely within or outside of this article, or whether or to what extent this article should be applied to a portion of the transaction.

Absent UCITA, or a transaction subject to Article 9, more concrete lines will have to await case law development, and that even includes the above Official Comment, which it is submitted should include the words "other than in the case of smart goods," after the words " . . . and the transfer of rights in information" in the second sentence of the above quotation. In this period, perhaps the approach of the court in Specht v. Netscape Communications Corp. (2002) is most appropriate: the court found it unnecessary to decide if UCC Article 2 applied to the transaction, as it determined UCITA furnished, even though not enacted, suitable insight from which to fashion a common law rule.

Ultimately, as was the case for the law of sales and of leases of goods, statutory provisions will be necessary to provide adequate certainty of law with predictable rules to govern rights and duties so people can plan, and to reduce transaction costs and litigation. UCITA is such a law. Much of it is drawn from UCC Article 2 and the Restatement of Contracts, much of it codifies the developing case law, and the balance adapts current rules to electronic commerce and reflects the significant differences between transactions in goods and licenses of computer information. As one study of UCITA stated, economic well-being is likely to be enhanced with the passage of UCITA. There is a lack of compelling alternatives. If the states develop their own regulations for computer information contracts, the lack of uniformity will create burdens. Moreover, there is no good reason to expect their design to be superior to UCITA.

4. PRICE DEFINED; RENT

Normally the price in a sales contract is payable in money. If the price is payable in something other than money the transaction is one of barter. However, the distinction between a sale and a barter was not legally significant at common law and the UCC's definition of a sales transaction includes a barter. The UCC provides that the price can be made payable in money or otherwise. If it is payable in whole or in part in goods, each party is a seller of the goods which the party is to transfer. Section 2–304(1). For example, if the contract requires B to convey realty to S in return for S's promise to transfer goods to B, the UCC clearly provides that Article 2 applies to the transfer of goods by S and to all of the obligations connected with this transfer. It is made equally clear, however, that B's transfer of the realty, and the obligations involved, generally are not governed by Article 2. Section 2–304(2). If S agrees to transfer goods to B in return for B's promise to perform services for S, S is the seller of the goods which he or she proposes to sell to B and, therefore, at least S's promise would be governed by Article 2. It is not explicitly stated, however, whether B's promise is so governed; presumably it is only to a degree consistent with the approach described in Official Comments 2 and 3 to the section. This could be extremely important in connection with the possible application, for example, of the statute of frauds and the statute of limitations sections (Sections 2–201 and 2–725).

Article 2A does not contain many of the provisions that appear in Article 2 dealing with contract formation and interpretation. For example, there is no "battle of the forms" provision (Section 2–207) and "gap filling" provisions (Sections 2–305–2–311) are absent. In large part this is because leases are more structured, and the informality of sales transactions that makes such provisions desirable is absent. Thus Article 2A contains no similar provision to Section 2–304, but the definition of "lease" in Section 2A–103(1)(p), which states it is a transfer of the right to possession and use of goods for a term for "consideration", should lead to results similar to those under Article 2 in the rare case where goods are leased, not for money (rent), but in return for other goods or property or services.

5. TERMS USED TO DESCRIBE GOODS

In order to determine the rights and obligations of the parties under a contract of sale or lease, it is important to understand the meaning of certain adjectives used to describe goods in Article 2 and to some degree in Article 2A.

a. Identified Goods

The term "identified" is not defined specifically in the UCC. It is used, however, by the courts and throughout Articles 2 and 2A to describe that process by which goods are specified as the goods to which the contract refers. Once particularized by earmarking or otherwise, the goods become "identified." Existing goods may be identified at the time the contract is made. If, for example, S and B agree to buy and sell or to lease a painting owned by S, the contract is one for "identified" goods. Sections 2–501(1)(a) and 2A–217(1). On the other hand, the goods may not be identified until after the contract is made. In such a case, identification occurs through some act such as shipment, marking, or otherwise, which designates the goods as those to which the contract refers, or it occurs when crops are planted or unborn young are conceived. Sections 2–501(1)(b) and (c), 2A–217(2) and (3). It is possible for the parties to agree when and in what manner identification shall occur. These provisions apply when the parties have not "explicitly" agreed otherwise. Some of these provisions will be considered later in connection with a discussion of the legal incidents of identification.

b. Future Goods

"Future goods" are described under the UCC as "goods which are not both existing and identified." Section 2–105(1). Thus, even though the seller owns goods which meet the description of those to be delivered to the buyer, the goods would be described as future goods until identified to the contract. Under Article 2A, the same concept is built into the definitions of "goods" and "lease" in Section 2A–103(1)(n) and (p). See Official Comments to definitions of "lease agreement" and "lease contract" in Section 2A–103.

c. Existing Goods

The term "existing goods," even though widely used in the UCC, is not defined, but is used to describe goods which are owned or possessed by the transferor. Sections 2–105(1); 2A–103(1)(n) and (p).

d. Fungible Goods

"Fungible goods" are those of which any one unit is the equivalent of any other unit either by reason of its nature or commercial usage. See Section 1–201(b)(18), which applies both with respect to Article 2 and Article 2A. Sections 2–103(3), 2A–103(4).

In the early case of Kimberly v. Patchin (1859), the court held that wheat of the same grade was a fungible good. One bushel of the wheat was by its very nature the equivalent of any other bushel in the mass. Similar decisions have been reached regarding goods such as coal, corn, hay, and oil. In some cases it has been held that although the individual units of the mass of goods may vary somewhat in size, weight, or appearance, the goods will be treated as fungible because of commercial usage. Thus in United States v. Amalgamated Sugar Co. (1934), bags of sugar stated to contain 100 pounds were treated as fungible goods because the evidence showed that this was the custom of the trade. In some cases the primary question is whether the parties intend to treat the goods as fungible. The Code makes it clear that the parties may expressly agree to treat non-fungible goods as fungible. Section 1–201(b)(18). If they have not expressed their intention the court must look at the nature of the goods and commercial usage.

The legal significance of treating goods as fungible is discussed in Chapter 7.

6. MERCHANT DEFINED

Generally speaking, neither common law decisions nor the provisions of the former Uniform Sales Act distinguished between the rules applicable to merchants and those applicable to non-merchants. In other words, prior to the UCC the basic law of sales and leases drew no distinction between the professional and the non-professional. That is not to say that some separate law might not apply special superseding rules to protect non-merchants in specialized cases. This certainly was true by the time of Article 2A for both consumer lessees and consumer buyers. See Sections 2–102 and 2–108, and Section 2A–104 and, for example, Unif. Consumer Credit Code, 7A U.L.A. 1 (1974), the Consumer Leasing Act, 15 U.S.C.A. § 1667 et seq., and the Magnuson–Moss Act, 15 U.S.C.A. § 2301 et seq.

Article 2 of the UCC may have been the first commercial statute to recognize that in some transactions special rules should apply to merchants or that, in other instances, merchant rules are inappropriate for non-merchants. Article 2A continues and expands this approach, but revised UCC Article 9 is the most extensive example of the approach while still leaving much consumer protection law outside the UCC. Because some rules and customs which might be suitable for professionals are not satisfactory or acceptable to the non-mercantile community, certain provisions of the UCC apply only to transactions "between merchants" and some apply only "against merchants." See Comment 1 to Section 2–104. When studying the provisions of the UCC one must, therefore, remain alert to this distinction between the professional and the non-professional. In addition, other Articles to a greater extent than Article 2, contain some provisions that apply only to, or which except, consumer transactions. See, for example, Sections 2A–503(3) and 9–109(d)(13). Even in Article 2, see Section 2–719(3). The additional Article 2A provisions are discussed in the next section of this chapter.

The definition in the UCC of a merchant is quite broad. Section 2–104(1) (made applicable to Article 2A through Section 2A–103(3)), defines a merchant as "a person that deals in goods of the kind or otherwise holds itself out by occupation as having knowledge or skill peculiar to the practices or goods involved in the transaction or to which the knowledge or skill may be attributed by the person's employment of an agent or broker or other intermediary that holds itself out by occupation as having the knowledge or skill." Official Comment 2 to Section 2–104 explains that by this provision a person may be classified as a merchant because of specialized knowledge of the goods, of business practices, or of both. The same comment explains that because of specialized knowledge of relevant business practices, banks or universities may be classified as merchants in certain transactions for the purpose of various of the UCC's sections which rest on normal business practices or broad concepts of fairness, such as the statute of frauds (Sections 2–201 and 2A–201), firm offers (Sections 2–205 and 2A–205), the definition of good faith (Section 2–103(1)(j), also applicable under Section 2A–103(3) in Article 2A), and responsibility to follow instructions (Sections 2–603 and 2–605, 2A–511 and 2A–514), but not for other purposes such as the implied warranty of merchantability (Sections 2–314 and 2A–212, and note these sections highlight that distinction). The same analysis holds for Article 2A. See Official Comment to Section 2A–101, Relationship of Article 2A to Other Articles.

A number of cases have involved whether a party to a contract is a merchant within the meaning of the UCC. Of these cases, a large number have involved farmers. One opinion held that a farmer was not a merchant in a transaction in which he sold soybeans raised by him to a grain company. Cook Grains, Inc. v. Fallis (1965). On the other hand, see Sierens v. Clausen (1975) where the court reached a different conclusion. Some states have dealt with this issue by statute. See, e.g., 6 Neb.Rev. Stat. UCC § 2–201(2)(b) (excluding certain sellers of their own crops from merchant coverage). Other, less difficult, cases on who is a merchant include a boat builder who agreed to construct a mast for a buyer's yacht and was held to be a merchant (Mercanti v. Persson (1971)), and high school band mothers selling food at an annual fund raising luncheon who were held not to be merchants. Samson v. Riesing (1974).

7. CONSUMER LEASE AND FINANCE LEASE DEFINED; RELATION OF UCC TO OTHER LAW

Article 2A, in addition to providing certain special rules for merchants as does Article 2, to a greater degree than Article 2 also provides certain special rules for consumers. To illustrate, see Sections 2A–106, 2A–108, 2A–109, 2A–221, 2A–406, 2A–407, and 2A–516 which have no counterpart in Article 2. Article 2 also has special rules for consumers. As a consequence, both Articles define a consumer contract. The definition in Article 2A originally was drawn from the federal Consumer Leasing Act and the 1974 Uniform Consumer Credit Code, and included a lease made by a professional (it is unlikely that a non-merchant would have the bargaining leverage to pose the dangers to consumers that are sought to be avoided) to an individual who takes under the lease primarily for a consumer purpose and where, if the enacting state elects, the lease obligation does not exceed a designated amount (the federal act uses a $25,000 cut off). The current definitions in Sections 2–103(1)(d) and 2A–103(1)(f) do not provide for a dollar limitation. However, for protections beyond those provided in the UCC, other state law may define a consumer contract more narrowly. For example, see Unif. Consumer Credit Code, 7A U.L.A. 1 (1974) and the Uniform Consumer Leases Act, both of which contain dollar limitations.

Both Articles explicitly subject their rules to other separate consumer rules of law. Sections 2–102 and 2–108, and Section 2A–104. Of course, a federal law, such as Magnuson–Moss Act, applies and its effect cannot be controlled by state law (but see Sections 2–108(4) and 2A–104(4) as to the federal "E-sign" act). Both Article 2 and Article 2A also may interact with many other types of state laws. Literally the type and number of such laws is too comprehensive to do more than provide an illustration or two. Thus, for example, see Sections 2–108(1)(a) and 2A–104(1)(a) as to certificate of title laws (and Saturn of Kings Automall, Inc. v. Mike

Albert Leasing, Inc. (2001) (under former Article 2);
Consolidated Aluminum Corp. v. Krieger (1986) (relation to a statute defining what is encompassed within a signed writing); and, where enacted, the Uniform Electronic Transactions Act; Matter of Great American Veal, Inc. (1985) (relation of trust fund under 7 U.S.C. § 196(b) to claims of unpaid sellers); Bailey v. LeBeau (1986) (relation to deceptive trade practices act); "lemon laws," specifying particular consumer rights where vehicles cannot be repaired ("lemons"), are another example). See generally Sections 2–108 and 2A–104.

A somewhat similar issue throughout the UCC is when does a UCC provision "displace" other law and when does other law "supplement" the UCC? See Section 1–103(b). It is clear, for example, that whether a purported agent's signature binds the principal in reference to Sections 2–201 and 2A–201 is determined by the law of agency and not Article 2 or Article 2A. But if Section 2–725 bars a claim for revocation of acceptance under Article 2, it is less clear whether the law permitting rescission for mutual mistake of fact is displaced. If that law would allow a different result, arguably it is. See Firestone & Parson, Inc. v. Union League (1987) and Donovan v. RRL Corp. (2001). In contrast, only a few courts have held the UCC displaces strict liability in tort. See Morrow v. New Moon Homes, Inc. (1976) (displaces in part) and Childs v. Westinghouse Elec. Corp. (1988) (enactment of Section 2–318 precludes judicial adoption of strict liability in tort). Some guidance on the issue exists in the Official Comment to Section 1–103, and further discussion appears in Miller, The ABCs of the UCC: Revised Article 1 General Provisions, Chapts. 4 and 5 (American Bar Association 2002).

Where the other law is federal the issue is one of preemption, and the standard, unless expressed by Congress, depends upon the circumstances; it may depend on whether the court believes Congress intended to occupy the entire field or, if not, whether the state law impinges on the Congressional purpose or, simply, whether compliance can be had with both laws. See, Forster v. R.J. Reynolds Tobacco Co. (1989) (relation of state tort law and warranty claims against cigarette manufacturers and the Cigarette Labeling and Advertising Act, 15 U.S.C. §§ 1331–41); Matthew Bender & Co., Inc. v. Jurisline.Com LLC (2000) (action for fraud and breach of contract was state law claim and not equivalent to an attempt to create a copyright so as to constitute a matter of federal jurisdiction). See also Rokicsak v. Colony Marine Sales & Service, Inc. (2002) (an implied warranty disclaimed in violation of Magnuson–Moss Act does not give rise to state action for warranty).

Article 2A draws a distinction between finance and other leases. Many leases are two party transactions; for example, a lessee leases an automobile for four years from a dealer. Other true leases, however, are the product of a three party transaction where a person who wishes to acquire a particular good contracts with a supplier of the good but for various tax or business reasons the supplier sells or leases the good to a leasing company or to a bank, which leases or releases the good to the person who seeks to acquire it. Many sales and leaseback transactions also involve similar considerations. See Official Comment to the definition of "finance lease" in Section 2A–103. The leases in these latter transactions are "finance leases," so called because the function of the lessor normally is limited to supplying the financing rather than the goods. Under Article 2A, as generally under the law prior to it (compare the majority and dissenting opinions in Sawyer v. Pioneer Leasing Corp. (1968) and see Citicorp Leasing, Inc. v. Allied Institutional Distributors, Inc. (1977)), the finance lessor generally is not held to the same responsibility as to the goods as is a "merchant" lessor. See Sections 2A–209, 2A–211, 2A–212, 2A–213, 2A–219, 2A–220, 2A–221, 2A–405, 2A–407, 2A–516, and 2A–517.

The definition of "finance lease" in Section 2A–103(1)(*l*) reflects the purpose behind the distinction. Thus, the lessor cannot select, manufacture, or supply the goods and must acquire the goods or the right to possess and use them in connection with the lease, although a re-lease at the end of a finance lease other than to a consumer may still qualify as a finance lease. Since the lessee's rights primarily will be with reference to the supplier of the goods rather than the lessor, for statutory finance lease treatment the lessee also must be afforded, prior to being bound under the lease, adequate information about the rights of the lessor under the contract with the supplier of the goods pursuant to which the lessor acquires the goods.

Consistent with one of the major reasons Article 2 is the primary model for Official Article 2A (see Comment to Section 2A–101, Statutory Analogue), the same results that flow from finance lease status by statute may be reached by the agreement of the parties consistent with the principle of freedom of contract. Official Comment to the definition of "finance lease" in Section 2A–103.

CHAPTER 2

FORMATION OF THE CONTRACT

---

1. INTRODUCTION

Generally speaking, the formation of contracts for the sale or for the lease of goods is governed by the same rules as those governing the formation of other types of contracts. In some instances, however, Article 2 and Article 2A, in an attempt to carry out the stated purpose of modernizing the law governing commercial transactions, formulated special rules applicable only to these contracts. In short, Articles 2 and 2A modify general contract law to the extent necessary to adopt it to sales or leases of goods, but general contract law, such as the doctrine of consideration, supplements or fills in what the UCC rules do not displace. Section 1–103(b).

For a further discussion of general contract law, see
C. Rohwer and A. Skroki, Contracts (5th ed. West
Group 2000).

2. THE OFFER

Both a present sale of goods and a contract to sell
goods as well as a lease of goods require mutual
manifestation of assent for their formation. The
seller or lessor must manifest its intent to sell or
lease; the buyer or lessee must manifest its intent
to buy or lease. This intent may be manifested by
words, by actions, by a combination of words and
actions, by the interaction of electronic agents or of
an electronic agent and an individual or, where
there is a duty to speak, by silence. Sections 2–
204(1) and 2A–204(1). See also Sections 2–204(4)
and 2A–204(4) (on electronic agents), and 2–211–2–
213 and 2A–222–2A–224 (on legal recognition of
electronic contracts, records and signatures, attribution, and electronic communication), the latter
being supplemented by the Uniform Electronic
Transactions Act, where enacted. As to "E-sign,"
see Sections 2–108 and 2A–104. Ordinarily a contract is formed when one party makes an offer to
buy or sell or lease goods and the other party
accepts the offer. A sufficient agreement may be
found, however, even though the moment of the
making of the agreement is undetermined. Sections
2–204(2) and 2A–204(2). Moreover, even though one
or more terms are left open, a contract will not fail
for indefiniteness if the parties have intended to
make a contract and there is a reasonably certain

basis for giving an appropriate remedy. Sections 2–204(3) and 2A–204(3). Of course, the more terms left open the less likely it is that a binding agreement at that point was intended. Official Comment 3 to Section 2–204. As to what supplies the rule where a term is left open, see Sections 1–303, 2–305, 2–308, 2–309, 2–311. Generally speaking, formation issues are less prevalent in leases than in sales because leases often are structured transactions where the entire agreement is negotiated and reduced to a record signed simultaneously by the parties and it is apparent that no agreement is contemplated until the writing is signed. See Computer Systems of America, Inc. v. International Business Machines Corp. (1986). To the contrary, sales contracts often involve the exchange of offers and acceptances that are separate and may differ and that may not cover all matters. Thus, while formation issues in leases are not unknown, Article 2A has fewer provisions in this area than does Article 2.

With some exceptions, an offer does not place the offeror under a contractual obligation until it is accepted, but only creates a power of acceptance in the offeree. This means that the offeror ordinarily is legally free to revoke the offer before it is accepted. Once the offer is properly accepted a contract is formed, and neither party may terminate it unilaterally without proper legal cause. In some circumstances, however, the offeror is contractually obligated not to revoke an offer. For example, S offers to sell goods to B in return for B's promise to pay five dollars for the privilege and promises to keep the offer open for ten days. Here S's promise is contractual as the promise to keep the offer open is supported by consideration; S is legally obligated not to revoke the offer. Also some courts have held an offer irrevocable on the basis of promissory estoppel. Sections 2–205 and 2A–205 create another means by which an offer to buy or sell or to lease goods may be made irrevocable. Section 2–205 provides (and Section 2A–205 is the same for leases):

An offer by a merchant to buy or sell goods in a signed record that by its terms gives assurance that it will be held open is not revocable, for lack of consideration, during the time stated or, if no time is stated, for a reasonable time not to exceed three months. Any such term of assurance in a form supplied by the offeree must be separately signed by the offeror.

The application of this provision is very circumscribed. First, it applies only to an offer to buy or sell or to lease "goods." Second, the offer must be made by a merchant. An offer made by a non-merchant, although meeting all the other requirements, would not come within the purview of the sections. "Merchant" is defined in Sections 2–104(1) and 2A–103(1)(z). Third, the offer must be in a record and signed by the offeror. An oral or an unsigned offer will not do. Fourth, the record must contain assurance that the offer will remain open. No guides are furnished as to what words are sufficient to constitute assurance. It is clear that the words "I will keep this offer open for ten days" would be sufficient. In one of the few cases in which the possible application of Section 2–205 was considered, the court held that the words "We are pleased to offer ... (structural steel at certain prices) ... Thank you for this opportunity to quote," were not sufficient to constitute assurance. E.A. Coronis Associates v. M. Gordon Const. Co. (1966). Fifth, no offer will remain irrevocable under this provision for longer than three months. For example, an offer meeting all the requirements of Section 2–205 or Section 2A–205 and giving assurance that it will remain open for four months would be irrevocable on the basis of these sections for only three months. See Official Comment 3 to Section 2–205 which, however, is equally applicable to Section 2A–205. As to that applicability, see Comment to Section 2A–101, Relationship of Article 2A to Other Articles.

3. THE ACCEPTANCE: BATTLE OF THE FORMS

Under traditional contract law, an effective acceptance must be unqualified and must not vary from the terms of the offer, the so-called "mirror image rule." Thus, if S sends B a letter offering to sell 100 units of a good at a stated price per unit, B's reply that it will take 75 units at that price does not constitute an acceptance of S's offer. It is a counteroffer, which S is free to accept or reject. The acceptance must be the "mirror image" of the offer. Some common law courts carried the rule to an extreme by holding that the slightest deviation in the attempted acceptance was a counter-offer and not an acceptance. Thus parties that thought they had a contract and acted accordingly until a dispute arose were at times surprised to learn they had no contract to govern the resolution of their dispute.

In sales transactions in the commercial world it is quite common for the parties to make use of various kinds of printed forms in consummating a sales contract. Often there is no one document designated as a contract. Several documents may be involved, with each bearing a different label, such as "purchase order," "invoice," or "confirmation of order," or "sales order." These forms will in most instances contain printed terms or conditions and will state that the order or sale is subject to these conditions. Moreover, the terms on the seller's form may vary from or be inconsistent with some of the terms of the buyer's form, and both parties, of course, use printed forms containing terms advantageous to themselves. Applications of the "mirror image" rule to fact situations in this commercial setting may produce some especially questionable decisions.

One such decision was Poel v. Brunswick–Balke–Collender Co. of New York (1915). There S's agent sent an offer to B's agent offering to sell a quantity of rubber. B's agent replied on B's own order form requesting shipment of the rubber. All terms in B's form were consistent with S's offer except that it contained a term providing: "The acceptance of this order ... in any event you must promptly acknowledge." S failed to acknowledge and later B withdrew from the deal for other reasons. In a suit by S against B for breach of contract, the court held that no contract had been formed between the parties. This conclusion was based on the theory that B's order form did not constitute an acceptance in that it contained a new proposition for a contract on the terms stated therein. As S had not acknowledged, B's proposal (counter-offer) remained unaccepted. The court reached this decision despite the fact that buyer had not objected, even at the time of withdrawal, to the lack of acknowledgment. It was within the context of the "mirror image" rule and decisions such as *Poel* that Section 2–207 was drafted.

Article 2A does not contain a similar provision. As discussed earlier, lease contracts tend to be formulated in more formal ways, and thus less need exists for such a provision. This is not to say that contract formation issues are absent in leases. See, e.g., Essex Crane Rental Corp. v. Weyher/Livsey Constructors, Inc. (1989). It is to say, however, that given the adverse experience under Section 2–207, it did not seem desirable to perpetuate its mistakes in a context where that approach is avoidable. For a detailed criticism of former Section 2–207, see Murray, A Proposed Revision of Section 2–207 of the Uniform Commercial Code, 6 Journal of Law and Comm. 337 (1986). For a road map to the section, see Frisch and Wladis, General Provisions, Sales, Bulk Transfers, and Documents of Title, 43 Bus. Law. 1259, 1266–67 (1988).

Former Section 2–207 provided:

(1) A definite and seasonable expression of acceptance or a written confirmation which is sent within a reasonable time operates as an acceptance even though it states terms additional to or different from those offered or agreed upon, unless acceptance is expressly made conditional on assent to the additional or different terms.

(2) The additional terms are to be construed as proposals for addition to the contract. Between merchants such terms become part of the contract unless:

(a) The offer expressly limits acceptance to the terms of the offer;

(b) they materially alter it; or

(c) notification of objection to them has already been given or is given within a reasonable time after notice is received.

(3) Conduct by both parties which recognizes the existence of a contract is sufficient to establish a contract for sale although the writings of the parties do not otherwise establish a contract. In such case the terms of the particular contract consist of those terms of which the writings of the parties agree, together with any supplementary terms incorporated under other provisions of this Act.

First, it should be observed that former Section 2–207(1) alters the mirror image rule and focuses on contract formation. A definite and seasonable expression of acceptance does not fail as an acceptance simply because it contains further or different suggestions or proposals such as "ship by Tuesday," "rush," and "ship draft against bill of lading inspection allowed." Official Comment 1 to former Section 2–207. In *Poel,* for example, B's order form contained an unequivocal request for the shipment of the goods described in S's offer. It seems this would be a definite expression of acceptance within the meaning of former Section 2–207, unless it can be concluded the acceptance was expressly made conditional on assent to the additional term, and it would not seem that "in any event you must promptly acknowledge" should be so construed as the policy of the section should require a clear expression. See, e.g., Dorton v. Collins & Aikman Corp. (1972). Compare C. Itoh & Co. (America) Inc. v. Jordan Int'l Co. (1977). Of course, at some point a varying "acceptance" perhaps should not be treated as an acceptance at all. Cf., e.g., Southern Idaho Pipe & Steel Co. v. Cal–Cut Pipe & Supply, Inc. (1977) (conflict in delivery dates). Thus, for example, an offer to buy 2000 pounds of number 1 grade sugar responded to with an offer to take 1000 pounds of number 2 grade sugar is not an acceptance.

The section also was intended to deal with the situation where an agreement has been reached, but the formal memoranda add terms not discussed. Official Comment 1 to former Section 2–207 and American Parts Co. v. American Arbitration Ass'n (1967).

The second thing to observe is that former Section 2–207(2) deals with *additional* term(s); it would not seem it deals with *different* terms, except where a confirmation of a prior agreement is involved, because the different term would be ejected under former Section 2–207(2)(c), and Official Comment 6 states what the contract is in that case. See discussion infra. The section distinguishes between additional terms which "materially alter" the offer and those which do not. As between merchants, unless the offeror has expressly limited acceptance to the exact terms of the offer, the terms which do not materially alter the offer become a part of the contract unless objection to them has already been given or is given within a reasonable time after notice of them is received, one of the rare cases where silence can constitute assent. Terms which materially alter the offer do not bind the offeror unless there is assent to them. Assent in this context usually must involve more than silence and often more than retention or even use. Compare Hill v. Gateway 2000 (1997) with Klocek v. Gateway (2000). Obviously, one difficulty in applying this provision to specific cases lies in determining whether an additional term "materially alters" the offer. Official Comments 4 and 5 to former Section 2–207 give examples of clauses which do or do not materially alter the offer. In Aceros Prefabricados, S.A. v. TradeArbed, Inc. (2002), the court found an arbitration clause did not create surprise or hardship, and thus was not material, where arbitration was a standard industry practice. A similar case is

Bayway Refining Co. v. Oxygenated Marketing & Trading A.G. (2000) (clause shifting tax liability, but also commenting that an arbitration clause was a per se material alteration, thus indicating the uncertainty of the "materiality" standard). See also Mid–State Contracting, Inc. v. Superior Floor Co., Inc. (2002) (addition of a term for payment of interest; addition of interest rates or other terms of credit not material). Of course the offeror can always protect itself, if it does not want to be bound by additional terms, by either stipulating in the offer that acceptance must be limited to the exact terms of the offer or by giving notice within a reasonable time that it objects to the additional term(s). If disagreement remains but the parties proceed as if there is a contract, former Section 2–207(3) recognizes that and determines its terms. See C. Itoh & Co. (America) Inc. v. Jordan Int'l Co. (1977).

A number of courts have dealt with the provisions of former Section 2–207. One of the earliest, best known and most criticized cases is Roto–Lith, Ltd. v. Bartlett & Co. (1962), subsequently overturned in Ionics v. Elmwood Sensors, Inc. (1997). There B mailed a written order for goods to S. S then mailed an acknowledgment and an invoice to B. Both contained language limiting S's liability for breach of warranty, and concluded with this sentence: "If these terms are not acceptable, Buyer must so notify the Seller at once." B did not protest S's attempt to limit its liability but accepted, used, and paid for the goods. In an action for damages for breach of warranty, B claimed that under former Section 2–207 the condition that there were to be no warranties "materially altered" the offer; therefore B was not bound by it. See Official Comment 4 to former Section 2–207. The court stated, however, that while the "no warranties" condition in S's invoice did materially alter B's offer, there also was no acceptance but instead there was a counter-offer and B accepted the goods by receiving and using them with knowledge of the condition and became bound by it.

If the court's position that a response which proposes a material alteration of the offer solely to the disadvantage of the offerer constitutes an acceptance only if there is assent to the additional terms so that any other response constitutes a counter-offer that will be accepted if the goods are used is correct, this means that former Section 2–207(2)(b) is meaningless. Rather, former Section 2–207(2)(b) seems clearly to embrace the idea that an offer can be accepted under subsection (1) when the response (acceptance) contains terms materially different from those in the offer; that is, in *Roto-Lith* the contract was formed upon the exchange of documents without consideration of the subsequent performance. Former Section 2–207(2) then normally dictates the terms. In contrast, in Dorton v. Collins & Aikman Corp. (1972), the court interpreted former Section 2–207(1) and (2) instead in such a way as to require "express consent" to material additional terms by the offeror before they become a part of the contract; mere acceptance of the offeree's performance would not suffice. See Official Comment 3 to Section 2–207. Thus the offeree can control its acceptance, but it must be done expressly. See McJunkin Corp. v. Mechanicals, Inc. (1989) (acceptance expressly conditioned so as not to constitute an acceptance without consent; contract formed and defined under former Section 2–207(3)).

The offeror also can control the acceptance under Section 2–207(2)(a) but interpretative problems exist; does the language used really fall within Section 2–207(2)(a) and (c) so that a contract results to the extent the acceptance contains all the terms of the offer and there is objection to any additional terms, or does the language instead say that no contract results since the offer can be accepted only by a response that contains neither additional nor different terms? In the latter case, it would seem the response should not be considered a counter-offer where use or other subsequent performance constitutes acceptance because it gives the party who happened to fire the "last shot" an advantage unrelated to substance; rather former Section 2–207(3) should be applied in accordance with Official Comment 7 to former Section 2–207. If there is no subsequent performance, there is no contract. See Koehring Co. v. Glowacki (1977).

A final issue is what is the result if an offeree's response contains different rather than additional terms. One view is the discrepant terms in both the offer and acceptance drop out, and UCC gap fillers come in. Perhaps a better view is that there should be no different treatment of different terms from the treatment of additional terms. The majority rule is the first—the "knockout" rule. Northrop Corp. v. Litronic Industries (1994).

Current Section 2–207 first separates the issues of whether there is a contract and, if so, what are its terms, by allocating former Section 2–207(1) to Section 2–206(3). Then Section 2–207 treats all cases, even beyond a battle of the forms, where there is a contract, whether by conduct or offer and acceptance and where a contract is confirmed, but there is an issue as to its terms, by providing the terms of the contract are (1) the terms that appear in the records of both parties, (2) the terms to which both parties agree, and (3) the terms supplied or incorporated under Article 2. Thus the issues under former Section 2–207(1) remain basically the same, but now arise under Section 2–206(3), and while Section 2–207 itself seems to avoid many issues under former Section 2–207(2), in fact some still exist as Official Comment 3 to Section 2–207 demonstrates (e.g., whether performance or conduct or repeated use of a term constitutes agreement; the effect of trade practice or course of dealing, which may indicate whether a difference is material and thus whether there is assent), but an important difference is the statute is less rigid and thus courts have greater discretion to reach an appropriate result in the enormous variety of circumstances that may be presented.

However, current Section 2–207 does not explicitly assist in the resolution of one situation over which there has been considerable litigation. That situation is the one where a customer acquires or orders and acquires a product, where that part of the transaction may or may not be sufficiently definite to constitute a contract, and the product then comes with terms under notice that retention or use will constitute acceptance of those terms. The issue can arise with any product (see, e.g., Hill v. BASF Wyandotte Corp. (1982) (limitation of liability on product label on cans of herbicide)) but recently has involved so-called "shrink wrap" licenses of software. See ProCD, Inc. v. Zeidenberg (1996) and Hill v. Gateway 2000 (1997) (upholding "later terms" where assented to by use where a choice existed between use and return) and Step–Saver Data Systems, Inc. v. Wyse Technology (1991) and Klocek v. Gateway, Inc. (2000) ("later terms" were proposals to be added but to which there was no express assent). Official Comment 5 to Section 2–207 states:

The section omits any specific treatment of terms on or in the container in which goods are delivered. This Article takes no position on whether a court should follow the reasoning in Hill v. Gateway 2000 (1997) (. . . the "rolling contract" is not made until acceptance of the seller's terms after the goods and terms are delivered) or the contrary reasoning in Step–Saver Data Systems, Inc. v. Wyse Technology (1991) (contract is made at time of oral or other bargain and "shrink wrap" terms or those in the container become part of contract only if they comply with provisions like Section 2–207).

It is submitted the two cases in the Official Comment are not really inconsistent, as there was no intent in *Hill* to have a final contract prior to review of the later terms and acceptance, while in *Step-Saver* the facts were held not to support this analysis. Thus if there is an intent to contract at the time of order or receipt and no intent for a "rolling contract," *Step-Saver* reaches the right result; if there is no contract at time of order or receipt due to inadequate definiteness or an intent for a "rolling contract," then the analysis in *Hill* is correct. See Brower v. Gateway 2000 (1998). Moreover, even if acceptance must wait, ultimately it must exist for the "later term" to be binding. See Specht v. Netscape (2002) and compare the Uniform Computer Information Transactions Act Sections 112, 202–205, and 209–212.

4.   THE ACCEPTANCE: OTHER PROBLEMS

Section 2–206 of the UCC provides:

(1) Unless otherwise unambiguously indicated by the language or circumstances:

(a) an offer to make a contract invites acceptance in any manner and by any medium reasonable in the circumstances; and

(b) an order or other offer to buy goods for prompt or current shipment invites acceptance either by a prompt promise to ship or by the prompt or current shipment of conforming or nonconforming goods, but the shipment of non-conforming goods is not an acceptance if the seller seasonably notifies the buyer that the shipment is offered only as an accommodation to the buyer.

(2) If the beginning of a requested performance is a reasonable mode of acceptance, an offeror that is not notified of acceptance within a reasonable time may treat the offer as having lapsed before acceptance.

(3) A definite and seasonable expression of acceptance in a record operates as an acceptance even if it contains terms additional to or different from the offer.

Section 2A–206 is the same except it deletes subsections (1)(b) and (3) as largely unnecessary in lease transactions.

a.   Means of Acceptance: Generally

Sections 2–206(1) and 2A–206(1) are intended to liberalize the means by which the offeree can accept an offer. Unless the offeror has specified clearly that acceptance must be made in a given manner, such as: "if you desire to accept, it must be by telegram to X by 5:00 on Friday," these provisions allow the offeree to accept in any reasonable manner. This is intended to reject former technical rules requiring acceptance to be communicated in a way identical with that used to communicate the offer.

For example, telegraphed offers need not be accepted by telegraph if the means of acceptance fulfills the same apparent needs as to place, time and form. Official Comment 1 to former Section 2–206.

b. Act or Promise as Acceptance

When an offeror communicates an offer to the offeree there may be some doubt in the latter's mind as to exactly what is being requested. The offeror may be bargaining for a promise (a bilateral contract) or for an act (a unilateral contract). In many instances, however, the offeror probably does not care what means of acceptance is used.

There are many cases holding that if the offeree attempts to accept with a response other than that prescribed in the offer there is no contract. If the offer calls for a promise, the mere performance of the act envisaged in the promise ordinarily is not an acceptance. If the offer calls for the performance of an act, a promise to perform the act will not suffice. Normally if the offer solicits a promise, the offeree must communicate the promise to the offeror; on the other hand if the offer calls for the performance of an act as the acceptance, the fact that the act has been performed often does not have to be communicated to the offeror.

In Port Huron Machinery Co. v. Wohlers (1928), the defendant sent the plaintiff an order for a piece of farm machinery, requesting immediate shipment. Two days after receiving the order the plaintiff shipped the machinery but did not notify the defendant of this fact. Two days after the goods were shipped the plaintiff received a telegram from the defendant attempting to revoke the offer. The defendant contended that the order called for a promise from the plaintiff and that the shipment of the machinery was not of itself an acceptance of the offer. It was contended, therefore, that the offer had been revoked before the plaintiff accepted it. The court held, however, that the offer had been accepted as soon as the machinery was shipped, because the offeror had bargained for an act and not a promise.

Sections 2–206 and 2A–206 reject a formal approach to determining what type of acceptance the offeror had in mind, and resolve any doubt as to the offeror's intentions in favor of the offeree. Unless clearly indicated otherwise, the offeree may accept by any reasonable means, and specifically in cases where the offeror's offer in ordinary commercial understanding contemplates current shipment, the offeree may accept either by prompt shipment or by prompt communication to the offeror of a promise to ship. If, however, the act of shipment is chosen, the offeree must within a reasonable time follow the beginning of performance with an unambiguous notice of acceptance to the offeror. Otherwise, the offeror may treat the offer as having lapsed before acceptance.

c. Acceptance and Non–Conforming Goods

Suppose in the *Port Huron Machinery Co.* case the defendant had not attempted to revoke the offer and had in due course received the machine, shortly thereafter discovering that the machine was not the one ordered or that it was in some way defective. Suppose also that the buyer brought suit against the seller and the seller defended on the ground that no contract was formed, because the shipment of nonconforming goods was not the act bargained for by the buyer and did not constitute an acceptance. Some courts upheld such a defense.

Section 2–206(1)(b) expressly provides that the shipment of nonconforming goods constitutes an acceptance and normally a breach unless the seller "reasonably notifies the buyer that the shipment is offered only as an accommodation to the buyer." If the seller takes that action, the shipment of the nonconforming goods constitutes a counter offer only, and the buyer is free to accept or reject the goods. To illustrate: Suppose B orders a certain quantity of aluminum screening from S. S ships steel screening. S has accepted the offer. There is a contract between the parties, but at the same time S's shipment of nonconforming goods is a breach. S could have protected himself by reasonably notifying B that the shipment was made only to accommodate B. In such a case S would not have accepted the offer and would not be in breach.

It would not appear a different result should be reached if the goods were leased rather than sold even though Section 2A–206 does not deal with this fact situation explicitly.

d.　Acceptance in Unilateral Contracts

Where an offeror makes an offer for a unilateral contract, it has been held by some courts that while the beginning of performance by the offeree does not constitute acceptance it does preclude the offeror from revoking the offer. This rule may allow an unscrupulous offeree to begin performance so as to bar the offeror's power of revocation, and then wait and watch market conditions. If market conditions develop favorably the offeree will proceed to complete performance and bind the offeror; if, on the other hand, market conditions develop unfavorably, the offeree is free to halt performance and prevent the formation of a contract.

Sections 2–206(2) and 2A–206(2) attempt to remove this gamesmanship by providing that unless the offeree notifies the offeror of the acceptance within a reasonable time after beginning performance, the offeror is free to treat the offer as having lapsed. An Official Comment to Section 2–206 explains that this provision is not intended to change any common law rule which might temporarily bar the offeror from revoking the offer; rather, the notice requirement tends to shorten the time within which the offeree, having begun performance, is free to decide whether to complete or abandon it.

CHAPTER 3

STATUTE OF FRAUDS, PAROL EVIDENCE, AND MODIFICATION

A. THE STATUTE OF FRAUDS

B. PAROL EVIDENCE

C. MODIFICATION

———————

A. THE STATUTE OF FRAUDS

1. INTRODUCTION

Generally speaking, a record (information inscribed on a tangible medium, as in a writing, or stored in an electronic or other medium, and that is in perceivable form–see Section 2–103(1) (m)) is not necessary to make a promise legally enforceable unless required by statute. Such a statute which is applicable to sales contracts or leases is called the statute of frauds. An original statute of frauds was enacted in England in 1677 in part in an attempt to prevent false assertions that a contract existed when one in fact was never concluded by the parties. This original statute contained twenty-five sections, of which eight imposed a general requirement of a writing to make the types of promises involved in those sections legally enforceable. One of the those sections applied to the sale of goods.

With some variations this section was adopted in almost all American jurisdictions. It was incorporated in substance in Section 4 of the Uniform Sales Act. In general, all of these statutes required that sales contracts for goods of a certain value were enforceable only if in writing, unless the buyer had accepted at least part of the goods or paid at least part of the price.

For some time the impact of the statute has been under criticism. It is argued that although the statute was originally enacted to curb fraud and perjury, it promotes more fraud than it prevents and its quantity term corrupts the substantive provisions of Article 2. It is open to debate whether it has prevented fraud in the proof of the making of a contract, but the statute generally has prompted more reliable forms of record keeping. It also is argued that the main reason for the enactment of the statute in 1677 has since ceased to exist. At the time of its original enactment litigants in civil cases could not testify in their own behalf in English courts. This disqualification meant that before the enactment of the statute an unscrupulous plaintiff could have induced a third party to testify that he or she was present when the defendant orally agreed to buy goods from the plaintiff. Even if this were completely false the defendant was disqualified from testifying to the contrary. The rule that parties to an action were disqualified as witnesses was repealed around the middle of the nineteenth century. In the 1930's the English Law Revision Commission recommended the complete repeal of the statute of frauds, and in 1954 many of the sections, including the sale of goods provision, of the English statute were repealed. As the 2003 amendments to Article 2 were prepared, there was no agreement that the statute of frauds in Article 2 should be deleted, perhaps because it did prompt record keeping. However, it was the opinion of most that it did need adjustment and clarification. Part of that adjustment came through the Uniform Electronic Transactions Act and the federal E-sign act, that allow an electronically signed record rather than a signed writing, and Section 2–201, as amended, not conforms. The remainder of the revision of the statute comes through amendment to Section 2–201 itself.

Section 2–201 now provides:

(1) A contract for the sale of goods for the price of $5000 or more is not enforceable by way of action or defense unless there is some record sufficient to indicate that a contract for sale has been made between the parties and signed by the party against which enforcement is sought or by the party's authorized agent or broker. A record is not insufficient because it omits or incorrectly states a term agreed upon, but the contract is not enforceable under this subsection beyond the quantity of goods shown in the record.

(2) Between merchants, if within a reasonable time a record in confirmation of the contract and sufficient against the sender is received and the party receiving it has reason to know its contents, it satisfies the requirements of subsection (a) against the recipient unless notice of objection to its contents is given in record within 10 days after it is received.

(3) A contract that does not satisfy the requirements of subsection (a) but which is valid in other respects is enforceable:

(a) if the goods are to be specially manufactured for the buyer and are not suitable for sale to others in the ordinary course of the seller's business and the seller, before notice of repudiation is received and under circumstances that reasonably indicate that the goods are for the buyer, has made either a substantial beginning of their manufacture or commitments for their procurement;

(b) if the party against which enforcement is sought admits in the party's pleading, or in the party's testimony or otherwise under oath that a contract for sale was made, but the contract is not enforceable under this paragraph beyond the quantity of goods admitted; or

(c) with respect to goods for which payment has been made and accepted or which have been received and accepted pursuant to Section 2–606.

Section 2A–201 is the same, except the cut-off figure is $1000 rather than $5000, and Section 2A–201 in addition requires the record to describe the goods leased and the lease term, adjusts the payment exception due to the difference between a sale and a lease, and omits the merchant exception which was viewed as having a very limited role to play in lease transactions according to Official Comment 1 to Section 2A–201.

2.   CONTRACTS COVERED

Section 2–201 is applicable only to contracts for sale of goods for the price of $5000 or more and Section 2A–201 is applicable only where the total payments to be made under the lease, excluding payments for options to renew or buy, are $1000 or more. Unless the thing being bought and sold or leased is a "good" as defined in the UCC, these sections are not applicable. Suppose, for example, S contracts to sell B a small building located on, and attached to, S's land and to be severed and removed by B. The contract is not one for the sale of goods under Section 2–107; therefore, Section 2–201 does not apply. Of course, another statute of frauds outside the UCC may apply to the real estate sale, and another provision of the UCC, for example Section 9–203, may apply where the sale is of certain other kinds of personal property. See also Bridgewater Washed Sand & Stone Co. v. Bridgewater Materials, Inc. (1972), where S agreed to sell a sand and gravel plant to B and agreed orally to replace, prior to the transfer, that portion of a stockpile of stone consumed in the ordinary course of business prior to the transfer. The court held the oral agreement was not a sale of goods within Section 2–201. On the other hand, if the contract requires S to sever, the contract is one for the sale of goods. Hence, if the price were $5000 or more, Section 2–201 would apply. However, another statute of frauds outside the UCC, for example, that requires a record if the contract is not to be performed within a year, will not apply; Section 2–201 is exclusive. Section 2–201(4).

Prior to Article 2A, a lease transaction might involve goods but not a contract for their "sale", and thus escape the UCC. In George F. Mueller and Sons, Inc. v. Northern Illinois Gas Co. (1973), the court held that a rental agreement providing for installation, servicing, and maintenance of vending machines was not a contract of "sale" within Section 2–201. If such a contract now is covered by Article 2A as a lease, Section 2A–201 could be applicable.

3. SUFFICIENCY OF THE WRITING

a. In General

If Section 2–201(1) or Section 2A–201(1) applies, or in common legal parlance, "if the contract falls within the statute of frauds," generally speaking a record signed by the party against which enforcement is sought is required to enforce the contract or to use its provisions in defense. Official Comment 5 to Section 2–201 explains this does not mean the agreement is non-existent for all purposes, such as whether a person in possession is a trespasser. On the other hand, a record only takes away the statute of frauds defense; the burden of persuading the trier of fact that a contract indeed was made and its terms is unaffected. In that respect, it will be observed that the statutes do not literally require that the contract be in record form. A record may be signed long after the parties have orally contracted in confirmation; the record need only indicate that a contract has been made. Nor need the record take any special form; it may be in a check, letter, telegram, or invoice, in electronic form in a computer, an entry in an account book, or an order blank. See Barber & Ross v. Lifetime Doors, Inc. (1987)

(written sales brochures deemed sufficient). In some instances a combination of two or more documents has been held sufficient even though any one of the documents alone would have been insufficient. In such cases, however, the documents must in some way show that they are related to each other; for example, they may be physically attached (pinned or stapled together) or one may expressly or impliedly incorporate the contents of the other(s) by reference. See Joseph E. Seagram & Sons, Inc. v. Shaffer (1962).

b. Must Be Signed

Subject to the exception discussed below, the record must be signed (see Section 2–103(1) (m)) by the party against which enforcement is sought (usually the defendant) or by that party's authorized agent or broker. Whether the agent is authorized is determined by law outside the UCC. Though the risk of forgery may make such casual forms inadvisable, the signature may be written in pencil, typewritten, or stamped with a rubber stamp and may be on any part of the document. See Southwest Engineering Co. v. Martin Tractor Co. (1970). Signing also includes attaching to or logically associating with the record an electronic sound, symbol, or process. A signature does not have to be the complete name of the party signing; that party's given name or initials are sufficient. Any mark made personally or through an authorized agent, with intent that it constitute a signature, is a signature in the eyes of the law. Sections 2–103(1)(p) and 1–201(2)(kk). Note nothing requires delivery of the record. Official Comment 6 to Section 2–201.

c. Other Contents

Apart from the requirement that the record be signed by the party to be charged (or that party's authorized agent), pre-UCC law was both conflicting and confusing as to what else the memorandum had to contain. Section 2–201 imposes only two other invariable requirements: the writing must indicate that a contract for sale has been made between the parties (see Gestetner Corp. v. Case Equipment Co. (1987) (letter which stated Case looked forward "to its continuing role as exclusive dealer for Gestetner" was sufficient)), and the contract is not enforceable under subsection (a) beyond the quantity shown in the record. Such terms as price, time and place of payment and delivery, and warranties may all be omitted. See Official Comment 1 to Section 2–201. Section 2A–201 requires a bit more given the different nature of a lease: the record also must describe the goods and the lease term. See, in elaboration of what will meet these requirements, Section 2A–201(2) and (5).

Under both sections, a record is not insufficient because a term is omitted or incorrectly stated. If, however, quantity is incorrectly stated in either case or the lease term in the case of a lease, the contract is not enforceable *on the basis of the record* beyond the quantity or lease term stated. In short, the only terms which must appear are these terms. Official Comment 1 to Section 2–201. See Global Truck & Equip. Co. v. Palmer Machine Works, Inc. (1986) (oral discussions covered 25 trailers, the writing was an order for 5) and Simmons Foods, Inc. v. Hill's Pet Nutrition, Inc. (2001) (no enforceable contract due to missing quantity terms; contract set forth an express quantity for first year of contract, but no quantity for last two years). Arguably courts should liberally construe the quantity requirement because once it is clear some contract has been made, its alleged terms, including quantity, can be proven in the usual way. Perhaps for this reason, courts tend to structure the rigor of this requirement to the circumstances. See, e.g., Jo–Ann, Inc. v. Alfin Fragrances, Inc. (1989) (statement of definite quantity not required in requirement and distributorship contracts), and PMC Corp. v. Houston Wire & Cable Co. (2002) (writing that referred to purchase of "major share" or "major portion" of seller's products sufficient). However, a record which merely states an offer or indicates negotiations between the parties is not sufficient. For example, one court held a memo insufficient which stated that a recited payment was a "deposit on tentative purchase." Arcuri v. Weiss (1962).

Pre–UCC courts generally agreed that the identity of the party other than the signer also had to be shown in the memo. Whether this is necessary under the UCC is not clear. Sections 2–201 and 2A–201 state that the record must indicate that a contract was made *between the parties*. This would seem to require that the memo in some way identify the non-signer. Comment 1 to Section 2–201 explains, however, that it is not necessary for the record to indicate which party is the seller and which the buyer.

4.   EXCEPTIONS

Section 2–201(2) and (3) and Section 2A–201(4) provide several exceptions to the general requirement that to be enforceable a contract "falling within" subsection (a) be evidenced by record signed by the party against whom enforcement is sought. The exceptions are discussed below.

a.   Record Signed Only by Party Seeking Enforcement

Normally, a memorandum, even though signed by one party and sufficient to make the contract enforceable against that party, is not effective against a party who has not signed it. In some cases this is unjust. For example, suppose S and B, both merchants, agree by telephone to buy and sell $800 worth of goods. It is understood that S is to confirm the agreement by letter. The following day S sends a letter to B confirming their conversation and setting out all the terms of the agreement. B does not reply. Under pre-UCC law the agreement is enforceable against S, but not against B. The UCC seeks to eliminate this inequity. Thus under Section

2–201(2) the letter would be a sufficient memorandum against B as a merchant even though B did not sign it. The provision may still operate harshly, however. Thus in Polygram, S.A. v. 32–03 Enterprises, Inc. (1988), the buyer who failed to read invoices packaged with the goods was bound by the terms of the invoice. Section 2A–201 does not contain a similar provision, not because the concept is inappropriate in a lease context, but because the fact situation would be rare in that context and a court should in those rare cases reach a result consistent with that under Section 2–201(b) by applying its principle. See Official Comment to Section 2A–101, Relationship of Article 2A to other Articles.

Several courts have dealt with the application of this provision. One of the first and best known cases is Harry Rubin & Sons, Inc. v. Consolidated Pipe Co. of America (1959). There B, in response to two oral agreements between the parties, sent two written memoranda to S, confirming the oral agreements. Each writing was signed by B's agent. S did not respond to either communication. The court held that both memoranda were sufficient to satisfy the statute of frauds as to B, and, as both parties were merchants, the contracts also were enforceable against S. In a more recent case, Cook Grains, Inc. v. Fallis (1965), a court held that Section 2–201(2) did not apply because S, a farmer-grower of soybeans was not a merchant. There is a difference of opinion on this point, and some states have addressed the matter by statute. See Sierens v. Clausen (1975) (farmer who had been engaged in farming for 34 years and who for at least five years had sold his soybean crop to grain elevators was held to be a merchant subject to this provision of the statute of frauds) and Nebraska Section 2–201(2)(b). See also American Plastic Equip., Inc. v. CBS, Inc. (1989) (one who has knowledge of relevant business practices involved is a merchant) and Official Comment 4 (a farmer should be considered a merchant).

b. Specially Manufactured Goods

Suppose S contracts to sell or lease goods which are not in existence at the time the contract is made, but which are to be manufactured by S for B. The contract envisages not only the transfer of ownership or possession and use of goods from S to B but the performance of services by S. Absent a more specific rule, if the contract is primarily for services, regardless of the value of the goods the goods provision of the statute of frauds would not apply. See the discussion in Chapter 1 on goods versus services issues generally. Section 2–201(3)(a) and Section 2A–201(4)(a) adopt a more specific rule. If the seller or lessor has made either a substantial beginning of the manufacture of the goods or commitments for their procurement, and the goods are to be specially manufactured for the buyer or lessee are not suitable for sale or lease to others in the ordinary course of the seller's or lessor's business, the special rule is applicable; that is, an oral contract is enforceable regardless of the amount involved. If the seller or lessor has taken no steps toward performance, however, and if the price involved is $5000 or more, or the total payments are $1000 or more in the case of a lease, the general rule applies even though the goods assertedly are to be specially made for the buyer or lessee and are not suitable for sale or lease to others in the ordinary course of the seller's or lessor's business. To illustrate: assume B orally orders for purchase 5000 calendars at one dollar each from S. The calendars are to be used for advertising purposes and are to have B's name and address and a picture of B's plant printed on the front. B repudiates four days after S accepts the offer but before S has in any way commenced performance. The agreement would be unenforceable under Section 2–201(1). On the other hand, assume B does not repudiate until the calendars have been completed but before their delivery. The agreement is enforceable under Section 2–201(3)(a). See Kalas v. Cook (2002). However, the design and manufacture of a prototype for which payment is made is not sufficient beginning of performance. Chambers Steel Engraving Corp. v. Tambrands, Inc. (1990).

c. Admission in Pleadings, Testimony or Otherwise under Oath

In a complaint, answer, or other pleading, or in a deposition, testimony or otherwise under oath, a party to an oral contract may admit making the contract. There is no reason why such an admission should not be sufficient against the party who makes it; the policy behind the statute of frauds is served.

There was much confusion in the pre-UCC cases on the question whether, under the above circumstances, an oral contract coming within the statute of frauds should be enforceable. The UCC seeks to avoid all doubt in these cases by the provisions of Sections 2–201(3)(b) and 2A–201(4)(b), which make admission in pleading or testimony equivalent to memoranda in record form (to the extent of the quantity admitted). One issue, however, is whether judgment may be rendered on pleadings which show a failure to meet the statute of frauds, or whether the matter should await the completion of discovery on the ground an admission may occur. A minority view represented by Triangle Marketing, Inc. v. Action Industries, Inc. (1986) allows judgment on the pleadings; a majority represented by Garrison v. Piatt (1966), denies judgment on the pleadings before discovery.

d. Partial Performance

Even if there is not a sufficient record, the contract may be enforceable in whole or in part on the basis of partial performance under Section 2–201(3)(c) and Section 2A–201(4)(c). Section 2–201(3)(c) declares that the acceptance of payment for, or the receipt and acceptance of, goods will make an oral sales contract, otherwise unenforceable because of the statute of frauds, enforceable "with respect to goods for which payment has been made and accepted or which have been received and accepted." To illustrate, suppose S orally contracts to sell B 5000 bushels of wheat for a price of $1 per bushel. At the time the contract is made B pays S $500. Under the UCC the contract would be enforceable only with respect to 500 bushels of wheat. Or, suppose instead of the partial payment by B, S delivers and B accepts 500 bushels of the wheat. The contract is enforceable with respect to the 500 bushels of wheat delivered.

A difficulty in the application of Section 2–201(3)(c) exists where partial payment has been made and an issue exists over whether the court can justly apportion the goods. See Official Comment 3 to Section 2–201. For example, in a case decided by a Pennsylvania county court, Williamson v. Martz (1956), the following fact situation appeared: S orally agreed to sell B two vats for a total price of $1600, of which B paid $100 at the time the contract was made. Later B repudiated the contract and refused to accept the vats or pay the balance of the price. S resold the vats at a loss of $800 and sued B for damages. B pleaded Section 2–201 as a defense, and S argued that the partial payment made the contract enforceable. The court held, however, that as a just apportionment of the goods could not be made, the contract was totally unenforceable. On the other hand, in Lockwood v. Smigel (1971), the buyer made a down payment of $100 on an $11,000 Rolls Royce. The court held the oral contract was enforceable on the basis of Section 2–201(3)(c).

The provision in Article 2A, Section 2A–201(4)(c), does not allow an accepted payment to indicate the asserted contract because in a lease rent is paid usually only for one or more months, unlike in a sale where payment is tendered in full or toward full payment for goods delivered. Official Comment 1 to Section 2A–201.

5. ESTOPPEL

There are a number of pre-UCC cases in which courts used the doctrine of estoppel to preclude a party from using the statute of frauds as a defense when there was no writing and none of the other exceptions applied. Although the courts have not been in agreement as to the circumstances which create an estoppel, the doctrine has been generally stated as follows:

> The vital principal is that he who by his language or conduct leads another to do what he would not otherwise have done shall not subject such person to loss or injury by disappointing the expectations upon which he acted. Such a change of position is sternly forbidden. It involves fraud and falsehood, and the law abhors both. (See Carpy v. Dowdell (1897)).

The application of this general principle may be illustrated by the facts in Moore v. Day (1954). There B, a broker and merchant, orally agreed to buy a quantity of beans from S, a grower, at a price that would bring the agreement within the statute of frauds. Delivery was deferred from time to time at B's request who claimed an overload and shipping difficulties. He assured S, however, that he would take the beans at the agreed price. The assurances continued for several months, and S continued to await performance. Then the price broke badly and B refused to take the beans. S sued B for damages and the latter pleaded the statute of frauds. The appellate court in affirming the trial court's judgment for S stated:

> (W)e believe the court's finding (B) was estopped from availing himself of the statute of frauds is supported by the evidence and the law ... (R)elying upon (B's) assurances, (S) refrained from selling the beans to others and altered their position to their damage and loss. Under such circumstances, the court had a right to believe that (B) was attempting to use the statute of frauds as a sword and not as a shield.

It will be noted that estoppel is not included in Section 2–201 or in Section 2A–201 as one of the exceptions to the writing requirement. Does this imply its preclusion, or is it still applicable by virtue of Section 1–103(b) which provides that, unless displaced by the particular provisions of the UCC, other principles of law and equity including the law relative to estoppel shall supplement the provisions of the UCC. A number of courts have held that the doctrine is applicable despite its omission. See, e.g., Mosekian v. Davis Canning Co. (1964). Other courts deny the exception either generally or under the facts of the case. See, e.g., Futch v. James River–Norwalk, Inc. (1989); Hoffmann v. Boone (1989).

Official Comment 2 to Section 2–201 now indicates the former court decisions are to be followed.

B. PAROL EVIDENCE

1. THE GENERAL PROBLEM

Whether required by the statute of frauds or not, a large percentage of sales transactions and an overwhelming percentage of leases are evidenced by some sort of writing or other record. If there is a record and suit is brought, a problem that may arise is whether some alleged agreement between the parties and not contained in the record may be placed in evidence. In legal parlance this is called a "parol evidence rule" problem. The policy under this rule is to exclude from consideration by the trier of fact evidence of prior or contemporaneous understandings concerning matters contained in the record when those understandings are offered for the purpose of altering or contradicting the record, and also to exclude asserted understandings not contained in the record if the parties intend the record to be a complete and exclusive final statement of their legal relationship. The theory is that all the preliminary negotiations and agreements, oral and otherwise, were superseded and merged in the record. Thus the parol evidence rule operates to protect the record as the evidence of the agreement of the parties; it does not serve to preclude evidence of fraud such as deliberate oral misrepresentations that induce a buyer or a lessee. See Thompson v. E.W. Jones, Inc. (1941).

There is some lack of clarity and consistency in the case law and discussion dealing with these problems. There are, however, things about the "rule" as to which there is agreement. Thus:

(1) Extrinsic (parol) evidence is admissible to show that the record was not intended by the parties to be a contract until the occurrence of some condition. Here the extrinsic evidence is offered not for the purpose of altering the terms of the record but to show that the record does not constitute a contract between the parties. This aspect of the analysis is consistent with the UCC. King v. Fordice (1989).

(2) Evidence of subsequent agreements between the parties, altering or even rescinding the contract in the record do not violate the parol evidence rule. Such an agreement necessarily could not have been merged into the record and is not, therefore, within the policy of the rule. See, however, Sections 2–209 and 2A–208.

(3) Extrinsic evidence is admissible to show that the record is void or voidable because of fraud, duress, illegality, unconscionability, or mistake. See the *Thompson* case noted above. See Official Comment 4 to Section 2–202.

(4) Extrinsic evidence is admissible to explain ambiguities on the face of the contract. For example, if a sales contract contains a term calling for delivery of the goods "F.O.B. Plant" and both parties own a plant, extrinsic evidence would be admissible to explain whether the parties intend-

ed the seller's or the buyer's plant. See Official Comment 5 to Section 2–202.

(5) The parol evidence rule is applicable to exclude extrinsic evidence that conflicts with a record that is final and exclusive on a matter, or, even if there is no conflict, if the record is a complete and exclusive "integration" of the agreement between the parties. An agreement is completely integrated where the parties adopt a record or records as the final, complete and exclusive expression of their agreement on a matter, or as to their entire agreement. The integration is the record or records so adopted. For example, a "sales slip" handed to a buyer with the goods in a retail sale normally would not be an integration of their agreement (but it could serve as a partial integration that is complete and exclusive as to the price). By the same token, if an alleged prior or contemporaneous agreement is not germane to the subject covered in the record, the parol evidence rule may not forbid proof of the oral understanding, even if the record otherwise is an integration. But if the oral agreement is subsidiary to, and does concern the subject of the record, even if the agreement is a consistent additional term the parol evidence rule forbids proof of the oral understanding if the record is intended as a complete and exclusive statement of the agreement.

Most of the difficulty which the courts have had with the parol evidence rule lies in determining when qualification five is applicable. With reference to what constitutes an integration, for example, some courts took the position that the record itself should be the sole criterion of whether it is a complete and final expression of the agreement between the parties. Under this view if the record is an apparently complete contractual document, prior or contemporaneous oral understandings are not admissible, if subsidiary to the record, even to supplement the record.

It should be kept in mind that whether or not the evidence is admissible is a question of law. If found admissible, it is allowed to be considered by the trier of fact, and the trier of fact is still free to believe or disbelieve the evidence.

2. UCC PROVISIONS

The UCC deals with the parol evidence rule as it relates to sales transactions in Section 2–202 which provides:

(1) Terms with respect to which the confirmatory records of the parties agree or which are otherwise set forth in a record intended by the parties as a final expression of their agreement with respect to the terms included therein may not be contradicted by evidence of any prior agreement or of a contemporaneous oral agreement but may be supplemented by evidence of:

(a) by course of performance, course of dealing, or usage of trade under Section 1–303; and

(b) consistent additional terms, unless the court finds the record was intended also as a complete and exclusive statement of the terms of the agreement.

(2) Terms in a record may be explained by evidence of course of performance, course of dealing, or usage of trade without a preliminary determination by the court that the language used is ambiguous.

Section 2A–202 reads the same in substance.

It is helpful to discuss this rule within the context of two fact situations which commonly have arisen.

The first involves a situation where the extrinsic evidence contradicts some term of the record. Assume in a dispute between S and B involving a sales transaction that S submits as evidence a record signed by both parties which among other provisions contains a term that the goods are sold "as is". B offers as evidence in oral or in record form that before the record produced by S, S expressly warranted the goods against defects for 90 days. If the court finds that the record introduced by S was intended by the parties as a final expression of their agreement with respect to warranties, B's offered evidence is not admissible. However, the agreement on warranties in the record may be supplemented by course of dealing, usage of trade and course of performance. See Official Comments 2 and 5 to Section 2–202. Compare Apple Valley Red–E–Mix, Inc. v. Mills–Winfield Engineering Sales, Inc. (1989) (lease of machine containing express warranty as to merchantability, a disclaimer of implied warranties and a merger clause precludes evidence of asserted warranty of fitness for a particular purpose) with Intercorp, Inc. v. Pennzoil Co. (1989) (parol admitted to contradict terms of extensively negotiated and signed contract where evidence indicated the writing was not intended to be a final expression of agreement).

The UCC also recognizes that the parties may have intended a record to be final on some matters but not on all. For example, a conclusion by the court that the agreement between S and B was final with respect to warranties would not preclude it from finding that the record was not intended to be final as to another term, such as time for performance. Thus evidence as to that could be admitted. Official Comments 2 and 3 to Section 2–202. The question of finality is one of law for the judge to decide. Official Comment 3 to Section 2–202. That fact situation will be taken up next. In this first fact situation, the judge should decide that the agreement submitted by S and admitted into evidence by the court was intended to be final on the warranty term, as the evidence offered by B is precluded as it admittedly preceded the evidence of S.

As to the second situation, assume that in a suit by S against B, S introduces an agreement in record form for the sale of goods signed by both parties. The agreement contains terms usual to such transactions, but is silent as to time for performance. B offers to prove a prior or contemporaneous oral agreement calling for delivery within 5 days. This problem is dealt with in Sections 2–202(1)(b) and 2A–202(1)(b). If B's proffered evidence is that of a "consistent additional term," it is admissible, unless the record produced by S was intended by the parties as a "complete and exclusive statement" of all the terms of the agreement. The basic question is whether the record was intended to be complete and exclusive. However, an initial difficulty lies in determining the meaning of the word "term(s)"; does it refer only to terms appearing in the record? It is recognized that terms can be implied even though the record is silent on the matter. For example, nothing more appearing, here it would be implied from the record that S and B intended for performance to take place within a reasonable time. See Section 2–309 and Official Comment 1. Accordingly, it could be argued that performance within a reasonable time is a term of the record and thus the asserted oral agreement setting a specific time is contradictory (unless it could be argued as explanatory of what the parties considered reasonable). Some authority seems to support the theory that the word "terms" as used in Section 2–202 (and thus by implication in Section 2A–202) means those in the record and not those that could be implied. In Hunt Foods & Industries, Inc. v. Doliner (1966), for example, the court stated: "To be inconsistent the term must contradict or negate a term of the writing. A term or condition which has a lesser effect is provable." On the other hand, see Alaska Northern Dev., Inc. v. Alyeska Pipeline Service Co. (1983). On the basis of the *Hunt Foods* authority it would seem that the oral evidence offered by B is evidence of a "consistent additional" term. Official Comment 3 to

Section 2–202, indicating evidence of terms that certainly would have appeared in the record should be excluded, arguably does not contradict this conclusion, given the above analysis. See Anderson & Nafziger v. G.T. Newcomb, Inc. (1979). In your author's opinion, the agreement should be considered to include both express and implied terms (see Section 1–201(b)(3)), but the evidence should be admissible to show what the parties considered as reasonable.

A basic question is, was the record produced by S intended by the parties to be a "complete and exclusive statement of all the terms." If so, B's extrinsic evidence is inadmissible even though the oral agreement concerns a consistent term. How does a court determine the intention of the parties on this question? Is there a presumption that a record apparently complete as a contract was intended as a total integration and the judge should not look beyond the four corners of the writing to determine the intention of the parties? Sections 2–202 and 2A–202 should be interpreted to reject this so-called "four corners" rule. See Official Comment 3 to Section 2–202, and Michael Schiavone & Sons, Inc. v. Securalloy Co. (1970).

Since Sections 2–202 and 2A–202 reject the four corners test, what evidence might be relevant in determining whether the record is intended as an integration? As the court in Whirlpool Corp. v. Regis Leasing Corp. (1968) put it, the more complete a record appears to be on its face, the less likely it is that any extrinsic term was agreed upon, even if consistent with the record. But what of a "bare-bones" memorandum? In Conner v. May (1969), S and B signed the following agreement of sale:

> Bought approximately 222 angus yearling steers for delivery April 24 to May (buyer's option) with unmerchantables out and 5% cut of need with 3% shrinkage weighed at railroad pens at 24½¢. At part payment of $2250.00 will be deducted off total price.

At time for delivery, B inspected and rejected the cattle because they had been fed improperly by S after the agreement was signed. In a suit by B against S for damages, the trial judge allowed B to testify that S made an oral promise the first time B saw the steers to continue them on the same feed until delivery. B further testified that at the time the agreement was signed he pointed out that the feeding term was not included (S denied making the oral promise). B also testified that he and S intended for the sale agreement to include only "the meat of the contract" so that if either got killed "our folks can settle it." On the other hand, an experienced cattle dealer testified that the feeding term is always the first thing discussed in cattle transactions, and if agreed on and whether written or oral is always understood to be a part of the contract. But he also stated that many terms in cattle sales contracts are not written. The trial court allowed all of this testimony to go to the jury, and it returned a verdict for B. S on appeal contended that all the testimony concerning the oral feeding agreement should have been excluded as violative of the parol evidence rule. In affirming, the appellate court stated that the evidence showed that agreements concerning the manner of feeding steers were commonly oral and collateral to any writing between the parties; therefore, the oral feeding term was not one which "certainly would have been included in the writing."

Often the record will include a merger clause; that is, a clause that states that the record is intended as a complete and exclusive statement of the terms of the agreement. Sections 2–202 and 2A–202 do not deal with the evidentiary strength of a merger clause; that determination depends on the particular circumstances of the case. Official Comment 3 to Section 2–202.

Evidence of course of dealing, usage of trade, and course of performance is admissible to explain the record even though the court finds the record to be unambiguous and to be a complete and exclusive statement of the agreement. Thus, the so-called "plain meaning rule" is rejected to this extent. Course of dealing, usage of trade, and course of performance are discussed in Chapter 4. Such evidence gives meaning to the words used in the record. For example, in Decker Steel Co. v. Exchange Nat. Bank (1964), the court admitted evidence of a trade usage to show that the words "thirty-six inch steel" had acquired a special meaning which allowed delivery of thirty-seven inch steel. The premise is that the record must be read on the assumption that the course of prior dealings between the parties and the usages of trade were taken for granted when the document was phrased. Course of performance is considered the best indication of what the parties intended in the record for it shows how they themselves have interpreted the words used. Section 1–303. The record itself should be able to negate course of dealing, usage of trade and course of performance, if this intention is clearly expressed. Section 1–303(e) (and see Official Comment 2 to Section 2–202). Nevertheless, evidence of course of performance may be admissible to show modification or waiver of an inconsistent term in the record. Section 1–303(f).

Issues of interpretation generally are left to the courts. However, the statute takes no position, other than with respect to evidence of course of performance, course of dealing, or usage of trade, whether any a preliminary determination of ambiguity is a condition to the admissibility of evidence drawn from any other source. Official Comment 5 to Section 2–202.

C.   MODIFICATION

1.   THE GENERAL PROBLEM

In Western Lithograph Co. v. Vanomar Producers (1921), S agreed in a written contract to sell B at specified prices all the can labels which the latter might need in its business during the next five years. During the first year, 1916, the contract was performed at the specified prices; however, at the middle of the following year S requested a flat increase of thirty-five cents per thousand on the contract prices because of increasing labor and material costs. B assented to the proposed increase and paid the higher price for subsequent deliveries during 1917. In 1918 all requested deliveries were made but not paid for in full. The unpaid balance amounted to $6700 at the original contract prices and to $9400 at the increased prices. S brought suit for $9400 and B denied liability for any amount over $6700.

The trial court entered judgment for S in the amount of $9400 but the appellate court set aside the judgment on the ground that B's promise to pay the higher prices was not supported by consideration; S was already legally obligated to deliver the labels at the original prices, and therefore suffered no legal detriment in return for B's promise to pay the higher prices.

In contrast, in Schwartzreich v. Bauman–Basch, Inc. (1921), the defendant, on August 31, 1917, in a written contract agreed to employ the plaintiff for twelve months beginning November 22, 1917, at a salary of $90 per week. In October the plaintiff was offered a similar job at higher pay by another company. When informed by the plaintiff that he was considering acceptance of this new offer, the defendant company agreed to pay the plaintiff $100 per week rather than lose his services. The parties prepared and signed a new contract identical with the old one except for the salary, and then tore the signatures from the old contract. In November, as agreed in the contract, plaintiff began to work for defendant, but was discharged in December. Plaintiff brought suit for damages and the question arose whether his damages should be based on the old or new rate of compensation. The court held that damages should be based on the salary of $100 per week stipulated in the new agreement. This was based on the conclusion that the old contract had been terminated by mutual assent, thereby freeing plaintiff from his legal obligation to work for defendant at a salary of $90 per week; thus there was a consideration for defendant's subsequent promise to pay a salary of $100 per week since plaintiff, no longer legally obligated to work for $90, suffered a legal detriment by promising to work for $100 per week.

At common law the distinction between these two cases is that in the first, the parties attempted to change a term of the contract by simply modifying the original contract, while in the second case they sought to change a term by rescinding the original contract and substituting a new contract exactly like the early one except for the salary. If the modification method is used there must be a new and independent consideration for the promise to pay a higher price or wage. On the other hand, if the rescission method is used, the promisee, freed of the old obligation, gives consideration by once again undertaking the same obligation. Obviously this reasoning is somewhat tenuous and formalistic.

A subsidiary problem which may arise when the intent to abrogate the old contract is not so clear is whether the parties did in fact rescind the old contract; that is, was their subsequent agreement a new contract or merely a modification of the existing one? For example, see San Gabriel Val. Ready–Mixt v. Casillas (1956).

2.   UCC PROVISIONS

Section 2–209 provides that:

(1) An agreement modifying a contract within this article needs no consideration to be binding.

(2) An agreement in a signed record that excludes modification or rescission except by a signed record may not be otherwise modified or rescinded, but, except as between merchants, such a requirement in a form record supplied by the merchant must be separately signed by the other party.

(3) The requirements of Section 2–201 must be satisfied if the contract as modified is within its provisions.

(4) An attempt at modification or rescission which does not satisfy the requirements of subsection (b) or (c) can operate as a waiver.

(5) A party that has made a waiver affecting an executory portion of a contract may retract the waiver by reasonable notification received by the other party that strict performance will be required of any term waived, unless the retraction would be unjust in view of a material change of position in reliance on the waiver.

Under Section 2–209, the result in the *Western Lithograph* case would not depend on whether there was consideration for B's promise. Assuming the requirements of good faith and the statute of frauds (both discussed below) are met, B would be obligated to pay the higher price.

Section 2A–208 is the same for leases, except that it deletes subsection (3) on the basis that it is unfair to allow an oral modification to make the entire lease contract unenforceable if, for example, the modification takes it a few dollars over the dollar limit but, at the same time, it is not uniformly sensible to make the contract still enforceable in its pre-modification state. Thus Article 2A leaves this issue to resolution on a case by case basis. Official Comment to Section 2A–208. As will be seen, this may be a wise course since the application of Section 2–209(3) is less than clear.

3.   GOOD FAITH

The fact that modification agreements are enforceable without the control produced by the need for consideration might encourage an unscrupulous party to resort to tactics illustrated by the following example: S contracts to sell B certain described goods at a price of $2 per unit. A short time before the goods are to be delivered, S, who knows that the market supply of such goods is limited and that B is not likely to resort to litigation, threatens not to deliver the goods unless B agrees to pay $2.25 per unit. B, of course, may refuse to pay the higher price and insist on performance; if S refuses to perform B may sue for damages. Litigation, however, is at best unsatisfactory; the time and expense involved often do not make it worthwhile. Therefore, if the goods are needed badly, B probably will agree to pay the higher price.

Official Comment 2 to Section 2–209 explains that to discourage such attempts to extort a modification agreement, modifications must meet the test of good faith to be effective. Even technical consideration will not insulate a bad faith modification. "Good faith means honesty in fact and the observance of reasonable commercial standards of fair dealing." Sections 1–201(b)(20), 2–103(1)(j), and 2A–103(1)(m). To meet the test there should be some objectively demonstrable reason for seeking a modification. Changing market conditions may provide sufficient reason for requesting modification, although they may not be sufficient to discharge a party from the duty of performance. Official Comment 2 to Section 2–209.

4. MODIFICATION AND THE STATUTE OF FRAUDS

Certain formalities must be met in modifying some contracts. Sections 2–209(2) and 2A–208(2) allow the parties to write their own statute of frauds into the contract. If there is a written agreement signed by the parties excluding oral modification (or rescission, including abandonment or other change by mutual consent, but not including unilateral termination or cancellation according to Official Comment 3 to Section 2–209), the contract can only be modified by agreement in a record, provided, if the form is supplied by a merchant to a non-merchant, such a requirement was separately signed by the non-merchant party. Section 2–209(3) for sales also requires modification in record form if the contract "as modified" is within the provisions of Section 2–201 (the statute of frauds). If so, the requirements of that section must be met.

The exact meaning of Section 2–209(3) is not clear when applied to different fact situations. Consider the following cases:

(1) S and B have a written contract for the sale of goods at a price of $6000. They agree to reduce the price to $5000.

(2) S and B have a contract (oral or written) for the sale of goods at a price of $4000. They agree to increase the price to $5000.

(3) S and B have a written contract for the sale of goods at a price of $5000. They agree to reduce the price to $4000.

(4) S and B have a written contract for the sale of goods at a price of $5000, calling for delivery within 30 days. They agree to reduce the delivery time to 15 days.

It seems fairly clear that the modifying agreements in cases (1) and (2) should require a record or come within one of the exceptions articulated in Section 2–201. The answer to cases (3) and (4) is not as clear. One court has held that Section 2–201 applies to a situation similar to case (4). Asco Mining Co. v. Gross Contracting Co. (1965). As discussed below an attempted modification not meeting the requirements for a modification may constitute a waiver. One court has held that such a waiver includes waiving the requirement of a record itself. Double–E Sportswear Corp. v. Girard Trust Bank (1973).

5.   MODIFICATION AND WAIVER

Some problems which may arise under Section 2–209 or Section 2A–208 will require a court to distinguish between a modification agreement and a waiver. Suppose, for example, S contracts to sell B five carloads of ore, one carload to be shipped on the first day of each succeeding month. After the contract is made, S requests B to accept the shipments as late as the fifteenth of each month, and B assents. A short time later, and before S has in any way changed position on the later date, B insists that deliveries be made by the first day of each month. If B's agreement to accept deliveries effects a modification and the good faith and statute of frauds requirements are met, B is legally bound by the agreement and may not revoke it. On the other hand, if the agreement is no more than a waiver of the earlier delivery date, it may be revoked and delivery by the first of each month may be insisted upon "unless the retraction would be unjust in view of a material change of position in reliance on the waiver." Section 2–209(5) and Section 2A–208(4).

The concept of "waiver" is used in different ways by the Code. Under Section 1–306, a waiver can relate to the past; any claim or right arising out of an alleged breach can be discharged by agreement of the aggrieved party in an authenticated record without consideration (or orally with consideration—see Official Comment to Section 1–306). Thus there can be, for example, an effective waiver of the right to reject, and also of the right of revocation of acceptance for defective goods. Any claim for damages may also be waived.

Some of the most difficult problems arise, however, when the waiver affects an executory portion of the contract, as in the case above where B agrees to accept deliveries as late as the fifteenth of each month. Usually, under pre-UCC law it was held that B's agreement was retractable unless supported by consideration or unless there was an estoppel due to reliance in a substantial way on the promise by the other party. Normally if the promise was supported by consideration it would have been called an agreement to modify and, if not supported by consideration, a waiver. Since Section 2–209 and Section 2A–208 provide that in contracts consideration is no longer necessary to make agreements to modify legally enforceable, the chief pre-UCC distinguishing feature between waivers and modification agreements has been abolished. As used in Section 2–209 and Section 2A–208, "waiver" would include "an attempt at modification" which does not meet the requirements of Section 2–209(2) or (3), or of Section 2A–209(2). Thus, suppose S and B have a written contract for the sale of goods at a price of $6000, and orally agree later to reduce the price to $5000. Evidently the oral evidence would be admissible if B has alleged that the subsequent conduct of the parties constituted a waiver of $1000 of the price.

CHAPTER 4

TERMS OF THE CONTRACT

---

1.   INTRODUCTION

The basic question to be answered when a problem arises concerning a sale or a lease contract is, "what is the agreement between the parties." The reason is Articles 2 and 2A largely allow the parties to contract for their own rules. Preliminarily, answering the question of what the contract contains necessitates ascertaining the "agreement" between the parties. The UCC defines "agreement" in Section 1–201(b)(3) as follows:

"Agreement," as distinguished from "contract," means the bargain of the parties in fact, as found in their language or inferred from other circumstances, including course of performance, course of dealing, or usage of trade as provided in Section 1–303.

However, a further step then is necessary, and that is to determine if the "contract" is the same as the "agreement."

"Contract" is defined in Section 1–201(b)(12) as:

"Contract," as distinguished from "agreement," means the total legal obligation that results from the parties' agreement as determined by the Uniform Commercial Code as supplemented by any other applicable laws.

Thus what the parties in fact do helps to determine their agreement. What they say, what they don't say, and what they or others have done in the current and in former transactions may be relevant in determining the content (terms) of their agreement. On the other hand, only that part of the agreement which is legally enforceable constitutes the contract. One or more of the terms or all of the agreement may be unenforceable, and, therefore, non-contractual. And the law may impose certain obligations or grant certain rights based on the agreement that also become part of the contract.

2.   EXPRESS TERMS

It is common for the parties to an agreement to agree expressly on many of the terms of the contract. Certainly this is true for the negotiated terms such as price, quantity, the description of the goods, delivery, and so on. It is also true as to non-negotiated and run of the mine boiler plate for which agreement may be inferred. However, it can be argued that non-negotiated terms that produce unfair surprise are not part of the agreement. See R. Nordstrom, Law of Sales, 276 (West 1970). The same result may perhaps be more appropriately reached through the doctrine of unconscionability discussed later in this chapter.

In general, the parties are free to agree to terms as they see fit. Freedom of contract is the rule, not the exception under Articles 2 and 2A. This policy is declared in Section 1–103(a)(2), and is implemented in Section 1–302 of the UCC, as follows:

(a) Except as otherwise provided in subsection (b) or elsewhere in the Uniform Commercial Code, the effect of provisions of the Uniform Commercial Code may be varied by agreement.

(b) The obligations of good faith, diligence, reasonableness, and care prescribed by the Uniform Commercial Code may not be disclaimed by agreement. The parties, by agreement, may determine the standards by which the performance of those obligations is to be measured if such standards are not manifestly unreasonable. Whenever the Uniform Commercial Code requires an action to be taken within a reasonable time, a time that is not manifestly unreasonable may be fixed by agreement.

(c) The presence in certain provisions of the Uniform Commercial Code of the phrase "unless otherwise agreed," or words of similar import, does not imply that the effect of other provisions may not be varied by agreement under this section.

Application of this general rule in Articles 2 and 2A can be simplified by dividing the applicable UCC provisions into four categories. One category consists of those provisions which expressly state that they may be varied by agreement. The risk of loss provisions found in Section 2–509 are a good example of this category. Section 2–509(4) states in pertinent part: "This section is subject to contrary agreement of the parties...." This provision was not incorporated in the risk of loss provision for Article 2A, Section 2A–219, as it was believed to be unnecessary given Section 1–302. Most provisions falling within this category contain the phrase "unless otherwise agreed" or similar language. Such sections include Sections 2–401, 2–511, 2A–217, 2A–501 and 2A–502.

A second category are those provisions which expressly provide that their effect cannot be varied by agreement of the parties. The obligation of good faith imposed by Section 1–304 is such a provision. Section 1–302(b). See also Sections 2–316(1) 2–318, 2–719(3), 2A–106, 2A–214(1), 2A–216, and 2A–503(3). Some provisions of Sections 2–316 and 2A–214 fall into a third category. Those provisions allow the parties by agreement to disclaim implied warranties but, to do so, the language used must conform with the standards set out in those sections. Just any language will not suffice.

The fourth category includes the largest number of provisions and encompasses those provisions which do not expressly provide whether or not their effect may be varied by agreement. It is made clear by the language of Section 1–302(c) that the mere absence of the phrase "unless otherwise agreed" in a provision does not imply that its effect cannot be varied by agreement; this obviously indicates that most provisions in this group are variable. See Official Comment 3 to Section 1–302. Some are not, however, based on the Official Comments. For example, Official Comment 1 to Section 2A–209 indicates the extension of the supplier's promises and warranties to a finance lessee cannot be limited or excluded in a discriminatory manner, i.e., exclusion of the supplier's liability to the lessee with respect to warranties made to the lessor. By the same token, Official Comment 1 to Section 1–302 explains that while the text of Section 2–201, the statute of frauds section, is silent on the question of an oral waiver of the record requirement, the policy implicitly forbids such a waiver as part of the "contract" made unenforceable. Another example is Sections 2–302 and 2A–108, the unconscionable contract or clause sections.

3. COURSE OF PERFORMANCE, COURSE OF DEALING, AND USAGE OF TRADE

Beyond the express terms of the agreement of the parties as found in their language, course of performance, course of dealing, and usage of trade are relevant sources in determining the terms of the agreement between the parties.

a. Course of Performance

"Course of performance" is defined in Section 1–303(a) as follows:

(a) A "course of performance" is a sequence of conduct between the parties to a particular transaction that exists if:

(1) the agreement of the parties with respect to the transaction involves repeated occasions for performance by a party; and

(2) the other party, with knowledge of the nature of the performance and opportunity for objection to it, accepts the performance or acquiesces in it without objection.

It is clear from the language that this provision only applies when the contract calls for more than one performance. "Repeated occasions for performance" are required. An installment contract is the typical contract calling for more than one performance. Suppose, for example, that a contract calls for the delivery of goods in 24 installments, F.O.B. Seller's City. This would normally mean that B is obligated to pay the freight (former Section 2–319, so stating, is repealed as inconsistent with modern commercial practice, but such still is the common understanding of the F.O.B. term). S's payment of the freight on the first installment would not constitute a course of performance. Finally, for the course of conduct to be legally chargeable against a party, the party must have had knowledge of it, and have accepted or acquiesced in it without objection. Express assent is not required.

Assuming there is sufficient evidence of repeated occasions of conduct to constitute a course of performance, this only means the evidence is admissible. It still may not be accepted by the trier of fact as controlling the meaning of the contract. For example, suppose S contracts to deliver goods in 24 installments, F.O.B. Seller's City. Normally, as stated above, B would be obligated to pay the freight. S, however, pays the freight on the first 12 installments, but refuses to do so on subsequent deliveries. Assuming S's conduct is sufficient to show a course of performance, it is admissible; however, S may have some explanation. S might produce evidence of an agreement made subsequent to the contract in which S agreed to pay the freight on the first twelve installments in return for some concession by B, but with the understanding that B would remain responsible for freight on all remaining deliveries. See Section 1–303(d) and (e).

b. Course of Dealing

"Course of dealing" is defined in Section 1–303(b) as follows:

(b) A "course of dealing" is a sequence of conduct concerning previous transactions between the parties to a particular transaction that is fairly to be regarded as establishing a common basis of understanding for interpreting their expressions and other conduct.

While course of dealing is quite similar to course of performance, the former refers to a sequence of conduct prior to the time the agreement in question is entered into and the latter refers to a sequence of conduct under the agreement in question.

A sequence of previous conduct in order to be admissible as a course of dealing must be that which "is fairly to be regarded as establishing a common basis of understanding for interpreting their expressions and other conduct." Suppose, for example, that S contracts to sell and deliver to B 31,000 tons of phosphate each year for three years. The contract states the price per ton but is silent about adjusting prices and quantities to reflect a declining market. Phosphate prices soon plunge precipitously. B, unable to resell the phosphate at a competitive price, offers to take it at the current market price. S refuses and sues for breach of contract. B seeks to introduce evidence of its business dealing with S over a six year period preceding the current contract, showing that in periods of a declining market there had been repeated and substantial deviations from the amounts and prices stated in the written contracts between the parties. This evidence should be admissible as being relevant in establishing "a common basis of understanding for interpreting" their current contract. See Columbia Nitrogen Corp. v. Royster Co. (1971).

c.   Usage of Trade

Usage of trade is another type of extrinsic evidence which is admissible to determine the meaning of the agreement between the parties. Section 1–303(c) in part provides:

(c) A "usage of trade" is any practice or method of dealing having such regularity of observance in a place, vocation, or trade as to justify an expectation that it will be observed with respect to the transaction in question.

Official Comment 4 explains that admissibility of evidence showing a usage of trade should not be subject to the same stringent requirements as those applicable to the proof of "custom." At common law, the courts generally required, among other things, that a custom be well known, ancient, universal and certain. The UCC only requires that usage of trade have "regularity of observance" at the place or places of contracting, in the trade, or in the vocation involved. Usage embodied in a trade code will qualify. It is not even necessary that the usage be general to the trade. It may be particular to a special branch of the trade. Official Comment 6 to Section 1–303.

Official Comment 5 to Section 1–303 explains that a usage of trade must meet the test of conscionability under Section 2–302 and that this requirement carries forward the policy underlying the common law requirement that a custom be reasonable. In other words, Section 2–302 applies to implicit as well as explicit terms. For example, a dishonest or harsh practice such as that of setting back the odometers on used cars would not be recognized.

d. Legal Effect

Assuming any of the three types of extrinsic evidence discussed above is admissible, what are the possible legal effects on the terms of the agreement? First, the evidence may help to clarify the meaning of words in the agreement. Some pre-UCC cases held that extrinsic evidence was not admissible to explain or supplement a written contract unless the court found the writing ambiguous. The UCC reflects a more liberal policy. Sections 2–202 and 2A–202 explain that course of performance, course of dealing, or usage of trade may be used to supplement or explain the record of the agreement and there is no requirement of ambiguity. See Section 1–303(d), Official Comment 3 to Section 1–303; and Sections 2–202 and 2A–202. This means that extrinsic evidence is admissible to show a meaning for the words used in the agreement which may be contrary to the ordinary lay meaning of such words. Thus, a term calling for delivery of "steers not weighing over 625 pounds" may be qualified by a trade usage allowing for tender of steers averaging 625 pounds or less. See Major v. Bishop (1972). Suppose further, for example, that S contracts to sell B a certain quantity of "U.S. Fresh Frozen Chicken." Evidence would be admissible to show that the word "chicken" by course of performance, course of dealing, or trade usage meant "young chicken." That is, chicken suitable for broiling, frying or roasting but not for stewing. See Frigaliment Importing Co. v. B.N.S. Intern. Sales Corp. (1960).

Second, extrinsic evidence of course of dealing or usage of trade may add a term which is not in a record. Sections 2–314(3) and 2A–212(3), for example, state that implied warranties other than those stipulated in the UCC may arise from a course of dealing or usage of trade.

Third, evidence of course of performance or dealing or usage of trade may qualify a term which would otherwise be implied. A contract calling for S to sell B cattle would normally carry implied warranties; however, extrinsic evidence of course of performance, course of dealing or usage of trade would be admissible to exclude or modify the obligation of S. Sections 2–316(7) and 2A–214(7).

In some instances, there may be an apparent or actual conflict between the express terms of the agreement and proffered extrinsic evidence. Section 1–303(d) provides in part:

(d) . . . the express terms of an agreement and an applicable course of performance, course of dealing, or usage of trade must be construed whenever reasonable as consistent with each other. If such a construction is unreasonable:

(1) express terms prevail over course of performance, course of dealing, and usage of trade;

(2) course of performance prevails over course of dealing and usage of trade; and

(3) course of dealing prevails over usage of trade.

Even when there is a conflict with an express term, a course of performance may evidence an intention by the parties to waive or modify the written term. Section 1–303(f) provides that, subject to Section 2–209 (the statute should include Section 2A–208 as well) course of performance is relevant to show a waiver or modification of any term inconsistent with such course of performance.

4. OPEN PRICE AND OTHER TERMS

Because of the way contracts for the sale of goods often are formed through the exchange of forms as previously discussed, matters that would normally be covered in an agreement may inadvertently be overlooked and be left uncovered. This may also occur in a lease, although it is less likely because lease transactions seldom are formed through an exchange of forms. Where an important term is left open, the contract may fail for indefiniteness, unless some method to supply the missing term exists. The UCC seeks to avoid this result in both the sale and lease context by providing in Sections 2–204(3) and 2A–204(3) that although one or more terms are left open, a contract will not fail for indefiniteness if the parties have intended to make a contract and there is a reasonably certain basis for giving an appropriate remedy. Article 2 also attempts to avoid the consequence of an open term by providing statutory "gap-fillers." Because this problem is of a lesser nature in lease transactions, such provisions largely are absent in Article 2A. Nonetheless, as the Official Comment 3 to Section 2–204 notes, commercial standards on the point of indefiniteness are intended to be applied, and consequently Section 2A–204(3) should furnish in the lease context all the general authority a court may need to salvage the occasional lease with an open term or two, provided the parties intended to conclude a binding agreement.

The price term perhaps is the most material part of any sales contract. Hence, if the parties do not intend to be bound unless they agree on a price, they have not contracted; or, as it is commonly stated in the cases, "the agreement is void for indefiniteness." Section 2–305(4). This does not mean, however, that the parties must expressly agree on a price. Often the price term is supplied by implication. For example, suppose B, a retail grocer, calls S, a wholesaler, and says "Send me one hundred bushels of No. 1 Idaho potatoes today," and S replies "O.K." and immediately sends a truck to B's store with the potatoes. There is no doubt that the parties intend a contract to buy and sell the potatoes even though nothing has been said about the price. The price is supplied by implication; the price is a reasonable price at the time for delivery. Section 2–305(1). While no explicit provision like Section 2–305(1) appears in Article 2A, under similar circumstances and in accordance with Section 2A–

204(3), a court should supply a reasonable rent at the time the lease becomes enforceable. The same should be true generally speaking in the other situations discussed hereafter in relation to sales contracts.

Usually the parties to a sale expressly agree on price at the time the contract is made; however, in many circumstances a rigid contract price may be too risky. The market is full of uncertainties; therefore, in order to avoid these risks the parties may leave the price term open. UCC Section 2–305 contains the following provisions regarding such cases:

(1) The parties if they so intend can conclude a contract for sale even if the price is not settled. In such a case the price is a reasonable price at the time for delivery if:

(a) nothing is said as to price; or

(b) the price is left to be agreed upon by the parties and they fail to agree; or

(c) the price is to be fixed in terms of some agreed market or other standard as set or recorded by a third person or agency and it is not so set or recorded.

(2) A price to be fixed by the seller or by the buyer means a price to be fixed in good faith.

(3) When a price left to be fixed otherwise than by agreement of the parties fails to be fixed through fault of one party, the other party may at the party's option treat the contract as cancelled or the party may fix a reasonable price.

Thus, Section 2–305 recognizes that the price term may be left open in any one of the following situations:

(1) price is not mentioned, as discussed above;

(2) the price is left to be agreed on later by the parties and no agreement occurs;

(3) the price is to be set by a third party pursuant to some market or other standard and it is not set; or

(4) the price is to be set later by the seller or buyer in good faith and it is not so set.

If the agreement between the parties says nothing about price but is complete in all other respects, it is enforceable and does not fail for indefiniteness as the price is to be a reasonable price at the time for delivery. Unless otherwise indicated by the agreement, the normal intention of the parties is to conclude a contract despite their silence as to price.

When the parties agree that the price is to be later agreed upon by them, there is no problem if they in fact later agree. The difficulty lies in those situations where they cannot agree. If the parties intend to conclude a contract, their subsequent failure to agree on a price again does not cause the bargain to fail for indefiniteness. Again, the price is a reasonable one at the time for delivery.

In some cases the parties agree that the price is to be fixed by a third person or agency. If the chosen party acts and selects a price there is no problem. Generally, the selected price is held to be binding in the absence of fraud or mistake. If the valuation is not set or recorded by the third party, at common law the bargain failed for indefiniteness. Under the UCC, if the failure to set or record the price is not the fault of either party, and the parties intended to be bound despite the third party's failure to set the price, the bargain does not fail and the price is a reasonable one at the time of delivery. To illustrate, suppose the contract is for 300 bales of cotton of a specified grade with the price to be the closing price for that grade set by the New Orleans Cotton Exchange on the day the cotton is to be delivered. However, on that date the Cotton Exchange is closed because of a hurricane and no prices are set. The price is a reasonable one at the time of delivery.

Official Comment 4 to Section 2–305 discusses further in what cases this provision should apply, and when it should not as the parties would not intend to be bound despite the failure to set the price since the particular person's judgment was a condition to the contract. Thus, for example, if the contract were for the sale of a Van Gogh painting with the price to be set by an art dealer trusted by both parties who dies before the price is set, the agreement may be viewed as not attaining contract status at all since the dealer was chosen not merely as a barometer or index of a fair price.

Should the third party's failure to set the price result from the fault of one of the parties to the contract, UCC Section 2–305(3) gives the other party the option either to treat the interference as a repudiation and cancel the contract or to itself fix a reasonable price. Thus, suppose, for example, S and B agree to buy and sell a certain quantity of wheat at a price to be set by C. If B later decides it doesn't want the wheat and induces C not to set a price, S may either cancel the contract or set a reasonable price.

If the parties leave the price term open to be fixed later by either of them, there is no problem if the price is set fairly by the party indicated or is set and consented to by the other party. The difficulty most often arises when the party to set the price refuses to do so and repudiates the bargain, or the other party repudiates the bargain before the price is set. According to pre-UCC authority, in that case the bargain is void for indefiniteness since an essential term is left to the sole determination of one of the parties who might set any price. In Weston Paper Mfg. Co. v. Downing Box Co. (1923), for example, the parties made a contract for the sale of 900 tons of strawboard to be shipped at the rate of 75 tons per month during 1921. The price was to be fixed by the seller in advance for each quarter-year, and was to be "seller's market price then existing under the seller's standard form of quarterly fixing contract." Several deliveries were made after which the buyer refused to accept any more deliveries, claiming the agreement was not binding because of the price term. The court held that the executory part of the agreement was void for indefiniteness, although with respect to the goods already accepted the buyer was liable for the price determined by the standard named in the agreement.

The UCC rejects this result and takes the position that any price to be fixed by either party "means a price to be fixed in good faith." Official Comment 3 to Section 2–305 indicates that "good faith includes observance of reasonable commercial standards of fair dealing, but in the normal case 'posted price' or a future seller's or buyer's 'given price,' 'price in effect,' 'market price' or the like satisfies the good faith requirement." In the above case, under the UCC the buyer would not be able to escape the executory part of the bargain. If, in the same case, the seller had wrongfully refused to set the price, thereby seeking to avoid the bargain, Section 2–305(3) controls, and the buyer may either cancel the agreement or set a reasonable price itself.

There may be terms other than price which also are left open by the parties who intend a contract nonetheless. This may occur when the express agreement is silent and there is no applicable usage of trade, course of dealing, or course of performance. Various provisions of Article 2 may supply the missing terms in such cases. See Official Comment 3 to Section 2–204. Under the comparable provision in Article 2A, Section 2A–204(3), even though Article 2A generally does not contain such "gap-filling" provisions, the appropriate commercial standards on the point of indefiniteness may be used by the court to complete the agreement. Most of the Article 2 "gap-filler" provisions are discussed elsewhere and only a listing is given here. It must be emphasized that the parties may vary these provisions by agreement; they apply only when the agreement is silent.

(a) place for delivery: Section 2–308.

(b) time for delivery: Section 2–309.

(c) time and place for payment: Section 2–310.

(d) passage of title: Section 2–401 (irrelevant for leases, see Section 2A–302).

(e) manner of identification: Section 2–501 (see Section 2A–217).

(f) tender by seller: Sections 2–503, 2–504.

(g) risk of loss: Section 2–509 (see Section 2A–219).

While not a gap filler in the same sense, Section 2–306 serves a similar function to legislatively define obligations within the generality of an output or requirements contract. Thus Section 2–306(a) specifies the output of the seller or the requirements of the buyer will mean the actual output or requirements as may occur in good faith, excluding a quantity unreasonably disproportionate to any estimate or, absent estimate, to any normal or otherwise comparable precedent. Section 2–306(2) also imposes within a contract for exclusive dealing a best efforts obligation. Whether a buyer of a business is bound is determined by other law but, if so, the sale itself is not grounds for sudden expansion or decrease. Official Comment 4 to Section 2–306.

5.   UNCONSCIONABLE TERMS

a.   **Introduction**

Under Articles 2 and 2A, the parties are generally free to agree to what terms they wish. Section 1–302. The principle counter balances on this freedom are the general and specific duties to perform or enforce the contract in good faith (Section 1–304), various specific provisions such as Sections 2–305, 2–306 and 2A–109, and the power of a court to refuse to enforce an unconscionable contract or clause of a contract as stated in Sections 2–302 and 2A–108. Section 2–302 provides:

(1) If the court as a matter of law finds a contract or any term of the contract to have been unconscionable at the time it was made, the court may refuse to enforce the contract, enforce the remainder of the contract without the unconscionable term, or so limit the application of the term as to avoid an unconscionable result.

(2) If it is claimed or appears to the court that a contract or any term thereof may be unconscionable, the parties must be afforded a reasonable opportunity to present evidence as to its commercial setting, purpose, and effect to aid the court in making the determination.

Section 2A–108 is the same, except that for consumer leases, as defined in Section 2A–103(1)(f) (a lease by a person regularly engaged in the business of leasing or selling makes to an individual who leases or contracts to lease goods primarily for a personal, family or household purpose), unconscionable inducement and enforcement also are covered, and a successful litigant may recover attorney's fees as well as be awarded appropriate relief sought. The Official Comment to Section 2A–108 illustrates a possible application of these additional provisions: inducement by a statement with the intent to invoke an integration clause should the lessee assert reliance upon the statement, and enforcement by using or threatening to use force or violence.

Certain observations concerning these sections are in order. First, the question of unconscionability is one of law for the judge. See Official Comment 3 to Section 2–302. A purpose is to build a body of case law interpretation as to what constitutes unconscionability. Second, it must be shown that the contract or term was unconscionable at the time of contracting; later unconscionability in the application of a term is theoretically not sufficient. See Lecates v. Hertrich Pontiac Buick Co. (1986). However, while the court in Kentucky West Virginia Gas Co. v. Interstate Natural Gas Co. (2000) agreed, it also stated § 1–103 allows a court to supplement the UCC and the court affirmed reformation of the contract on a charge of subsequent unconscionability. Third, the setting, purpose and effect of the contract or term are relevant in the determination of unconscionability. Fourth, the court, after a finding of unconscionability as to the contract or term, has three choices: (1) it may refuse to enforce the entire contract if it finds that unconscionability pervades the whole contract; (2) it may refuse to enforce the offending term or terms and enforce the remainder of the contract; and (3) it may so limit the application of the offending term as to avoid an unconscionable result. In the case of inducement or enforcement, the court may grant appropriate relief. Use of the doctrine by the victim of an unconscionable bargain to obtain damages generally does not seem to be within the purview of the section, however. Best v. United States Nat. Bank (1986) and Mitchell v. Ford Motor Credit (1998). But see Langemeier v. National Oats Co., Inc. (1985) (no error in awarding damages for breach of contract where enforcement of contract without the unconscionable clause led to that result).

b. Historical and Commercial Setting

The right of courts to refuse to enforce all the terms agreed to by the parties has been recognized for centuries. Fraud is one of the oldest doctrines used by the courts in this policing process. Another is duress and yet another is the term is against public policy. There are many circumstances, however, where the conduct of a party may not violate public policy or constitute legal fraud or duress but may still be sufficiently egregious to shock the court's conscience and amount to a bargain that "no man in his senses and not under delusion would make on the one hand, and as no honest and fair man would accept on the other." Earl of

Chesterfield v. Janssen (1750). It is a rule of long standing that equity courts will refuse to grant performance of a contract in these circumstances; a person who comes into equity must come in with clean hands. One of the leading cases involving such a fact situation is Campbell Soup Co. v. Wentz (1948). There the plaintiff sought specific performance of a contract for the sale of a special type of carrot against the seller, a farmer. The form contract, prepared by the buyer, contained a provision which excused the buyer from taking the goods under certain circumstances, but prohibited the seller from selling them elsewhere without the buyer's written consent if the buyer refused to take the carrots because of one of the specified contingencies. The court refused to grant specific performance on the basis of the unconscionability of this provision.

Nonetheless, generally speaking it has not been recognized formally that courts have broad discretion in denying or granting legal remedies. Traditionally they have used various other means by which to avoid enforcing harsh contract provisions. One approach has been to hold a term void as contrary to public policy. See Henningsen v. Bloomfield Motors, Inc. (1960). Another common device has been the judicial act of strict construction of the language against the seller especially where the buyer is a consumer who signs a form contract furnished by the seller. See Official Comment 1 to Section 2–302 and Bekkevold v. Potts (1927). Sections 2–302 and 2A–108 are intended to allow courts to deal directly with these problems and to exercise discretion analogous to that traditionally exercised by courts sitting in equity. As a part of Official Comment 1 to Section 2–302 states, "This section makes it possible for a court to police explicitly against the contracts or terms which the court finds to be unconscionable. . . ."

The inclusion of Sections 2–302 and 2A–108 in the UCC reflects sensitivity to some realities of modern commercial life. One of the cornerstones of classical contract theory is that a contract is a bargain in which the terms have been worked out freely between parties who are equals. This premise is invalid in many modern commercial transactions, especially those involving consumers. Standard form contracts, usually supplied by the seller or lessor, are in widespread use. Seldom does a consumer-buyer or lessee understand all the terms. Frequently he or she signs without even a cursory reading. When is the last time you read a video rental contract or documentation that came with a purchase of goods? Almost never does a buyer or lessee seek legal advice before signing. Almost always the terms are advantageous to the party supplying the form. In the absence of specific consumer law involving disclosure (such as the Magnuson–Moss Warranty Act, 15 U.S.C.A. §§ 2301–2312) or explicit statutory controls on contract provisions (such as Mass.Ann.Laws Ch. 106 § 2–316A, which renders disclaimers in consumer sales unenforceable), Sections 2–302 and 2A–108 furnish the courts a means to police adhesive consumer and even commercial transactions.

c. Application in the Courts

Few successful cases have arisen to date under Section 2A–108. Thus in Siemens Credit Corp. v. American Transit Ins. Co. (2001), a term in a finance lease that obligated a company to make all payments regardless of the condition or performance of the lease equipment was upheld. But see First Federal Financial Service, Inc. v. Derrington's Chevron, Inc. (1999) (forum selection clause under circumstances in case was unconscionable). And, even before Article 2A, the results were similar. In Dillman & Associates, Inc. v. Capitol Leasing Co. (1982), the court applied Section 2–302 by analogy to a lease of equipment, a process no longer necessary upon enactment of Article 2A, but refused under the circumstances to declare a lease between businessmen of equal sophistication for a copier selected by the lessee and which lease disclaimed warranties in conspicuous language to be unconscionable. See also John Deere Leasing Co. v. Blubaugh (1986), applying Article 2 by analogy to an excessive damage recovery clause favorable to the lessor where there also was an element of unfair surprise.

In sales cases, a number of courts have refused to enforce contracts or terms on the basis of Section 2–302, almost exclusively in consumer transactions. In some of these cases courts have found an excessive price as the basis for unconscionability. In American Home Improvement, Inc. v. MacIver (1964), the plaintiff agreed to make certain home improvements for the defendant for a contract price of $1,759. The court found that $959 was the value of the goods and services and the balance of $800 was a sales commission paid by the plaintiff to the salesman. However, the defendant signed a document obligating him to pay a total of $2,568.60. The balance of $809.60 consisted of interest and carrying charges. After a negligible amount of work had been performed, the defendant told the plaintiff to cease work and the latter complied. The plaintiff sued for damages, but the court held that the contract was unenforceable. First, the court found that the plaintiff had failed to comply with a state disclosure statute, and second the contract was unconscionable because of the excessive price. Other excessive price term cases include Jones v. Star Credit Corp. (1969), Frostifresh Corp. v. Reynoso (1966), State ex rel. Lefkowitz v. ITM, Inc. (1966), and Toker v. Westerman (1970). See also Carboni v. Arrospide (1991) (analogizing interest rate on loan of 200% to price for goods sold).

These cases arguably are examples of what is characterized as "substantive unconscionability"; that is, a provision (or contract) that is so one-sided as to be oppressive in light of the general commercial background and the commercial needs of the particular trade or case, perhaps due to inequality of bargaining power, unfair surprise, lack of meaningful choice, or the like. See Official Comment 1 to Section 2–302 and, e.g., Johnson v. Mobil Oil Corp.

(1976) (factors involved include age, intelligence, business acumen, experience, relative bargaining power, absence of explanation of terms, lack of alternatives, and commercial reasonableness of terms). In many, perhaps most, substantive unconscionability cases so-called "procedural unconscionability" also is involved, where the provision (or contract), whether or not it is substantively unconscionable, proves unfairly surprising to the party against whom enforcement is sought due to the obscure language used, placement of the clause, the guile practiced by the other party, or similar causes. Some believe that a provision (or contract) may fail on either basis alone. See Frank's Maintenance & Engineering, Inc. v. C.A. Roberts Co. (1980). But see Gillman v. Chase Manhattan Bank (1988) (contract must be both procedurally and substantively unconscionable when made). Nonetheless, the presence in the same case of both problem areas obviously makes the case more compelling, and tends to explain why most unconscionability litigation in a commercial context either fails (see Salt River Project Agricultural Improvement and Power District v. Westinghouse Electric Corp. (1983), exclusion of warranty and limitation of liability clauses not unconscionable when there was no disparity in bargaining power, no surprise, and purchaser signed willingly, Intergraph Corp. v. Intel Corp. (1999), unconscionability is a remedy normally reserved for protection of the unsophisticated and uneducated and in agreement negotiated between commercial entities it is not the judicial role to rewrite the contract, and Taylor Investment Corp. v. Weil (2001), same), or results in a poor decision (see A & M Produce Co. v. FMC Corp. (1982), disclaimer and limitations of remedy clauses struck even though conspicuous and buyer intentionally selected cheaper machine that turned out not to be suitable for needs). But see, where there is evidence of procedural unconscionability, Industralease Automated & Scientific Equip. Corp. v. R.M.E. Enterprises, Inc. (1977).

Other cases in which Section 2–302 has been applied fall into several basic categories. One involves contractual attempts to limit the buyer's remedies. See Unico v. Owen (1967), clause in a retail installment sale contract in which the consumer buyer agreed not to assert any defenses against the seller's assignee unconscionable under the circumstances; Jefferson Credit Corp. v. Marcano (1969), disclaimer clause in contract for retail sale of automobile unconscionable even though it seemed to comply with the requirements of Section 2–316, however, the contract was in English, and the buyers could only read Spanish, Fairfield Leasing Corp. v. Techni–Graphics, Inc. (1992), waiver of jury trial; Brower v. Gateway 2000, Inc. (1998), arbitration clause that involved prohibitive costs; Varner v. B.L. Lanier Fruit Co., Inc. (1979), liquidated damage clause may be so inadequate as to justify recovery of actual damages; and Eastern Air Lines, Inc. v. McDonnell Douglas Corp. (1976), exculpatory clause (see UCC Section 2–615) excusing performance for circumstances that make performance difficult subject to UCC limitations for good faith, reasonableness and unconscionability. A second category involves contractual attempts to grant excessive creditor advantage. Compare Williams v. Walker–Thomas Furniture Co. (1965), cross-collateral clause buried in obscure language in form allowing repossession until all debt paid from low income, unsophisticated buyer, with In re MacDonald (1989), cross collateral clause common in industry; and see Seibel v. Layne & Bowler, Inc. (1982), inconspicuous merger clause excluding oral warranty; Capital Associates, Inc. v. Hudgens (1984), hidden acceleration clause allowing recovery of unaccrued and unearned rent; Sections 2–718(1), 2–719(3), 2A–503(2) and (3); and Paragon Homes, Inc. v. Carter, (1968), clause granting exclusive jurisdiction in inconvenient forum; Leasing Service Corp. v. Carbonex (1981), charges of 15–20% of amounts owing for attorney's fees were unconscionable.

CHAPTER 5

DOCUMENTS OF TITLE AND LETTERS OF CREDIT

---

1. INTRODUCTION

Goods often are shipped in a documentary transaction that involves a bill of lading or stored and perhaps sold utilizing a warehouse receipt. This chapter is directed to a brief discussion of those kinds of documents of title, which to the extent state law applies are covered in Article 7 of the UCC. At times payment for goods sold is accomplished through a letter of credit, which are covered in Article 5. See definition of document of title in Section 1–201(b)(16) and of letter of credit in Section 5–102(a)(10). The most common documents of title in a sale are bills of lading (Section 1–201(b)(6)), and warehouse receipts (Section 1–201(b)(42)). These documents represent or purport to represent goods which have been deposited with a bailee for transportation or for storage. They facilitate the exchange and transfer of goods. Bills of lading are especially helpful when the seller lacks faith in the buyer's credit and thus does not wish to give up control of the goods until the price has been paid. If the seller delivers a bill of lading consigning the goods to the seller, but with an indorsement and instructions permitting and directing the carrier to deliver the goods to the bearer of the document on presentation of the document, to the seller's bank along with a sight draft drawn on the buyer (see Section 3–104), the seller can collect the price through the banking system. The reason is that to obtain the document in order to obtain the goods the buyer must pay the draft when it is presented by the bank to which it has been sent for presentation to the buyer. Thus through the banking system as agent (Section 4–201), the seller retains, by use of the bill of lading and the duty of the carrier to deliver in accordance with its terms, control over the goods until payment is obtained, and the buyer likewise is assured of receiving the goods upon making payment. See Farnsworth, Documentary Drafts Under the Uniform Commercial Code, 22 Bus.Law. 479 (1967).

Of course, the buyer may refuse to pay the draft on presentation. In that case, the seller may be forced to dispose of the goods in a distant market, or reship them at additional expense for redisposal. If the seller has the right to draw under a letter of credit in this instance risks such as this are largely eliminated. Sections 5–103(d) and 5–109.

This chapter briefly discusses these matters.

2. BILLS OF LADING

The law governing bills of lading is not found only in Article 7. For example, the Federal Bills of Lading Act, 49 U.S.C.A. § 81 et seq., governs bills of lading in exports and interstate shipments. To the extent of the brief discussion here there is no significant difference between the two statutes. Accordingly, all references are to the UCC.

A bill of lading is a document issued by a railroad or other carrier when goods are delivered to it for shipment. Section 1–201(b)(6). The bill recites not only the fact that goods have been received, but also the terms of the contract of carriage between the shipper (consignor) and the carrier. The bill may be either negotiable or straight (non-negotiable). A negotiable bill of lading is one in which the carrier agrees to deliver the goods to "the order of" some named party (the consignee) or to "bearer." Section 7–104(a). In a straight bill of lading (non-negotiable) the carrier undertakes to deliver the goods to a named consignee. Thus, a bill of lading calling for delivery "to the order of John Buyer" is negotiable; a bill calling for delivery "to John Buyer" is a straight bill and non-negotiable.

The concept of "holder" is important to an understanding of the rights and obligations connected with the use of negotiable bills of lading and other documents of title. The UCC defines a "holder" of a document of title as "the person in possession of a negotiable tangible document of title if the goods are deliverable either to bearer or to the order of the person in possession" or "a person in control of negotiable electronic document of title." Section 1–201(b)(21)(B) and (C). Under this definition then, a holder is the person who has possession or control of a document that runs to the person. A bill of lading runs to the person who has possession or control if it either calls for delivery of the goods to bearer or, in the case of a tangible document of title, is indorsed to bearer or in blank, that is, the indorser signs the indorser's name without more on the back, or if it is issued to or indorsed to the order of the person in possession. "Control" in the case of a negotiable electronic document of title is defined in Section 7–106 and means the single authoritative copy of the document identifies the person to whose order the document was issued or, if transferred, the most recent transferee. In contrast, if B has possession of an unindorsed negotiable tangible bill of lading calling for delivery to the order of P, B is not a holder. The document runs to P not B.

The process by which a negotiable document of title is transferred so as to make the transferee a "holder" is called negotiation. A negotiable tangible bill of lading calling for delivery of goods to the order of B requires, for negotiation to P, B's indorsement plus delivery to P. Section 7–501(a)(1). Once B has indorsed it in blank or to bearer any person can negotiate the document by delivery alone. Section 7–501(a)(2). Likewise, if the bill of lading by its original terms calls for delivery to bearer, it can be negotiated by delivery alone. Section 7–501(a)(2). A negotiable electronic document of title is negotiated through voluntary transfer of control and no indorsement is required. Section 7–501(b)(1).

A negotiable bill enables the holder to control possession of the goods. This is because the carrier's obligation is to deliver the goods to the "holder" of the document, which means it cannot safely deliver the goods without obtaining possession or control of the bill of lading. Sections 7–403(a) and (c) and 7–502(a). For example, suppose S ships goods to B under a bill of lading calling for delivery to the order of B and sends the bill to B. Before the goods arrive B sells the goods to P by indorsing the bill of lading in blank, that is, signing B's name, without more, on the back and delivering it to P. The bill now has been "negotiated" and P becomes the "holder." The carrier's obligation under the bill of lading is to deliver the goods to P. Should it deliver them to B instead it would be liable to P for conversion of the goods. Sections 7–403 and 7–404.

If the seller ships goods under a negotiable bill, whether the bill calls for delivery to the order of the seller, the order of the buyer, the order of some other party, or bearer, the seller has a security interest in the goods as long as the seller retains control of the bill of lading. Section 2–505(1)(a). A security interest gives the seller recourse against the goods in order to secure the performance of one or more of the buyer's duties, usually payment of the purchase price, as well control of the goods until the buyer pays. Sections 1–201(b)(35), 7–403 and 7–502.

As a straight bill of lading calls for delivery of the goods to a named party, the carrier's contract is normally fulfilled by delivering the goods at destination to the named consignee and obtaining possession or control of the document of title is not necessary. Thus the carrier may safely deliver the goods to the buyer if the buyer is consignee without determining if the buyer has possession or control of the bill of lading. Sections 7–403 and 7–504.

Accordingly, if a seller ships goods under a straight bill the seller can retain a security interest under the document and control the goods only by naming seller as consignee. Otherwise the seller loses control of the goods as against the carrier unless the seller has a right to stop the goods in transit under Section 2–705. The carrier has a right (in fact may be obligated) to deliver the goods to the named consignee even though the seller retains possession or control of the bill of lading.

As mentioned, use of a bill of lading is especially helpful in sales transactions where goods are shipped and the seller lacks faith in the buyer's credit or has bargained otherwise for payment when the goods are delivered. Suppose, for example, S in Philadelphia contracts to sell goods to B in Chicago. S does not want to extend credit to B. S ships the goods to Chicago and has the carrier issue either a negotiable bill of lading calling for delivery to the order of S, the order of B, or bearer, or a straight bill of lading calling for delivery to S. S then sends the bill to S's agent in Chicago. The agent tenders the document to B and requests the purchase price.

When B pays the price to the agent the latter negotiates the bill to B if a negotiable document is being used, or if a straight bill is being used the agent transfers the document to B and gives the carrier written instructions to deliver the goods to B. Or S can achieve the same result by having a sight draft drawn on the buyer collected through the banking system with the document then released to the buyer. Thus in the above example if S does not have an agent in Chicago, S may use a draft with the bill of lading, commonly called "a bill of lading with draft attached." In such case S would draw a draft on B for the purchase price, attach it to the bill of lading, and deliver them to S's bank in Philadelphia. The Philadelphia bank would then send the documents to its correspondent bank in Chicago and the latter would hold the bill of lading until B pays the draft.

3. WAREHOUSE RECEIPTS

In many instances it is convenient for the owner of goods to store them with a bailee, a warehouse, "a person engaged in the business of storing goods for hire." Section 7–102(a)(13). In return the warehouse may issue a warehouse receipt. The receipt acknowledges receipt of the goods, describes the goods stored, and contains the terms of the storage contract. Section 7–202 provides that unless it contains the terms listed in that section the warehouse is liable for damages to any person injured by the omission. If the document calls for delivery of the goods to bearer or to the order of a named person it is negotiable. If it calls for delivery to a named party it is non-negotiable. Section 7–104(b).

As in the case of a bill of lading, a bailee under a negotiable warehouse receipt is obligated to deliver the goods to the "holder" of the receipt, and under a non-negotiable receipt is obligated to deliver either to the person to whom delivery is to be made by the terms of the receipt or pursuant to written instructions under the document. Section 7–403(a) and (c).

Warehouse receipts are helpful in sales transactions in allowing a seller to make delivery of the goods without the need for physical delivery of the goods. Rather, delivery is made by transferring the warehouse receipt to the buyer. Section 2–503(5). For example, S stores 5000 bushels of wheat with W and receives a warehouse receipt calling for delivery "to the order of S." S contracts to sell the wheat to B and makes delivery by indorsing the receipt in blank or to the order of B and delivering it to B. A "sale" has been consummated without moving the wheat.

Warehouse receipts also are frequently used as collateral for a loan. In the above case S, instead of selling the wheat to B, may wish to keep it, but is in need of cash. S's local bank is willing to lend the needed money but requires sufficient security. S indorses the warehouse receipt "to the order of the Bank" or "to bearer" and delivers it to the bank which makes the agreed loan. If S defaults in the obligation to repay, the bank may take possession of the wheat and sell it and use the proceeds to satisfy the debt.

4.   LETTERS OF CREDIT

Letters of credit may be issued by persons other than banks (Sections 5–102(a)(9) and (10)), but for this discussion a bank issuer is assumed. Suppose, to utilize the previous hypothetical, S in Philadelphia contracts to sell goods to B in Chicago, but is worried about whether B will pay the draft when it is presented for payment. S might require B to procure a letter of credit. B, the "applicant" (Section 5–102(a)(2)) (also called an "account party") will apply to B's bank ("issuer" under Section 5–102(a)(9)) to issue a "letter of credit" or "credit" (Section 5–102(a)(10)) in favor of S as "beneficiary" (Section 5–102(a)(3)). The credit normally will be irrevocable (Section 5–106(a)) and will contain an expiration date ("expiry"). See Section 5–106(c). The letter will provide that if S submits the draft and bill of lading, the bank will pay the draft. Sections 5–102(a)(8) and 5–103(d) and 5–108. Thus S is better assured of payment because the irrevocable obligation of B's bank runs to S and is independent of the sale transaction. Section 5–103(d).

That obligation must be performed, with very limited exceptions for fraud and forgery (see Sections 5–108, 5–109, 5–111), even if a dispute arises between S and B in the sales transaction and B requests the bank not to pay, or seeks a court order denying the bank the right to pay. Sections 5–103(d) and 5–109(a). A failure by the bank to pay when the conditions of the credit are met is wrongful dishonor. Sections 5–102(a)(5), 5–108–5–111. The bank must pay even though B is insolvent and cannot, or otherwise refuses to, carry out the duty to reimburse the bank for payment to S. Sections 5–103(d) and 5–108.

Many credits are made subject to the Uniform Customs and Practice for Commercial Documentary Credits, which are operating rules, and some substantive rules, prepared by the International Chamber of Commerce. As such, the "UCP" may vary the effect of or supplement the rules of Article 5 by agreement. Sections 5–103(c) and Official Comment 2 and 5–116(c). Thus in a number of instances rules other than those of Article 5 may apply.

CHAPTER 6

PERFORMANCE

---

1. GENERAL OBLIGATIONS

Once the parties have concluded a contract, there is an obligation in a contract for sale on the seller "to transfer and deliver" the goods and an obligation on the buyer "to accept and pay" the price. Section 2–301. No exactly similar provision appears in Article 2A, but from the definition of "lease" in Section 2A–103(1)(p) it can be deduced that in an enforceable lease contract the basic obligation of the lessor is to transfer possession of the goods for the lease term and that of the lessee is to pay the agreed rent in money or other value. Of course, by agreement, the parties to either a sale or a lease can

135

assume additional obligations; for example, a lessor may agree to maintain leased equipment during the lease term.

Whatever obligations are assumed must be performed in accordance with the contract. Section 2A–301 makes that explicit for leases as does Section 2–301 for sales. As pointed out in Chapter 4, the parties are free, within limits, to agree as to how, when, and where these obligations are to be performed. A determination of what the parties have agreed involves not only consideration of their language and usage of trade, course of dealing and course of performance, but also consideration of the surrounding circumstances under which the words are used. Official Comment to Section 2–301.

If, however, the parties have not otherwise agreed, various provisions of Article 2 describe the obligations of the parties in the absence of agreement. These provisions are designed to reflect the presumed intent of the parties on the topic; that is, what they would have provided had they focused on the matter. Article 2A contains few such provisions. This is because in some instances the topic is not relevant to leases, as opposed to sales, and in other instances because lease agreements customarily are formulated through a structured process that normally leaves less to be filled in by statute as there is more likely to be agreement. Nonetheless, to the extent the lease contract does not cover a topic, the proper answer usually can be inferred from the nature of a lease. Moreover, the answer presumably will accord with any express statutory resolution of the matter supplied in Article 2 for sales, to the extent the matter is relevant to both sales and leases, because, as noted, the statutory resolutions of Article 2 are intended to reflect what the parties presumably would have agreed had the matter been considered by them, and are based on what may be inferred from the nature of a sale. The previously noted obligations to deliver and pay merely are explicit examples of the result of this process.

The seller's obligation to tender delivery and the buyer's obligation to tender payment are concurrent conditions, unless otherwise agreed, such as in the case of a credit transaction. Sections 2–507(1), 2–511(1). This means that the buyer's obligation does not arise until the seller tenders delivery and the seller's obligation does not arise until the buyer tenders payment. If neither party tenders performance as provided in the contract, there is no breach. See In re S.N.A. Nut Co. (S.N.A. Nut Co. v. The Haagen–Dazs Co.) (2000) (under course of dealing nut supplier did not deliver until maker ordered; thus supplier established tender of delivery for contracts with proof buyer stopped ordering before contracts expiration, and consequently buyer was obligated to pay for nuts that should have been ordered.)

The same principle extended in time can be implied in a lease, unless otherwise agreed and except as qualified in a finance lease (Section 2A–103(1)(*l*)) that is not a consumer lease (Section 2A–103(1)(f)), where the statutory "hell or high water" clause of Section 2A–407(1) makes the lessee's promises under the lease contract irrevocable and independent (of the lessor's performance) upon the lessee's acceptance of the goods.

2. TENDER OBLIGATIONS

Section 2–503(1) states two primary requirements for proper tender by the seller:

(a) The seller must "put and hold conforming goods at the buyer's disposition."

(b) The seller must "give the buyer any notification reasonably necessary enable the buyer to take delivery."

Note, as discussed above, where payment is due upon delivery the buyer's disposition is qualified by the seller's right to retain control of the goods until payment. Official Comment 2 to Section 2–503. Again, this obligation and its details is implied in a lease under Article 2A.

It is necessary to know where the seller must "put and hold conforming goods" in order to determine whether a proper tender has been made. The parties may, and usually do, agree where tender of delivery is to be made. If they do not, Article 2 sets out specific rules for making that determination. Article 2A does not, leaving the matter to the courts to resolve in those infrequent cases where it is not covered in the lease contract.

The Article 2 default rules were formulated with the realization that sales contracts generally fall into two categories: those in which the seller assumes no responsibility for transporting the goods to the buyer, and those in which the seller does. Article 2 also contains specific rules for the manner of tender. Thus, tender must be at a reasonable hour and the buyer generally must furnish facilities to accept the goods. It should be observed that notice to the buyer of a tender is not required in all instances, but only when reasonably necessary to allow the buyer to take delivery. It will be noted in the discussion of shipment contracts below that, unless otherwise agreed, prompt notice to the buyer of shipment is mandatory. Whether it is required in other instances varies with the circumstances. Suppose, for example, B contracted to buy a used car from S, and the latter agreed to repaint the automobile and make certain repairs. It would seem reasonable to require S to notify B when the work was completed so as to enable B to pick up the car. On the other hand, if the contract did not require S to do anything to the car, notice should not be necessary. S's tender obligation would be met merely by holding the car ready for B to pick up.

Section 2–503(5) contains further explicit rules where the goods are in the possession of a bailee and are to be delivered without being moved, and subsection (6) discusses the tender rules for the delivery of documents of title.

Under Section 2–307, unless otherwise agreed all goods called for by the contract must be tendered in a single delivery, unless circumstances give either party the right to make or demand delivery in lots as, for example, where the contract calls for the

shipment of 10 carloads of coal but only three cars
are available at a given time or the contract is for
brick to build a building and the buyer's storage
space is limited so that it is impossible to receive
the entire amount of brick at once.

a. Non–Shipment Contracts

Where delivery by a carrier such as an airline,
railroad, or shipping or trucking line (delivery by
the seller's own truck normally is not considered to
be delivery by a carrier) is not required or authorized, the place for delivery is the seller's place of
business if the seller has one; otherwise, it is the
seller's residence. Section 2–308(1). This means
that the buyer must call for and pick up the goods
at the place for delivery; the seller's tender obligation is met by holding conforming goods at that
place ready for the buyer to pick up at the time
agreed. Of course, the parties can agree on another
place. In Crowder v. Aurora Co-operative Elevator
Co. (1986), the seller agreed to deliver grain at the
buyer's elevator. When the seller failed to haul the
corn to the elevator the court found no tender had
occurred. Where the seller is to supervise installation of the goods, tender nonetheless occurs when
the goods are delivered and is not postponed until
installation. Long Island Lighting Co. v. Trans-
america Delaval, Inc. (1986).

There are no such explicit rules in Article 2A, and
the appropriate rule is determined by agreement
and circumstances. For example, circumstances

would indicate that the lessor would deliver and install a heavy leased fixture to the lessee's premises, but that a weekend lease of a car would involve pickup by the lessee at the lessor's location.

The rule allowing delivery at the business or residence of the seller does not apply in those instances where the parties contract for identified goods and know at the time of contracting that the goods are at a location other than the seller's residence or place of business. In such cases the place for delivery is where the goods are located. Section 2–308(2). Suppose, for example, S contracts to sell B a large number of bricks known by both parties at the time of contracting to be stacked on a vacant lot owned by S. Unless otherwise agreed, S's tender obligation is met by holding the bricks at the lot ready for B to pick them up at the time agreed. See Haken v. Scheffler (1970).

In a similar situation, the parties may have knowledge at the time of contracting that the goods are in the hands of a bailee. Normally in such instances delivery by way of documents, such as warehouse receipts or bills of lading, will either be required or authorized. If not, the place where the goods are located is the place for delivery. Simply keeping the goods at the location is not sufficient tender of delivery, however. The seller, in addition, must obtain acknowledgment from the bailee of the buyer's right to possession. See Section 2–308(3) and Official Comments 2 and 3 to Section 2–308.

b. Shipment Contracts

A contract for sale may require or authorize the seller to transport the goods to the buyer. Authority to ship may be implied from usage of trade, course of dealing, course of performance, or the surrounding circumstances. The fact that the parties are at a distance should alone give implied authority to ship, as where B whose place of business is in Pittsburgh contracts to buy goods from S whose business is in Philadelphia.

It is necessary to distinguish a "shipment" from a "destination" contract. While a "shipment" contract authorizes the seller to transport the goods to the buyer, it does not obligate the seller to deliver the goods at point of destination as does the "destination" contract. The Official Comment 5 to Section 2–503 explains that the shipment contract is the normal one and the destination contract is the exception. See also Pestana v. Karinol Corp. (1979). In other words, the contract is a "shipment" one unless it explicitly requires the seller to deliver at a particular destination.

Exactly what language is sufficient is difficult to determine in some cases. One court has held that the words "ship to" followed by the buyer's address are not sufficient. Electric Regulator Corp. v. Sterling Extruder Corp. (1968). In contrast, see National Heater Co. v. Corrigan Co. Mechanical Contractors, Inc. (1973) ($275,640.00 price for delivery to rail siding at construction site constituted destination contract). Official Comment 5 to Section 2–503 explains that a term obligating the seller to pay the cost of transportation, with nothing more, does not obligate the seller to deliver at the named destination. The use of mercantile terms in the contract to indicate delivery obligations is discussed below.

In a shipment contract, unless otherwise agreed, the seller is obligated under Section 2–503(1) and (2) and Section 2–504 to:

(1) place conforming goods in the possession of a carrier and make a proper contract for their transportation considering the nature of the goods and other circumstances of the case,

(2) obtain and promptly deliver or tender in due form any document necessary either to enable the buyer to obtain possession of the goods or otherwise required by the agreement or by usage of trade, and

(3) promptly notify the buyer of the shipment.

A proper contract for transportation of the goods is an especially important obligation of the seller. What is a proper contract depends on "the nature of the goods and other circumstances of the case." For example, in the case of livestock, a proper contract might include arrangements for watering and protection against cold; in the case of fresh meat it would include arrangements for proper refrigeration. See Official Comment 3 to Section 2–504. Failure of the seller to make a proper transportation contract is illustrated by the pre-UCC case of Miller v. Harvey (1917). S contracted to sell 43 automobile tires, to be sent by express to B. The price of $95.43 was paid in advance. The transportation contract limited the express company's liability to $50 unless a greater value was declared and paid for at the time of shipment. S failed to declare a higher value and the goods were lost in transit. B demanded a duplicate shipment; it was made, and the question presented to the court was whether duplicate payment was required also. The court held that duplicate payment was not required because S had breached a duty to B and must bear the loss of the first shipment.

The seller must promptly notify the buyer of the shipment even though there is no express term in the contract requiring it. In open credit sales notice is usually given by sending an invoice, and in the case of documentary contracts by forwarding the documents. While it is usual to send a straight bill of lading, this is not required. However, good faith would require the seller to send such a document if it should prove necessary or convenient to the buyer in pursuing a claim against the carrier in case of loss. Official Comment 7 to Section 2–503.

Should the seller fail either to make a proper contract for the transportation of the goods or to notify the buyer, the latter may reject the goods for that reason under Section 2–504(2) only if material delay or loss ensues. See also Section 2–601. The limitation is designed to preclude rejection for trivial reasons. In shipment cases, rejection by the buyer when the goods are received can prove economically wasteful. The seller has to incur additional expense either to reship or to resell at the destination point.

Special problems are presented when the goods are perishable; these are discussed at a later point.

c. Destination Contracts

So-called "destination" contracts not only authorize the seller to transport the goods to the buyer, but also require delivery at a particular place, the destination point. For example, S who is located in Philadelphia contracts to sell and deliver goods to B at the latter's warehouse in Chicago. Here, in the absence of contrary agreement, S's tender obligations are the general ones discussed earlier only of putting and holding conforming goods at B's disposition, but to do so at B's warehouse, and to give B any notice reasonably necessary to enable B to take delivery of the goods. In addition, as with the shipment contract, the destination contract may necessitate the delivery of documents to B. Tender of documents is required either if necessary to allow B to obtain control of the goods or if the contract expressly requires it. Section 2–503(1), (4) and (5).

d. Under Mercantile Terms

Many sales contracts contain mercantile symbols or terms to indicate the obligations of the parties. The UCC previously defined some of the most common of these terms in order to avoid the diversity of meaning given to them by some courts. Much of this diversity of meaning occurred because of the failure of the Uniform Sales Act to define these terms. Nonetheless, definitions enshrined in the statute could not change when mercantile custom changed. As a result, amended Article 2 deletes these definitions and provides in an Official Comment to former Section 2–319 (now "reserved") the reason: they are inconsistent with modern commercial practices. Rather the effect of a party's use of shipment terms must be interpreted in light of applicable usage of trade and any course of performance or course of dealing between the parties. On that, see Roszkowski, Shipping Terms Based on Incoterms 2000: A Statutory Proposal, 34 UCC Law Journal 169 (2001). Therefore, unless otherwise agreed, use of these terms in a sales contract will establish the meaning and impose the obligations indicated by those sources. Compare In re Daewoo International (America) Corp. (2001) (seller under "cost and freight" terms pursuant to § 2–504(a) and its mandate of a reasonable contract for shipping had no duty to ensure the seaworthiness of the vessel).

e.   Time for Tender

If the parties have not agreed otherwise, delivery is due within a reasonable time. Section 2–309. While there is no explicit rule for leases, the applicable principle is the same. What is a reasonable time depends on what constitutes "acceptable commercial conduct" in view of the type of contract involved and the kind and nature of performance required under the circumstances. Official Comment 1 to Section 2–309. For example, if the goods are in existence and identified at the time the contract is made, a reasonable time within which to tender delivery would be considerably shorter than when the goods are to be manufactured by the seller. The seller's knowledge of the buyer's intended use of the goods may be relevant in determining a reasonable time. One court held that failure to deliver a motor vehicle until August is too late when the contract was made in May, and S knew B intended to use the vehicle for camping that summer. Hedrick v. Goodwin Bros., Inc. (1975). The obligation of good faith requires reasonable notification before a contract may be treated as breached or in default because a reasonable time for delivery has expired. When both parties let an originally reasonable time go by in silence, the course of conduct may be viewed as enlarging the reasonable time. Official Comments 5 and 6 to Section 2–309.

If the parties have agreed on a time for delivery, then delivery is due at that time. The contract may expressly stipulate a definite time for delivery, or a definite time may be implied by the usage of the trade, a course of dealing between the parties or other circumstances of the case.

The seller's failure, without legal cause, to tender delivery by the required time constitutes a breach of contract, for which the buyer has a right of action. Section 2–711(1). The same is true for a lease; there is a default. Section 2A–508(1). Unexcused delay in delivery, however, raises the question whether time is of the essence. If time is of the essence, unexcused delay in tendering delivery gives the aggrieved party not only a right of action for any loss from the breach of contract or default, but also complete relief from its own duty to perform. Suppose, for example, S contracts to deliver goods to B on July 1, and in return B agrees to pay $200. If S tenders delivery on July 3 and time is of the essence, B not only may recover damages from S for failure to deliver on the 1st but also is freed of the legal obligation to accept and pay for the goods. If, however, time is not of the essence, B is not relieved of the obligation to take and pay for the goods, although B may recover damages for any loss directly and proximately caused by the delay. Sections 2–711 and 2A–508.

The older sales cases seemed to presume that time was of the essence in actions at law. The modern contract rule, however, is more flexible. Unless the nature of the contract is such as to make performance on the exact day agreed upon of vital importance, or the contract in terms otherwise provides, failure by a promisor to perform a promise on the day stated in the promise does not discharge the duty of the other party. Thus where the goods are specially made by the seller for the buyer and have relatively little value to anyone else, the courts have been less inclined to hold time is of the essence when tender by the seller is late. Moreover, even in some cases in which the parties have agreed that time is of the essence, courts have allowed slight extensions when justice requires. On the other hand, when the contract has not expressly dealt with the matter courts have been more likely to find that time is of the essence where the contract called for delivery on a specific day and the goods were readily marketable elsewhere because, in such cases, the buyer's refusal to accept the goods following late tender of delivery is not likely to cause great injury to the seller.

The same issue may also arise with respect to other aspects of performance. Indeed the general issue can be stated as follows: does the failure of S to make a perfect tender not only give B a cause of action for damages, but also the right to reject the goods.

Section 2–601 provides:

Subject to the Sections 2–504 and Section 2–612 and unless otherwise agreed under Sections 2–718 and 2–719, if the goods or the tender of delivery fail in any respect to conform to the contract, the buyer may:

    (1) reject the whole;

    (2) accept the whole; or

    (3) accept any commercial unit or units and reject the rest.

Section 2A–509(1) is substantially the same, but the section cross references are to the comparable Article 2A sections.

Ostensibly these sections adopt the perfect tender rule in non-installment contracts unless otherwise agreed. Or, from the standpoint of time for tender of performance, "time is of the essence unless agreed otherwise." Several sections of the UCC which are discussed elsewhere qualify these sections, however. See Sections 2–504, 2–508 and 2A–513, 2–612 and 2A–510, and 2–614 and 2A–404.

Article 2 explicitly and Article 2A by implication require that the goods not only be tendered on a proper day, but also at a reasonable hour. Section 2–503(2)(a). What is a reasonable hour varies with the facts of each case. The nature of the goods and the usages governing the transaction are important factors. Tender of a small item may be perfectly reasonable at an hour when it might be unreasonable to tender a large, complicated item requiring dismantling or assembly. A particular hour might be reasonable for tendering an article to a farmer but unreasonable for tendering goods to a merchant in the center of a commercial district.

In John Manners & Co. v. S. Hirshenhorn & Sons (1952), the parties contracted on December 12, 1950 for the sale of certain goods. The goods were en route to New York by ship and were to arrive there on December 23. The contract called for payment within ten days after December 12 upon presentation by the seller of two copies of bills of lading and certain other documents. At 3:30 p.m. on December 22nd, after the close of banking hours and without prior notice, the documents were tendered to the buyer and payment was demanded. The trial court held as a matter of law that tender had been properly made. The appellate court reversed and ordered a new trial saying:

Laying aside anything resembling courtesy as legally necessary to business relations, the question remains whether the contract required plaintiff to keep $64,000 in cash in its office after banking hours and until the close of business hours (for even a certified check would not be legal tender if the seller were disposed to be technical).... If not, then it made no difference whether the plaintiff had the necessary funds in its bank account if it could have raised them upon short notice in order to meet the purchase price.

While this is not a UCC case, the same result should follow under the UCC. See also Section 2–511(2).

3. OBLIGATION TO PAY THE PRICE OR THE RENT

The buyer's basic obligation is spelled out in Section 2–507(1):

Tender of delivery is a condition to the buyer's duty to accept the goods and, unless otherwise agreed, to the buyer's duty to pay for them. Tender entitles the seller to acceptance of the goods and to payment according to the contract.

In Article 2A, the lessee's basic obligation is to pay in accordance with the lease contract the agreed consideration in return for the right to possession and use of the goods. This obligation is derived from Sections 2A–103(1)(r), 2A–508(1), 2A–509(1), and 2A–516(1).

It should be noted that the buyer or the lessee has two obligations: (1) to accept the goods, and (2) to pay the price or the rent. Acceptance (or non-acceptance) is of importance primarily in determining the remedies available to the seller or lessor. See the In re S.N.A. Nut Co. case, discussed earlier. What constitutes acceptance and the legal significance of acceptance and failure to accept are discussed in subsequent chapters. Discussion here is restricted to the obligation to pay.

As discussed previously in this chapter, duty to tender payment and the duty to tender delivery are concurrent conditions, unless otherwise agreed. This means that there is no duty to pay the price or rent until tender of delivery, and no duty to deliver arises until tender of agreed payment. Extension of credit to the buyer represents the usual commercial transaction in which the parties have "otherwise agreed" in a contract for sale. See Official Comment 1 to Section 2–511. The same would be true where the lessor allows use of the goods in advance of rent due at the end of the month, rather than rent being due on the first of the month. When credit is extended there is a duty to deliver without tender of any payment or only upon tender of any down payment or security deposit as a condition to the duty to deliver. The delivery to the seller of a proper letter of credit under an agreement that the primary method of payment will be by letter of credit suspends the buyer's obligation to pay, but if the letter of credit is dishonored the seller may on reasonable notification to the buyer require payment directly. Section 2–325.

Special mention should be made regarding the buyer's obligation of payment in non-credit transactions where the goods are to be shipped by the seller to the buyer. The Uniform Sales Act contained a provision that in shipment contracts "delivery of the goods to a carrier ... is deemed to be delivery of the goods to the buyer." Section 46(1). Some courts interpreted this as obligating the buyer to pay the price as soon as the seller delivered the goods to the carrier. Most courts held, however, that the buyer is obligated to pay the price only when the goods have been received. The UCC adopts the latter view: "Unless otherwise agreed, the following rules apply:"

(1) "Payment is due at the time and place at which the buyer is to receive the goods even if the place of shipment is the place of delivery." Section 2–310(1).

The principal reason is that, unless otherwise agreed, the buyer should have an opportunity to inspect the goods before being required to accept or pay for them.

a. Right of Inspection

The right to inspect the goods before payment in a non-credit sale is very important from the buyer's standpoint. Usually inspection will reveal whether the goods are conforming. If they are non-conforming the seller has not made a proper tender and there is no obligation to pay the price. The buyer is at a serious disadvantage if payment is required before inspection. While payment could be recovered if later inspection showed the goods to be nonconforming, this might require bringing a legal action against the seller. Furthermore, there is always the chance that the seller is insolvent, making a judgment of little value. While these same considerations may exist for a credit buyer or lessee, the amount initially payable is less than the price or full rent. For this reason and because lease transactions often occur in a way that minimizes this issue, no explicit provision on inspection exists in Article 2A.

Article 2 provides for the buyer's right to inspect before payment unless the parties have agreed otherwise. Section 2–513(1) provides:

(1) Unless otherwise agreed and subject to subsection (c), if goods are tendered or delivered or identified to the contract for sale, the buyer has a right before payment or acceptance to inspect them at any reasonable place and time and in any reasonable manner. If the seller is required or authorized to send the goods to the buyer, the inspection may be after their arrival.

It will be observed that the details as to when, where, and how the inspection is to be made are not spelled out. The single criterion is that of "reasonableness" which must be determined from the facts of each case. However, where the seller is required or authorized to send the goods to the buyer, the inspection may be after the arrival of the goods. In cases, where the buyer must pay to obtain the bill of lading to gain delivery of the goods (but the contract does not provide for payment against documents), the right of inspection should be noted on the document. Official Comment 2 to Section 2–310.

The inspection place is the destination point if the buyer wishes. Although not stated in the UCC, it would seem the buyer could insist upon inspection at the shipment point if desired since the right to wait until the arrival of the goods is for the buyer's own benefit. Indeed, where the right to inspect is contracted away because the buyer agrees to pay against documents of title, that is tender of delivery is agreed to be made by way of documents, the buyer may wish to contract for inspection by a third party at the point of shipment, and then to pay against an inspection certificate as one required document. Inspection at destination point is consistent with Section 2–310(1), which makes payment due at the time and place at which the buyer is to receive the goods.

The parties are free to set the place, method, or standard of inspection in their contract. If they do so, their agreement will control. Section 2–513(4) recognizes that in some instances when the parties fix a place, method or standard of inspection in the agreement, compliance with these terms may subsequently become impossible. In such a case inspection is to be conducted in accordance with the rules provided in Section 2–513(1), unless it clearly appears that the parties intended that the place, method or standard agreed to were necessary conditions which if not met would cause the bargain to fail. See Official Comment 6 to Section 2–513.

Section 2–513(3) outlines three principal situations in which the general right of inspection before payment does not exist. Even in these situations, however, the parties are free to agree expressly that the buyer shall have a right of inspection. These three exceptions are discussed below.

(1) *Special problems in overseas sales.* Should a buyer at a distant port of destination inspect goods and then unjustifiably reject them as nonconforming, the seller is placed in an especially difficult position. The seller would be faced with taking possession and disposing of the goods at this distant point where in all likelihood the seller would have no agents and where the market would be unknown. Furthermore, any legal action against the buyer would be more onerous because of the possibility that it would have to be instituted at the point of destination where the buyer is located.

The seller normally avoids these difficulties by requiring the buyer to purchase and receive shipment under a C.I.F. or C. & F. contract. One of the seller's obligations requires that the seller procure any documents (usually a bill of lading) required to effect shipment and forward and tender such documents in proper form to the buyer. Because these documents, at least before air transportation, often arrived at the point of destination and were tendered to the buyer before the goods arrived, pre-UCC case law, following mercantile practice, obligated the buyer to pay in exchange for the documents even when the contract was silent as to the time for payment. This means payment would normally be required before the goods arrive and without any inspection.

Article 2 continues this same rule. Sections 2–513(3)(a) and (b)

(2) *Delivery C.O.D.* A second exception to the general right of inspection before payment is articulated in Section 2–513(3)(a) as follows: "Unless otherwise agreed, the buyer is not entitled to inspect the goods before payment of the price if the contract provides:"

(a) "for delivery on terms that under applicable course of performance, course of dealing, or usage of trade are interpreted to preclude inspection before payment."

C.O.D. is such a term "C.O.D." means "cash on delivery."

By consenting to this delivery term the buyer agrees that payment is to be made simultaneously with delivery and constitutes the carrier as the buyer's agent to receive and transmit the price to the seller. It has been the practice of carriers in C.O.D. contracts not to allow inspection before payment. The UCC accepts this commercial practice. See Liverpool v. Baltimore Diamond Exchange, Inc. (2002).

(3) *Cash against documents.* The third exception is stated this way: ". . . the buyer is not entitled to inspect the goods before payment of the price if the contract provides:"

(b) "for payment against documents of title, unless such payment is due only after the goods are to become available for inspection."

Section 2–513(3)(b). Official Comment 4 to Section 2–310 provides the example of cash against documents as a term of this type.

It is important to note that a contract for payment against documents is not the same as a contract in which the seller is merely required or authorized to ship the goods under documents. In both instances depending on the means of transportation the goods may travel more slowly than the documents so that the goods are not available for inspection when the documents arrive. If the contract calls for payment against the documents, payment is due when the documents are tendered unless otherwise agreed. In other cases, however, even though documents are used the buyer is not obligated to pay when the documents arrive and are tendered, but can wait until the goods arrive, inspect them, and refuse payment if they are nonconforming. This is the difference between the situations described in Section 2–310(2) and (3); the latter situation where the seller merely selects to ship with documents is the one covered in subsection (2) and thus, if the seller wishes to demand payment before inspection, the seller must put an appropriate term into the contract because the seller's unilateral selection of a means of shipment will not control the buyer's right of inspection.

Two specific examples will serve to illustrate the difference. Suppose S in Philadelphia contracts to sell and ship goods by rail "F.O.B. Philadelphia" to B in Chicago. There are no credit terms. S delivers the goods to the carrier, obtains an order bill of lading, attaches a sight draft drawn on B for the price, and forwards the bill of lading and draft through regular banking channels to B in Chicago. Three days after the goods are shipped and approximately one week before the goods will arrive in Chicago, the draft with bill of lading attached is presented for payment to B. B can refuse to pay the draft at that time. B is entitled to wait until the goods arrive in Chicago so that B can inspect them before payment. This is true despite the fact that use of documents was authorized. The contract did not call for payment against documents. Section 2–310(2).

Suppose, on the other hand, all the facts above remain the same except that there is a term in the contract providing: "Payment is due upon presentation of sight draft attached to bill of lading." This is a contract calling for payment against documents. B has no right to inspect the goods before payment. B must pay the draft when it is presented and a failure to do so constitutes a breach of contract and dishonor of the draft. Section 2–310(3).

In this situation it is possible for the parties to insert a provision in the contract for payment against documents "on arrival" of the goods. Section 2–513(3)(b). If this is done, the documents must be held until the goods arrive. Thus the goods become available for inspection, and B is entitled to inspect them before payment. Official Comment 5 to Section 2–513. Should the draft with attached bill of lading be presented for payment before the goods arrive, B is under no legal duty to honor it at that time. But if the contract calls for payment against documents and the goods nonetheless arrive before the documents, the buyer does not have the right to inspect the goods before payment. Official Comment 5 to Section 2–513. It is only when the term for payment against documents also contains an "on arrival" of the goods provision, as discussed above, that inspection before payment becomes proper.

If the contract calls for payment before inspection, Article 2 permits two instances in which the buyer is excused from making payment. One is where the non-conformity appears without inspection. Section 2–512(1)(a). For example, B orders a piece of fine crystal, C.O.D. The package arrives in a crushed condition, and it appears obvious the contents are not intact. B is not obligated to pay at that time. Should it be decided that risk of loss was on B while the goods were in transit, however, B would be liable for the price. The second exception is where despite tender of the required documents, the circumstances would justify injunction against honor under the provisions of Section 5–109(b).

Section 2–512(1)(b). Section 5–109(b) provides that in some instances where material fraud or forgery concerning documents is discovered, or that honor would facilitate a material fraud, a court order may be obtained enjoining payment against the documents presented under a letter of credit.

The right to inspect the goods before payment should not be confused with the right to inspect the goods before acceptance under Sections 2–606(1)(a) and 2A–515(1). Payment may be made before inspection as required by the contract, but this neither constitutes acceptance of the goods nor impairs the right to inspect before acceptance. Section 2–512(2). One difference between the two perhaps is that, as discussed above, it is contemplated that the right of inspection before payment may be contracted away, but courts should be very cautious to find that the right to inspect before acceptance is displaced by agreement. Cf. Rozmus v. Thompson's Lincoln–Mercury Co. (1966) (plaintiff accepted goods when he signed conditional sale contract acknowledging acceptance of goods in good order). Official Comment 1 to Section 2–513 suggests no agreement can displace the entire right of inspection except perhaps where the contract is simply for the sale of "this thing." Even then, however, the buyer would be entitled to examine the goods before acceptance to determine if it is "the thing" contracted for. If it is not there would be a right to reject. Section 2–601.

There is a relationship between the right of inspection and risk of loss are relevant here. A buyer or lessee may reject goods, before or after payment, because they are not in conformity with the contract and still be liable. Suppose B contracts to buy goods that then are shipped to B. Inspection reveals the goods are damaged and B rejects them. Subsequently B institutes suit for recovery of the price, if paid before inspection, or if not paid, S institutes suit for the price. S does not deny that the goods were damaged when inspected by B, but produces evidence that the damage was caused by the carrier in transit. This is a risk of loss question. If risk of loss was on B while the goods were in transit B is liable for wrongful rejection despite the damage.

Section 2–513(2) provides that the buyer must bear the expense of inspection unless the parties otherwise agree. If, however, the goods do not conform and are rejected the seller is liable for these expenses. They become a part of the buyer's incidental damages. Section 2–715(1). Section 2A–520(1) reads the same.

Suppose the seller tenders the goods and the buyer's right of inspection is not contracted away, but the seller refuses to allow the buyer to inspect them before payment. What are the buyer's rights? Is the buyer required to pay for the goods with only a right to reject if the goods prove to be nonconforming, or to sue the seller for damages. Or does the seller's refusal impair the tender of performance, giving the buyer the right to reject the goods and to refuse to pay for them.

The UCC does not answer these questions explicitly. The answer may depend on whether Section 2–601 is qualified by the last paragraph of Section 2–504 in this instance. One commentator concludes that the buyer may reject. See Nordstrom, *Handbook of the Law of Sales*, 361–363 (1970). This conclusion seems sound, and is based primarily on a Official Comment to Section 2–503. Official Comment 2 to Section 2–503 states in part that where the seller is demanding payment on delivery, the seller must first allow the buyer to inspect the goods *in order to avoid impairing the tender* (emphasis added) unless the contract for sale is on C.I.F., C.O.D., cash against documents or similar terms negating the privilege of inspection before payment.

It also seems clear that in this instance the buyer would not accept the goods. Section 2–606(1)(b) provides:

Acceptance of goods occurs when the buyer . . . fails to make an effective rejection under Section 2–602(1), but such acceptance does not occur until the buyer has had a reasonable opportunity to inspect them . . . .

See also by implication Section 2–512(2).

b. Manner of Payment

Section 2–511(2) provides:

(2) Tender of payment is sufficient when made by any means or in any manner current in the

ordinary course of business unless the seller demands payment in legal tender and gives any extension of time reasonably necessary to procure it.

Article 2A leaves this matter to agreement or to case by case resolution as it may infrequently arise.

Section 2–511(2) means that where the contract price has been expressed in money, a tender by the buyer of either cash or a check is proper. There are instances, however, when the seller will not want to accept the buyer's check, but will demand cash or a certified check. Should such demand be made, the seller must give any extension of time necessary for the buyer to procure the requested medium of payment. To illustrate, suppose S tenders goods to B on the last business day when tender is possible, during business hours, but after banking hours. B tenders a check for \$4,000, the amount of the purchase price. S demands cash. See John Manners & Co. v. S. Hirshenhorn & Sons (1952). Under the UCC evidently, S would be required to give B until the next banking day to obtain the cash if B did not have it on hand, unless B had been given sufficient advance notice that a check would not be acceptable. Should S refuse to grant the extension, B's tender of the check would be sufficient tender so that S's failure to deliver the goods would constitute a breach of contract.

Where payment is made by check, the payment, absent contrary agreement, is conditional and defeated as between the parties if the check is dishonored. Sections 2–511(3) and 3–310(b)(1). Conditional payment simply means that the check is taken on the condition that it will be honored (paid) by the drawee bank. The underlying obligation to pay is suspended until the check is presented for payment. If it is paid, the obligation for payment is discharged; if it is dishonored, the drawer may be sued either on the underlying obligation or on the check.

CHAPTER 7

TITLE AND RIGHTS OF THIRD PARTIES

A. PASSAGE OF TITLE

1. Introduction.
2. Manner of Identification.
   a. Specific Goods.
   b. Future Goods.
   c. Fungible Goods.
   d. Crops and the Unborn Young of Animals.
3. Rules for Passage of Title Under Article 2.
   a. Destination Contracts.
   b. Shipment Contracts.
   c. Other Circumstances.
4. Passage of Title and Reservation of a Security Interest.
5. Effect of Rejection or Revocation of Acceptance.
6. Sale on Approval and Sale or Return.
7. Consignments.

B. THE RIGHTS OF THIRD PARTIES

1. Introduction.
2. Entrusting.
   a. Generally.
   b. Apparent Ownership, Apparent Authority, and Estoppel.
   c. Delivery of Possession Without Indicia of Title or Authority.
3. Voidable Interests.
   a. Cash Transactions.
   b. The Impostor Problem.
   c. Voidable Interests and Entrusting Compared.

A. PASSAGE OF TITLE

1. INTRODUCTION

Who has title to the goods? This is the question which courts frequently were called upon to answer in pre-UCC sales cases. That law provided that generally risk of loss depended on who had title. This meant, for example, that in a sales transaction in which S was to ship goods to B and the goods were lost, stolen, or destroyed in transit, an action by S for the price required the court to determine if title had passed to B before the time the goods suffered casualty. If so, B bore the risk of loss and was responsible for the price; if not, S had the risk of loss and could not recover the price. Former law made another important question rest upon title; the right of the buyer to maintain an action to recover possession of goods wrongfully withheld by the seller usually depended on whether title had passed. If title had not passed, an action for money damages ordinarily was the buyer's only remedy. Other legal problems, some not directly involving sales transactions, also were dealt with by the courts by locating "title." For example, must seller or buyer pay a personal property tax imposed on the "owner" of goods? Did a "sale" take place in state

X or state Y when such sales are legal in X but not in Y? May S's creditor levy on goods in S's possession which S has contracted to sell to B? Many scholars believed that the "title" approach was not a satisfactory method for dealing with the sales problems above.

The Official Comment to UCC Section 2–101 states in part:

> The arrangement of the present Article is in terms of contract for sale and the various steps of its performance. The legal consequences are stated as following directly from the contract and action taken under it without resorting to the idea of when property or title passed or was to pass as being the determining factor. The purpose is to avoid making practical issues between practical men turn upon the location of an intangible something, the passing of which no man can prove by evidence and to substitute for such abstractions proof of words and actions of a tangible character.

See also Section 2–401: "The provisions of this article ... apply irrespective of title to the goods unless the provision refers to such title." See In re Kellstrom Industries, Inc. (2002) (even though goods were delivered constructively and title passed, they had not been received by buyer and seller had right to stop their physical transfer under Section 2–705).

Two important areas in which title is no longer relevant are remedies and risk of loss. Remedies and risk of loss are discussed in subsequent chapters.

Article 2A does not have a similar provision since title does not pass in a lease and, not surprisingly, issues like remedies and risk of loss are governed by specific provisions without regard to a title analysis. Indeed, with a few exceptions (Sections 2A–525, 2A–532 and 2A–309) title, that is to say the lessor's reversionary interest in the goods, is not addressed in Article 2A.

Despite the decreased importance of the passage of title in Article 2, there is a section to deal with the problem when it becomes relevant. That provision is Section 2–401. Courts have resorted to that section when answering some questions not explicitly covered by another Article 2 provision. See New England Yacht Sales, Inc. v. Commissioner of Revenue Services (1986) (taxation issue) and In re Victoria Alloys, Inc. (2001)) (in cash against documents transaction where buyer never paid for the goods, buyer had no basis for asserting an interest which would inure to the benefit of its bankruptcy estate). For another example, in Motors Ins. Corp. v. Safeco Ins. Co. (1967), B's son wrecked the automobile he was driving. Earlier in the day S, an automobile dealer, and B had agreed on a trade. B turned over his old car to S, and S gave B unqualified and unconditional possession of the new car which was wrecked by B's son. All that remained to be done was processing the title papers and payment of the price, both of which were done after the crash. B's insurance carrier denied coverage on the ground that title had not passed to B at the time of the accident; therefore, S's insurer was liable for the loss. The court relied on Section 2–401 and held that title passed at the time and place of delivery; hence, B was the "owner" of the automobile at the time of loss. A similar case is Allen v. Lynn Hickey Dodge, Inc. (2001) and a similar result was reached in Madrid v. Bloomington Auto Company, Inc. (2003) (determination of legal title controlled by UCC and not Indiana certificate of title act). In neither case did the court construe the certificate of title law to postpone passage of title under Article 2. This depends on general principles of statutory construction as Article 2 defers to such laws except with respect to the rights of a buyer in ordinary course of business under Section 2–403(2). See Nudi Auto RV & Boat Sales, Inc. v. John Deere Ins. Co. (2002) (broker bought 21 cars from auction house for resale, sold them to buyer, auction houses held titles until paid, they were never paid, and court entered judgment for buyer in claim of buyer against its insurance company under false pretenses coverage that broker had never acquired title and could not pass title under Section 2–403(2). Article 2A also does but also has additional provisions. See Sections 2A–104(1) and (2) and Sections 2A–105, 2A–304(3) and 2A–305(3).

Section 2–401 provides:

The provisions of this article with regard to the rights, obligations, and remedies of the seller, the buyer, purchasers or other third parties apply irrespective of title to the goods unless the provision refers to such title. Insofar as situations are not covered by the other provisions of this article and matters concerning title become material, the following rules apply:

(1) Title to goods cannot pass under a contract for sale before their identification to the contract under Section 2–501, and, unless otherwise explicitly agreed, the buyer acquires by their identification a special property as limited by this article. Any retention or reservation by the seller of the title in goods shipped or delivered to the buyer is limited in effect to a reservation of a security interest. Subject to this section and to Article 9, title to goods passes from the seller to the buyer in any manner and on any conditions explicitly agreed on by the parties.

(2) Unless otherwise explicitly agreed, title passes to the buyer at the time and place at which the seller completes performance with reference to the delivery of the goods, despite any reservation of a security interest and if a document of title is to be delivered at a different time or place; and in particular despite any reservation of a security interest by the bill of lading:

(a) if the contract requires or authorizes the seller to send the goods to the buyer but does not require the seller to deliver them at destination, title passes to the buyer at the time and place of shipment; or

(b) if the contract requires delivery at destination, title passes on tender there.

(3) Unless otherwise explicitly agreed, if delivery is to be made without moving the goods:

(a) if the seller is to deliver a document of title, title passes at the time when and the place where the seller delivers such documents; or

(b) if the goods at the time of contracting are already identified and no documents are to be delivered, title passes at the time and place of contracting.

(4) A rejection or other refusal by the buyer to receive or retain the goods, whether or not justified, or a justified revocation of acceptance revests title to the goods in the seller. Such revesting occurs by operation of law and is not a sale.

2.   MANNER OF IDENTIFICATION

Title to goods cannot pass until the goods have been "identified" to the contract. Section 2–401(1). Before identification, an attempted sale is effective only as a contract to sell. Therefore, it is necessary to discuss the Code provisions dealing with identification before considering Section 2–401.

It should be noted that identification is important not only in relation to transfer of title but may also be legally relevant in determining what remedy is available to an aggrieved party. See Chapters 11 and 12. Furthermore, once the goods are identified to the contract the buyer has an insurable interest in them even if the buyer neither has title nor bears the risk of loss. Section 2–501(1) and Spirit of Excellence, Ltd. v. Intercargo Insurance Co. (2002) (after transfer of insurable interest in goods from seller to buyer, seller lacked standing to recover for damage). Identification also plays a role in Article 2A even though the passage of title is not involved; for example, in relation to the acquisition by the lessee of an insurable interest. See Sections 2A–217 and 2A–218.

As indicated in Chapter 1, the term "identified" or "identification" is not defined specifically in the Code but is used in Articles 2 and 2A to describe the process by which goods are particularized as the goods to which the contract refers.

The parties are free to agree upon the time and manner in which existing goods become identified to the contract. Sections 2–501(1) and 2A–217, first sentence. For example, suppose S contracts to manufacture and sell or lease several dozen storm windows to B. The parties might agree that each storm window should be regarded as identified to the contract as soon as the glass is inserted in the frame, even though two or three additional operations are necessary before the window is complete and in a deliverable state. Section 2–501, Official Comment 4.

In the absence of an explicit agreement, the time of identification is determined by the particular rules set forth in Sections 2–501 and 2A–217.

a.   Specific Goods

If the contract is for specific goods, identification occurs as soon as the contract is made. Sections 2–501(1)(a) and 2A–217(1). For example, if B and S contract to buy and sell or to lease an original Van Gogh, identification occurs when the contract is made.

b.   Future Goods

When the contract is for future goods, identification normally occurs only when the goods are in some way designated or particularized by the seller or the lessor as the goods to which the contract refers. This particularization may be made by shipment, marking, or any other action sufficient to show that these are the goods to which the contract refers. Sections 2–501(1)(b) and 2A–217(2). To illustrate, if the parties contract for the sale or lease of goods of a certain description and S has a warehouse filled with goods answering that description, until identification the contract is a contract for future goods. Identification does not occur until S in some way particularizes a quantity of the goods as the goods to which the contract refers. Moreover, until identification takes place, title cannot pass to B in the case of a sale. An explicit agreement could give the buyer or the lessee the power to select the goods. Official Comment 3 to Section 2–501.

What if the lessor is both selling and leasing goods to the same person and has set aside goods for that person without designation between the contracts? Article 2A leaves this issue for the courts on the particular facts. Official Comment to Section 2A–217.

c. Fungible Goods

The parties may agree to buy and sell or to lease a certain number, weight, or measure from an identified mass of fungible goods. See Section 1–201(2)(r) for the definition of "fungible goods." In the absence of explicit agreement to the contrary, identification of the undivided share occurs as soon as the contract is made. Section 2–501(1)(a), Official Comment 5. So long as the mass from which the goods are to be taken is identified at the time the contract is made, the contract is for specific rather than future goods even though the goods contracted for have not yet been segregated from the mass. To illustrate, S owns a large tank of gasoline and contracts to sell B 500 gallons from it. The exact quantity of gasoline in the tank is unknown to the parties, though it exceeds 500 gallons. In the absence of explicit agreement otherwise, identification takes place as soon as the contract is made.

d. Crops and the Unborn Young of Animals

In order to be in a deliverable state, the goods must conform with the requirements of the contract so that the refusal to accept the goods after a proper tender will constitute a breach of contract. While it is possible for identification to occur before goods reach a deliverable state (see Official Comment 4 to Section 2–501), and while they are non-conforming, identification obviously cannot take place unless the goods exist. Sections 2–501(1) and 2A–217. The UCC does not define what is meant by the phrase "existing goods." Some goods are legally regarded as existing potentially and therefore capable of identification long before qualifying as deliverable under the terms of the contract. Both Articles 2 and 2A recognize this concept of potential existence in dealing with the identification of growing crops and the unborn young of animals.

If the parties agree to buy and sell growing crops, identification occurs as soon as the crop is planted if it is to be harvested within twelve months or the next normal harvest season after contracting, whichever is later. Section 2–501(1)(c). The operation of this provision may be illustrated with several examples:

Case 1. On January 30, 1980, S contracts to sell B all the corn to be raised on a certain tract of land. Identification occurs when the corn is planted on May 4, 1980, for the corn normally would be harvested in the fall of 1980.

Case 2. A contract is made on January 30, 1980, for the sale of corn to be raised on a certain tract during the 1981 season. Under the Code identification does not occur when the corn is planted in the spring of 1981, because it is not to be harvested within twelve months or the next normal harvest season after contracting.

Case 3. A field of corn is planted in May, 1980, and on June 10, 1980, S contracts to sell all the corn harvested from the field in the fall. Identification occurs when the contract is made.

In contracts for the sale or lease of unborn young animals, identification takes place as soon as the young are conceived, provided in the case of a sale that birth will take place within twelve months after the contract is made. Sections 2–501(1)(c) and 2A–217(3). Suppose that on June 14, 1980, S contracts to sell B the first foal to be born of a specified mare. The mare is bred a few days later. Identification occurs at conception. The gestation period for horses is eleven months; therefore, the foal normally would be born within twelve months after the contract is made. If, however, the mare had not been bred until sometime in November, identification would not occur at conception. Birth would not occur within twelve months after the contract was made.

3.   RULES FOR PASSAGE OF TITLE UNDER ARTICLE 2

As indicated earlier, except for unidentified goods the parties are free to agree as to when the title to the goods will pass to the buyer. Often it is difficult or impossible to determine when the parties intend title to pass. In cases where the parties have not otherwise explicitly agreed, the UCC lays down specific rules for determining when the title to identified goods passes in Section 2–401. The requirement of explicit agreement to vary these rules is an attempt to clear up some of the confusion and uncertainty which developed under the common law and the Uniform Sales Act as a result of judicial attempts to find the "implied" intention of the parties. See Official Comment 3 to Section 2–501.

Generally speaking, under the UCC title to goods passes from the seller to the buyer at the time and place at which the seller completes performance with reference to the physical delivery of the goods. Section 2–401(2). There are more detailed rules, however.

a. Destination Contracts

If the contract requires the seller to deliver the goods to a certain destination, such as the buyer's location, title passes when tender occurs at that destination. Section 2–401(2)(b). Suppose S in Chicago agrees to sell goods to B and to deliver them to B's warehouse in Miami. Unless otherwise explicitly agreed, title does not pass to B until the goods are tendered at B's warehouse in Miami.

b. Shipment Contracts

If the contract requires or authorizes the seller to send the goods to the buyer but does not require delivery at destination, title passes to the buyer at the time and place for shipment. Section 2–401(2)(a). For example, S in Philadelphia contracts to sell goods to B in Chicago. The contract provides that the goods will be sent by rail but does not require that they be delivered to any particular address in Chicago. Title passes when S delivers the goods to the railroad in Philadelphia.

It should be noted that sales contracts often contain the term "F.O.B.", which means free on board at a named place. The term may be F.O.B. city of shipment, F.O.B. city of destination, or F.O.B. some other point, such as "F.O.B. seller's warehouse" or "F.O.B. buyer's plant." Article 2 no longer provides statutory meanings for shipping terms. See Roszkowski, Shipping Terms Based on Incoterms 2000: A Statutory Proposal, 34 UCC Law Journal 169 (2001). However, generally if the term is F.O.B. place of destination, unless otherwise agreed the seller must at its own risk and expense transport the goods to the named place and tender delivery there. In other words, the term F.O.B. place of destination, in the absence of agreement to the contrary, makes the transaction a destination contract and title will not pass until the seller tenders delivery at that place. Section 2–401(2)(b). Suppose, however, the contract simply requires the seller to pay the freight to point of destination, nothing more. Such a term is not regarded as an agreement by the seller to deliver to the buyer or to an agreed destination, and therefore the transaction is a shipment contract.

Under an F.O.B. place of shipment contract, title passes to the buyer when the seller delivers the goods to the carrier, unless otherwise agreed. Section 2–401(2)(a). However, under a C.I.F. or C. & F.

place of destination contract, delivery occurs and title passes to the buyer at the place of shipment.

c. Other Circumstances

In some instances the contract contemplates transfer of title without moving the goods from the possession of a warehouse or other bailee, or even from the possession of the seller. If the seller is to deliver a document of title, title passes when and at the place where the document is delivered. Section 2–401(3)(a). If no documents are to be delivered and the goods are identified, title passes when the contract is made. Section 2–401(3)(b). Where the goods are not identified at the time of contracting, apparently title passes upon identification.

4. PASSAGE OF TITLE AND RESERVATION OF A SECURITY INTEREST

It is common for the seller to reserve a security interest in the goods until the purchase price has been paid. Chapter 4 discusses methods of controlling the goods by use of a bill of lading in non-credit transactions until the price is paid. Where credit is extended to the buyer, the seller may reserve a security interest by contract with the buyer under the provisions of Article 9 of the UCC in the goods until payment. Of course, since a lessor retains title as owner, and is not a secured party, a security interest is unnecessary to repossess the goods. Section 2A–525(2).

Regardless of the method used by a seller, however, reservation of a security interest does not of itself affect the rules discussed above governing passage of title. This is true even though the security device adopted expressly reserves title in the seller. Reservation of title in such cases is limited in effect to a security interest. Section 2–401(1).

5. EFFECT OF REJECTION OR REVOCATION OF ACCEPTANCE

Suppose that under a shipment contract, where title passes to the buyer at shipment, after the goods arrive at point of destination the buyer decides that it does not want the goods or that they do not conform to the terms of the contract, and therefore refuses to accept them. This action revests title in the seller regardless of whether the buyer's action is legally justifiable. Section 2–401(d). In some instances the buyer accepts the goods but later revokes acceptance. Such action, if justified, also revests title in the seller. Section 2–401(4). In both cases, the revesting of title is by operation of law and is not a sale.

6. SALE ON APPROVAL AND SALE OR RETURN

Among the various contractual agreements used in the marketing of goods are the "sale on approval" and the "sale or return." The type of arrangement that has been adopted in a given situation may be legally significant in determining who holds title to the goods and thus the rights of creditors. Both arrangements are transactions in which goods are delivered by the seller to the buyer with the understanding that they may be returned even though they conform to the contract. Section 2–326(1). If the transaction is a sale on approval, the goods must be delivered primarily for use and there is no "sale" until the buyer accepts the goods; that is, title does not pass to the buyer until the buyer indicates approval by accepting the goods. Section 2–326(1)(a) and (2). As to when acceptance of goods occurs, see Section 2–606 discussed in Chapter 10. Until acceptance by the buyer, the "sale on approval" is only a bailment with an option to purchase. On the other hand, if the arrangement is a "sale or return," the goods must be delivered primarily for resale and there is a present sale plus an option to return the goods. Title passes to the buyer until the buyer properly exercises the option to return, which revests title in the seller. Section 2–326(1)(b) and (2). Accordingly, in the latter case but not in the former the goods are not available to the buyer's creditors. Section 2–326(2).

In some cases the "or return" option may be disputed. Section 2–326(3) states this term constitutes a contract for sale within the statute of frauds and contradicts the sale aspect of the contract within the parol evidence rule.

7. CONSIGNMENTS

In some cases, the transaction may be structured as a "consignment" where no sale at all is intended but the goods are instead delivered to a person with the power in that person to sell them in the ordinary course to that person's buyers. This device ostensibly places the goods beyond the reach of the creditors of the person in possession even though it is economically equivalent to a sale or return and inventory financing of the person in possession where normally that person would acquire title subject to the inventory lender's security interest under UCC Article 9.

In order to protect the creditors of the person acquiring possession, such a consignment with respect to claims of the creditors of the person in possession is treated as a purchase money security interest, with some exceptions, such as it is established that the merchant conducting the business is generally known by that person's creditors to be substantially engaged in selling other's goods. Section 9–102(a)(20), 9–103(d), 9–109(a)(4) and 9–319. To be good against third parties, a financing statement must be filed under Article 9 of the UCC and, in addition, the party delivering possession may have a further duty of notice under Section 9–324.

If goods are not delivered to a person for sale but rather for another purpose such as storage or processing, the transaction may be a bailment or another form of transaction outside the scope of the UCC. But in CIBA–Geigy Corp. v. Flo–Lizer, Inc.

(1989), the court held that a delivery for storage, where the person taking delivery had apparent power to sell, subjected the goods to the UCC (then Section 2–326(3)). This reading is a generous interpretation of what constitutes "the purpose of sale." Compare In re Zwagerman (1991), which probably goes too far the other way. First National Bank of Blooming Prairie v. Olsen (1987) perhaps represents a sound analysis in these difficult cases. For an example of a clear bailment, see Eastman Kodak Co. v. Harrison (In re Sitkin Smelting & Refining, Inc.) (1981) (not delivered primarily for resale).

B. THE RIGHTS OF THIRD PARTIES

1. INTRODUCTION

In Anglo–American law there are two basic principles which govern the transfer of property interests. The first is that one can transfer no better interest than one has, and its converse rule that a transferee obtains the interest of the transferor. Section 2–403(a) and, subject to Section 2A–303, Sections 2A–304(1) and 2A–305(1).

The second principle is that one may not be deprived of one's interest without consent. To illustrate, suppose O loses his or her watch or it is stolen from him or her. Neither the finder nor the thief acquires title as against O. Furthermore, one who acquires the watch, however innocently, from the finder or thief, acquires no title as against O. In either of these cases O may assert his or her ownership and reclaim his or her watch. If he or she reclaims it from the innocent third party, the latter's only recourse is an action for damages against the person who sold the watch for breach of implied warranty. See Sections 2–312 and, for leases, 2A–211 discussed in Chapter 9.

In transactions involving goods, these two principles are subject to some exceptions which are discussed below.

2.   ENTRUSTING

a.   **Generally**

One of the most common legal relationships is that in which the owner entrusts goods to a bailee with authority to deal with them in accordance with certain terms agreed on between the parties. The bailee may be given authority to sell, repair, use or in some other way deal with the goods. Difficulty arises however, when the bailee, through either mistake or fraud, sells or leases the goods to an innocent third party in violation of the bailment agreement. Without question the owner has a right of action against the bailee for the value of the goods; however, in many instances this right is purely academic because the bailee has absconded or is so financially embarrassed that a judgment against the bailee is worthless. Commonly, then, the owner seeks to recover the goods from the innocent third party. These cases present a conflict between two interests which our society seeks to protect through law. One is the social interest in the security of acquisitions and the other is the social interest in the security of transactions.

b. Apparent Ownership, Apparent Authority, and Estoppel

In some instances, the owner of goods not only entrusts another with possession but is guilty of further conduct which makes it appear to third parties that the bailee either owns the goods or is authorized to sell or otherwise deal with them as agent for the owner. The mere separation of ownership and possession, however, is not normally such conduct. Article 2A makes this point in the case of a lease in Sections 2A–301 and 2A–302, and by not requiring filing or other public notice to protect the interest of the lessor against asserted claims of third parties. See Official Comment to Section 2A–101, Issues: Filing, and Mooney, The Mystery and Myth of "Ostensible Ownership" and Article 9 Filing: A Critique of Proposals to Extend Filing Requirements to Leases, 39 Ala.L.Rev. 683 (1988).

An old Pennsylvania case will serve as an example of apparent ownership. In O'Connor's Adm'x v. Clark (1895), O'Connor was a drayman who owned several wagons. One of his drivers was Tracy, who once had his own piano moving business. O'Connor, hoping to increase his own business by attracting some of Tracy's former customers, had the words "George Tracy, Piano Mover," painted on one of his wagons and gave Tracy possession of this wagon. Tracy, acting wrongfully and purporting to be the actual owner, offered to sell the wagon to Clark. Before paying the price, however, Clark, accompanied by Tracy, made inquiries at a police station and a saloon as to whether Tracy was in fact the person whose name appeared on the wagon. Various persons at these two places identified Tracy and the sale was consummated. The court refused to allow O'Connor to reclaim the wagon from Clark. The court reasoned that by painting Tracy's name on the wagon and giving him possession of it, O'Connor created appearances of ownership in Tracy, and because Clark purchased the wagon in reliance on these appearances, O'Connor should be barred from asserting his ownership against Clark.

Another typical kind of case in which courts have estopped the owner from asserting ownership against an innocent third party is where the owner gives an agent or some other person a document of title naming the latter as owner of the goods, and the person so named as owner, without authority and purporting to be the true owner, proceeds to sell or lease the goods to an innocent party who relies on the document.

In other cases the owner, while not creating an appearance of ownership in another, is guilty of conduct which makes it appear that the latter has the authority to sell or lease the goods as agent for the owner. The owner is said to have created an apparent authority in the faithless "agent," and if the latter sells or leases the goods to an innocent party who relies on the appearance of authority, the owner will be estopped to claim that the agent acted without authority. See Zendman v. Harry Winston, Inc. (1953).

These principles are not specifically spelled out in the Uniform Commercial Code; however, Official Comment 1 to Section 2–403 states an intention to continue unimpaired these general legal principles which should serve as authority to conclude they supplement the UCC under Section 1–103(b) rather than being displaced by its provisions. The same would be true with regard to the similar provisions of Sections 2A–304(1) and 2A–305(1).

c. Delivery of Possession Without Indicia of Title or Authority

As previously noted, the traditional view is that mere entrusting of possession does not cloak the bailee with apparent ownership or apparent authority to sell or lease even though the bailee may also be a dealer in goods of that kind. The old style factor's acts, enacted during the nineteenth century, were an early statutory exception to this general principle. They were designed to protect a good faith purchaser in the consignment setting discussed earlier. At that time, and today, a contractual device commonly used in the marketing of goods was the consignment, a transaction in which the owner delivers goods to a bailee who acts for the owner in selling and delivering the goods to customers. Such bailees commonly are called factors or commission merchants, and they often are also dealers who buy and sell goods on their own account. Assuming that the owner gives the factor no appearance of title or authority to sell, the common-law view was that a factor wrongfully pledging or selling the goods cannot give an innocent pledgee or buyer a title superior to the owner's. However, in those states which enacted old style factor's acts, innocent pledgees and buyers would prevail against the owner. The UCC, as discussed, now deals with consignments in Article 9.

Sections 2–403(2), 2A–304(2) and 2A–305(2) go further than the old style factor's acts and Article 9's consignment provisions in protecting innocent buyers and lessees for, unlike in those cases, the goods need not have been entrusted to the bailee for resale.

Section 2–403(2) provides:

(2) Entrusting of goods to a merchant that deals in goods of that kind gives the merchant power to transfer all of the entruster's rights to the goods and to transfer the goods free of any interest of the entruster to a buyer in ordinary course of business.

Two steps are essential before this subsection is applicable: (1) an entrusting of goods to a merchant who deals in goods of that kind and (2) a sale by such merchant to a buyer in ordinary course of business.

"Entrusting" is rather broadly defined in Section 2–403(3) as including "any delivery and any acquiescence in retention of possession regardless of any condition expressed between the parties to the delivery or acquiescence and regardless of whether the procurement of the entrusting or the possessor's disposition of the goods was punishable under the criminal law." This language means that there can be an entrusting even though delivery was obtained by fraud. There is no need for the party entrusted (bailee) to have any sort of title or even any right to retain the goods as against the entruster. While the entruster often is the owner, the entruster can have a lesser interest, such as a security interest.

The entrusting must be to a merchant who deals in goods of that kind. In Gallagher v. Unenrolled Motor Vessel River Queen (1973), the defendant sold and repaired boats as well as rented space to boat owners in his marina. The plaintiff rented a stall in the marina and delivered his boat to the defendant for storage. The defendant wrongfully sold the boat to a buyer and the plaintiff brought an action to recover it. The court decided that the plaintiff had not delivered the boat to a merchant who dealt in the goods of that kind as the boat had been delivered for storage, not for sale or repairs, and the defendant's storage business was separate and apart from his business as a repairman and boat merchant. This seems a very fine reading of the facts given the purpose of the section. Contrast Bank of New Hampshire v. Schreiber (1998) (car entrusted to dealer's service division for service and not to the sales division of dealership, and then sold to a customer of the dealership, was entrusted to a merchant who dealt in goods of that kind). The delivery of textile goods to a customs broker also has been held not to be a delivery to a merchant who deals in goods of that kind. Toyomenka, Inc. v. Mount Hope Finishing Co. (1970). On the other hand, delivery of an automobile to a dealer in new and used automobiles would constitute an entrusting within the meaning of this provision of the UCC. See Mattek v. Malofsky (1969). However, distinguish Superior Bank, FSB v. Human Services Employees Credit Union (2001), where the debtors transferred a car to the dealership they owned while it was subject to a security interest in a credit union given to secure the purchase financing, and the court upheld the security interest against a bank that had purchased the credit contract from the customer of the dealership; all the debtor's could "entrust" was their interest which was subject to the outstanding security interest.

There also must be a sale to a buyer in ordinary course of business. The UCC defines such a buyer as "a person that buys goods in good faith, without knowledge that the sale violates the rights of another person in the goods and in the ordinary course from a person, other than a pawnbroker, in the business of selling goods of that kind." Section 1–201(2)(i). Only a buyer that takes possession of the goods or has a right to recover the goods from the seller under Article 2 may be a buyer in ordinary course of business. A case in which the court dealt with whether or not a person was a buyer in ordinary course is Mattek v. Malofsky (1969). There plaintiff's son left her automobile with a licensed used car dealer with authority to display the car but not to sell it. Later the dealer drove the automobile with the dealer's license plate on it to defendant's used car lot and sold it to him. No certificate of title was delivered to defendant as required by the state motor vehicle code. Plaintiff brought a possessory action against defendant, and the latter's defense was based on Section 2–403(2). The court found that delivery of the automobile by plaintiff's son to the dealer constituted an entrusting within Section 2–403(2). It further concluded that defendant, even though a merchant, could be a buyer in ordinary course of business. The court found, however, that defendant did not meet the requirement of "good faith" and was not therefore a buyer in ordinary course of business. The court's reasoning was based on the theory that "good faith" under the UCC requires in the case of merchants at that time not only "honesty in fact," but also "the observance of reasonable commercial standards of fair dealing in the trade." Observance of reasonable commercial standards requires the merchant to have the knowledge of a merchant. Thus, defendant was chargeable with knowledge that the used car sold to him had a certificate of title outstanding, and that the dealer was required by law to transfer the certificate to him. On similar facts except the sale was to a consumer and the non-delivery of the certificate of title was explained, see Godfrey v. Gilsdorf (1970). A similar result was reached in Madrid v. Bloomington Auto Company, Inc. (2003).

Of course, for the buyer to obtain full title, the entruster must have had such title. See Barth v.

Protetch (1987), where that was not true. Another related type case is Executive Financial Services, Inc. v. Pagel (1986) (now codified in Section 2–403(2)). There a secured party entrusted several tractors to a John Deere dealership to lease to farmers, but instead the tractors were sold to a buyer in ordinary course of business. Because the security interest had not been created by the dealership, Section 9–307(1) (now Section 9–320(a)) did not apply, but the court held the rights of the secured party as such were transferred to the buyer in ordinary course of business.

Finally, Porter v. Wertz (1979), suggests there must be a unity of entrustment and sale. In the *Porter* case, the owner entrusted a painting to an art dealer for private use. The dealer delivered the painting to a friend, who was a restaurant worker, who in turn sold the painting to another art dealer. The court in part ruled against the second dealer because the owner did not entrust the painting to the person who sold it. One might argue that under the law at the time of the case that the first art dealer could pass on what he had, which was the power to transfer the owner's rights, thus giving the second art dealer power to transfer those rights when that dealer sold to its customer, but the language of amended Section 2–403(2) makes this argument difficult.

Another interesting case is Kahr v. Markland (1989), where plaintiff donated some bags of used clothing to a Goodwill store. One bag contained 28 pieces of sterling silver delivered by mistake. Defendant bought the valuable bag for $15. The court ruled the silver was not entrusted since no "voluntary transfer of possession" occurred due to the unknowing nature of the transfer. The silver was held to be lost property subject to recovery by its true owner. Perhaps a more acceptable basis for the result is defendant was not a buyer in ordinary course of business since he knew the silver was not stainless steel and thus arguably did not purchase in good faith. A similar case is Kenyon v. Abel (2001), where a valuable painting was delivered by movers moving the owner to a new home by mistake to the Salvation Army and sold by it for $25; there was no entrustment.

The results under Article 2A are similar. Suppose the third party is a subsequent lessee in ordinary course of business from a lessor to whom the existing lessee entrusted the goods; for example, a lessee of an automobile who has returned it to the dealer from whom it was leased for maintenance, and then the dealer re-leases the automobile to a second lessee in the ordinary course of the dealer's business. The subsequent lessee should prevail. See Sections 2A–304(2) and (3), 2A–104 and 2A–103(1)(t), and Official Comment 7 to Section 2A–304 which cites the *Gilsdorf* case.

As in the *Mattek* and *Gilsdorf* cases, above, many of the cases litigated have involved automobiles. These cases have been complicated by the fact that all states have statutes requiring that automobiles be "titled." This means that the state upon proper application will issue a certificate of title describing the vehicle and identifying the owner. If the vehicle is transferred these statutes generally require that the certificate be signed by the owner and delivered to the transferee. See, for example, Neb.Rev.St. § 60–105, which states, as applicable, that no person acquiring a motor vehicle shall acquire any right, title, claim, or interest in or to such motor vehicle until he shall have had delivered to him physical possession of such motor vehicle and a certificate of title or a manufacturer's or importer's certificate.

A conflict between a certificate of title act and Sections 2–403(2), or Sections 2A–105, 2A–304 or 2A–305, may arise when an automobile is entrusted to a dealer and the dealer wrongfully sells or leases the automobile to a buyer or lessee in ordinary course of business without complying with the state's certificate of title act. Which statute controls; that is, the UCC protects the innocent third party and the title acts protect the title holder. Under prior law the cases are not in agreement. See Godfrey v. Gilsdorf (1970) and Madrid v. Bloomington Auto Company, Inc. (2003) (Section 2–403(2) controls) and Messer v. Averill (1970) (certificate of title act controls). See, also Dugdale of Nebraska, Inc. v. First State Bank (1988) and Dartmouth Motor Sales, Inc. v. Wilcox (1986). Currently, both Article 2 and Article 2A specifically addresses the issue and, in the case of conflict (if that interpretation is reached by the court), generally subordinate the UCC rule to the certificate of title act. Sections 2–108(2) and 2A–104(2). But in this situation, the

UCC rule prevails. See Section 2–108(1)(a) and Sections 2A–104(2), 2A–105, 2A–304(3) and 2A–305(3). Not all potential issues of conflict involve certificate of title acts. See In re Wegner (1988) (required bill of sale to transfer title to livestock) and In re Gull Air, Inc. (1987) (compliance with Federal Aviation Act).

What if the owner of property leases it to a dealer, who then either leases it or sells it to a lessee or a buyer in ordinary course of business? This is a form of entrustment, and in Barco Auto Leasing Corp. v. Holt (1988), the court held that a buyer could prevail. See also Exxon Co., U.S.A. v. TLW Computer Industries, Inc. (1983). The same result would obtain under Section 2A–305(b) and (c), which covers both buyers and sublessees in ordinary course of business.

3. VOIDABLE INTERESTS

Absent the applicability of the above rules, as previously noted, normally a transferee of goods acquires only the interest that the transferor of the goods had. For example, and subject to Section 2A–303 on restrictions in the lease, if a lessor double leases the same goods, the second lessee takes subject to the first lease. If a lessee sells or subleases goods, the buyer or sublessee gets only the interest that the lessee had. Sections 2A–304(1) and 2A–305(1). See also Section 2–403(1) and Rohweder v. Aberdeen Production Credit Ass'n (1985).

In some instances, however, a seller or lessor will deliver goods to a buyer or lessee pursuant to contract but for a reason such as fraud the buyer or lessee will obtain only a "voidable" interest. Legal title or a leasehold interest is voidable when the title or interest is subject to a right in the seller or lessor to avoid the sale or lease and revest full title in the seller or lessor. It is commonly said that "voidable" means "valid until avoided." Suppose, for example, that B, who intentionally misrepresents B's financial condition, induces S to sell goods on credit. Delivery of the goods to B gives B "voidable" title only, and S, upon discovering the fraud, may rescind the sale and recover the goods. If that occurs before a good faith purchaser purchases from B, then title is in S and B has nothing to convey, but, if S has not recovered the goods, S has entrusted them and the purchaser may prevail under that analysis if a buyer in ordinary course of business. For a discussion of the seller's right to reclaim the goods on the buyer's insolvency, see Chapter 11. A similar analysis applies if B fraudulently induces S to lease the goods. In contrast, if the goods are wrongfully taken and are not delivered voluntarily because of mistake, Section 2–403 does not create a voidable title. Kenyon v. Abel (2001).

The problem becomes complex if B then resells the goods to P before S can avoid the sale. At common law, the courts protected P if P was a good faith purchaser. This is also the rule adopted by Section 2–403(1), which provides in part: "A person with voidable title has power to transfer good title to a good faith purchaser for value."

The same principle exists in Article 2A. Suppose instead (1) B leases the goods to P, or (2) itself leased the goods from S and then subleases them to P? In the first case, under Section 2A–304(1), a lessor with voidable title has power to transfer a good leasehold interest to a good faith subsequent lessee for value, and, in the second case, under Section 2A–305(1) a lessee with a voidable leasehold interest has power to transfer a good leasehold interest to either a good faith buyer for value or a good faith sublessee for value. There is some overlap between Sections 2–403(1) and 2A–304(1) and 2A–305(1) due to the definitions of "purchase" in Sections 1–201(2)(cc) and 2A–103(1)(bb) and "purchaser" in Section 1–201(b)(30), which include both a sale and a lease. See Official Comment 2 to Section 2A–304.

The question always is: did the transaction in which the goods were delivered result in a "voidable" interest? If the transaction vested no interest at all, as in the case of theft or other involuntary transfer, then the voidable principle is inapplicable, and in the absence of other circumstances (such as estoppel or an entrusting) the transferee does not have the power to transfer a good interest even to a good faith purchaser for value. See Suburban Motors, Inc. v. State Farm Mutual Automobile Insur. Co. (1990), where the court upheld this principle even though the certificate of title was facially valid, and the *Kenyon v. Abel* case discussed earlier. The problem of determining whether the interest is "voidable" or "void" has been especially difficult in two types of situations discussed below.

a. Cash Transactions

A sales agreement may not provide for an extension of credit to the buyer, or it may provide expressly that the payment term is "cash." In either case the transaction is commonly called a "cash sale," and the buyer is obligated to pay the price upon delivery of the goods. Section 2–507(1).

There are cases where despite an agreement for payment on delivery the goods are delivered but the buyer fails to pay the price. The early case of Leven v. Smith (1845) involved such a situation. There B agreed to buy certain boots and shoes from S to be delivered by S to B's store and to be paid for on delivery. S's employee took the goods to B's store, where B, after examining the goods, offered in payment of the price a small amount in cash and a promissory note for the balance. The employee took the money and note but informed B he could not accept payment in this manner without authority from S. The employee then left B's store with the understanding that he was to consult S as to whether payment in this manner would be satisfactory. S, when informed by his employee of the circumstances, refused to accept payment in that way and instructed the employee to return to B's place of business and bring back the goods. When the employee demanded the goods B refused to return them. The employee had left the goods with B no more than four or five minutes. The court allowed S to recover the goods on the theory that the sale was intended to be strictly for cash and that title thus was not to pass until payment was made (or the requirement was waived).

All courts at common law agreed that the cash term could be waived, although there was a difference of opinion as to what constituted a waiver. In some jurisdictions a waiver resulted if the seller did not expressly declare at the time of delivery a right to retake the goods if payment were not made later. Other courts disagreed, and looked to the seller's subsequent conduct in light of the circumstances. Failure for several weeks after delivery to take any steps toward collecting the price constituted a waiver according to one court. Hirsch Lumber Co. v. Hubbell (1911). Failure to take action to recover the goods after failure of the buyer to pay following repeated demands by the seller for payment constituted a waiver according to another court. Frech v. Lewis (1907).

The courts agreed that if the seller did not waive the cash term the seller could recover the goods *from the buyer* (emphasis added) if the price were not paid. This was on the theory that delivery was conditional and title would not pass to the buyer until payment. A more difficult question was raised when the buyer sold the goods to a good faith purchaser before the seller could recover them. Even here most courts protected the seller and allowed recovery of the goods from the good faith purchaser, on the theory that as the buyer had no title none could be transferred. Under the UCC, however, an entrustment analysis may apply, as discussed earlier.

The most frequent "cash sale" transaction which has come before the courts is where the buyer gives a "bad check," that is, a check drawn against insufficient funds and dishonored by the drawee bank. Most pre-UCC cases held that acceptance of the check was not a waiver of the cash term and delivery of the goods was conditioned on honor of the check. Thus the seller could recover the goods from the buyer if the check was dishonored. Most courts also allowed the seller to recover from a good faith purchaser.

Section 2–507(2) of the UCC deals with the cash sale situation by providing:

(2) If payment is due and demanded on delivery to the buyer of goods or documents of title, the seller may reclaim the goods delivered upon a demand made within a reasonable time after the seller discovers or should have discovered that payment was not made.

First, it should be observed that this subsection deals only with the rights of the seller against the buyer. The seller's rights against a good faith purchaser for value are determined by other provisions which are discussed below.

Second, in order for the transaction to be a "cash transaction", two conditions must be met: (1) payment must be due on delivery, that is, the parties must not have agreed that credit would be extended, and (2) even if payment is due it must, nevertheless, be demanded upon delivery. Delivery without demand would constitute a waiver and the transaction becomes a credit one.

There need be no demand for payment in cash. Acceptance of a check or demand for payment by check would not constitute a waiver, as payment in this manner is a commercially normal practice even in "cash transactions." Section 2–511(2) and Official Comment 4. Payment by check is not tantamount to payment in cash, however, but is only conditional. Section 2–511(3) provides that subject to the provisions of the UCC on the effect of an obligation under Section 3–310, payment by check is conditional and is defeated as between the parties by dishonor of the check on due presentment.

The same rule is stated generally in Article 3 at Section 3–310(b). Of course, if payment is not made the seller also may sue for the price under Section 2–709 or sue on any check given under UCC Section 3–414. It might be noted the bad check situation could also arise to a degree in a lease context where a bad check for a security deposit or rent would constitute a default and allow cancellation of the lease with similar results to those in a sale as discussed. See Sections 2A–523(1) and 2A–525(2). A lessor might then also sue for the rent under Section 2A–529, and would have the same rights as to a check because of the Article 3 rules.

Returning to the sale context, Official Comment 3 to Section 2–507 used to assert that the seller's right to recover the goods under former Section 2–507(2) was subject to the same ten day limitation to which a seller was subject in recovering goods from an insolvent buyer under former Section 2–702(2). Under the latter section, which deals with credit and not cash sales, if a seller discovered that a buyer had received goods on credit while insolvent, the seller could reclaim the goods only if the seller demanded their return within ten days after the buyer received them. Under current Article 2, these specific time limits are deleted as inappropriate, and a reasonable time is substituted; that is, excessive time that causes prejudice, waiver, estoppel, or ratification is not reasonable. However, there maybe a different limit in bankruptcy under Bankruptcy Code § 546(c). Official Comment 3 to Section 2–507, and Official Comment 2 to Section 2–702.

Now suppose the buyer or lessee resells or releases the goods to a good faith purchaser before the seller or lessor can recover them? The seller or lessor would still have an action for the price or the rent or an action on the check if a bad check had been given, but many times these rights would be purely academic as a judgment would be of little if any value. Recovery of the goods often is a much more satisfactory remedy. May the seller or lessor recover the goods from the good faith purchaser?

This question is addressed in Section 2–403(1), which provides in part that a person with voidable title has power to transfer a good title to a good faith purchaser for value. If goods have been delivered under a transaction of purchase, the purchaser has such power even though ... (b) the delivery was in exchange for a check that is later dishonored, or (c) it was agreed that the transaction was to be a cash sale.

Sections 2A–304(1) and 2A–305(1) are the same except for adjustments due to the different contexts. See also Section 2–507(3), which subjects the right to reclaim to the rights of a buyer in ordinary course or other good faith purchaser for value.

These provisions change the majority rule at common law and protect the good faith purchaser for value. Thus under the UCC in "cash sales" and "bad check" transactions, the seller or lessor may not recover the goods from the good faith purchaser, but is left to the remedies against the buyer or lessee.

In order to be protected under these provisions, the purchaser must be a good faith purchaser for value. "Good faith" is defined in Section 1–201(b)(20) as honesty in fact and the observance of reasonable commercial standards of fair dealing, and Sections 2–103(3) and 2A–103(4) incorporate that standard. Honesty in fact is to be determined by what the purchaser actually knew and not by what an investigation into the facts would have arguably disclosed. Johnson & Johnson Products, Inc. v. Dal Intern. Trading Co. (1986). A very cheap price, coupled with knowledge of thefts in the area and other uncustomary circumstances, may preclude good faith. Liles Brothers & Son v. Wright (1982). A purchaser is one who takes "by sale, lease, discount, negotiation, mortgage, pledge, lien, security interest, issue or re-issue, gift, or any other voluntary transaction creating an interest in property." Sections 1–201(b)(29), (30) and 2A–103(d). Value includes consideration sufficient to support a simple contract and taking of property in payment of or as security for a pre-existing claim. Section 1–204. Thus taking goods as a gift would not make one a purchaser for value, but paying for the goods in cash or by the exchange of other property would constitute giving value, as would taking goods in payment for a debt already owed by the transferor to the transferee.

Neither Section 2–403(1) nor Section 2A–304(1) or 2A–305(1) arguably make protection of a good faith purchaser necessarily turn on whether or not the person who transferred the goods to the purchaser had a "voidable" interest, as was the case many times at common law. Rather if the goods have been delivered "under a transaction of purchase" and in a cash sale or for a bad check arguably the purchaser may prevail. Since a transaction of purchase "includes taking by sale, lease, discount, negotiation, mortgage, pledge, lien, security interest, issue or reissue, gift, or any voluntary transaction creating an interest in property," it could be argued that a delivery of goods under a transaction which at common law vested no interest in a purchaser creates no property interest in the purchaser and, therefore, there is no delivery "under a transaction of purchase" and those provisions are not applicable to protect a good faith purchaser. See Weber, "The Extension of the Voidable Title Principle Under the Code," 49 Ky. L. J. 437, 455–457 (1961). This analysis is specifically repudiated to the extent statutes have extended the category of larcenous conduct from which no interest could be derived under the common law. See Mowrey v. Walsh (1828) and Official Comment 2 to Section 2–403; Sections 2–403(1)(d) ("criminal fraud"), 2A–304(1)(d) and 2A–305(1)(c) (same). This same argument also could be advanced with reference to "at a distance impersonation" discussed under the imposter problem. The argument seems strained, however, and the conclusion already stated, that the language of these provisions changes the majority common law rule and protects a good faith purchaser, seems the correct interpretation.

b. The Imposter Problem

Suppose B visits S and poses as X, a financially responsible citizen. Believing B to be X, S delivers goods to him or her on credit. B then resells the goods to P, a good faith purchaser. Subsequently, S discovers the fraud and attempts to recover the goods from P. Courts which have dealt with the problem have not allowed S to do so, on the theory that B's fraud was merely "collateral," S intended to sell to the person before S, whoever he or she was, and the latter person acquired voidable title which ripened into full title upon transfer to a good faith purchaser. See Dudley v. Lovins (1949); Phelps v. McQuade (1917).

Of course, an impersonation may not occur face-to-face. Suppose, for example, B writes to S and represents himself or herself as X and orders goods on credit from S. X is known to S as a responsible business person. S ships the goods addressed to X. B receives the goods and sells them to P, a good faith purchaser. Courts have refused to protect P in this case on the theory that S intended to deal with X and X alone; therefore, B received no title and could transfer none to P. See Newberry v. Norfolk & Southern R. Co. (1903); Cundy v. Lindsay (1878).

This distinction is formalistic and vulnerable to criticism. The UCC should be read to abolish the distinction between "face-to-face" and "at-a-distance" impersonation, and protect the good faith purchaser in both cases. Sections 2–403(1)(a), 2A–304(1)(a) and 2A–305(1)(a).

c. Voidable Interests and Entrusting Compared

In either the imposter or the cash sale and bad check situations a good faith purchaser might be protected under either the entrustment or the voidable interest rules. The following examples will serve to illustrate the various possibilities.

(1) S sells and delivers goods to B who pays for them with a bad check. Before S recovers the goods, B resells the goods to P and absconds.

(2) S sells and delivers goods on credit to B, relying on B's fraudulent representation that he or she is X. B immediately resells the goods to P and absconds.

(3) D, who owns a valuable watch entrusts it for repairs to B, who repairs and sells new and used watches. B wrongfully sells the watch to P and absconds.

In examples 1 and 2, P prevails if he or she is a good faith purchaser for value as the goods were delivered to B under a transaction of purchase. It is not necessary that B be a merchant dealing in goods of that kind or that P be a buyer in the ordinary course of business. If B were a merchant dealing in goods of that kind, however, delivery of the goods by S to B would constitute an entrusting under Section 2–403(3) and therefore, if P were a buyer in the ordinary course of business, Section 2–403(2) as well as Section 2–403(1) would protect P.

In example 3, P would prevail only by showing that Section 2–403(2) applied. Section 2–403(1) would not apply because there was no delivery to B under a transaction of purchase. While the facts show an entrusting to a merchant who deals in watches, P would also have to prove that he or she was a buyer in ordinary course of business. If P were a wholesale dealer, for example, he or she might qualify as a good faith purchaser for value, but might not as a buyer in ordinary course. Section 1–201(b)(9).

4.   POSSESSION AND RIGHTS
OF CREDITORS

Suppose S sells goods to B and title passes to B, but the latter leaves the goods in S's possession, perhaps because S must prepare them for delivery and will deliver them later, or perhaps because B leases the goods back to S in a sale-leaseback. S then wrongfully resells the goods to P, a good faith purchaser. P may prevail over B, usually on the theory that S's possession, coupled with prior ownership, gave S apparent ownership. While this theory is not altogether sound (since it evidently is applied even when P has no knowledge that S was the prior owner), the result seems sound enough from the standpoint of public policy. The UCC does not deal with the problem specifically, except the fact B has title does not necessarily even give B a claim to the goods (as opposed to damages for failure of the seller to deliver), because, while the rights of unsecured creditors of the seller with respect to goods that have been identified to the contract for sale are subject to the buyer's rights to recover the goods, the buyer has a right to recover the goods only under Section 2–502 (limited right to obtain goods from an insolvent seller) and Section 2–716 (limited right to specific performance). Moreover, if S also is a merchant dealing in the ordinary course of business, B's permitting S to retain possession constitutes an entrusting and P is protected under Section 2–403(2). Sections 2A–304(2) and 2A–305(2) follow the same principle. If, however, those sections are inapplicable a court dealing with the problem would have to rely on other rules of law in the jurisdiction pursuant to Section 1–103(b). Section 2–402(2).

Suppose, in the same fact situation, that S does not resell the goods to P but rather that C, S's creditor, attempts to levy on the goods so as to subject them to the payment of C's claim against S. B then intervenes, claiming the goods by virtue of the sale. C then argues that since S has possession of the goods any alleged prior sale is fraudulent and void. If C can prove as a fact that the transaction between S and B is merely a scheme to defraud, that is, an attempt to place the goods beyond the reach of S's creditors while still allowing their full use to S, the sale will be void as to C and C's rights in the goods are superior to those of B. On the other hand, if C cannot prove that the sale by S to B was in fact an attempt to defraud, opinion regarding the legal rights of the parties is widely divided. In some states the courts have held that S's retention of possession makes the sale, as to C, fraudulent as a matter of law except in a few narrow exceptions, such as the goods are too heavy to move. See Sturtevant and Keep v. Ballard (1811). This rule precludes B from introducing evidence to show that the sale by S to B was made in good faith and that S's retention of possession was commercially reasonable under the circumstances. However, even in those jurisdictions which follow this strict view, as noted in some narrow instances B has been allowed to prevail over the claim of C. Other states reject the "fraud in law" approach and take the view that

S's retention of possession is only presumed to be fraudulent and B is allowed to introduce evidence to prove good faith and thereby to rebut the presumption of fraud. This sometimes is called the "fraud in fact" theory. See Davis v. Turner (1848). Under the Uniform Fraudulent Transfer Act, which is the law in many states, retention of possession by the seller under Section 4(b)(2) is only a factor to be considered and does not establish a presumption. Finally, in some states, regardless of which of the above theories is followed, the seller's retention of possession is not regarded as fraudulent and C has no right to complain unless C is an existing creditor, that is, a creditor of the seller at the time of the sale. If C is a subsequent creditor (one who becomes a creditor of S after the sale to B), it is reasoned that C has no right to complain, since one who extends credit to another ordinarily has no right to assume that the latter owns all goods in that person's possession.

In view of the wide difference of opinion regarding C's right to goods retained by S after sale to B, the UCC does not propose any specific solution. Rather, Section 2–402(2) provides that:

(2) A creditor of the seller may treat a sale or an identification of goods to a contract for sale as void if as against the creditor a retention of possession by the seller is fraudulent under any rule of law of the state where the goods are situated. However, retention of possession in good faith and current course of trade by a merchant-

seller for a commercially reasonable time after a sale or identification is not fraudulent.

See also Section 2–402(3) and Section 2A–308(1) and (2) to the same effect where a lessor retains possession.

The UCC thus leaves the question whether retention of possession is fraudulent up to the law of each state, except that a buyer or lessee is protected when the seller or lessor is a merchant and the seller or the lessor retains the goods in good faith and current course of trade for a commercially reasonable time, such as for the period to prepare the goods for delivery or to deliver the goods. In addition, because sale-leasebacks have a recognized commercial validity, Section 2A–308(3) insulates this transaction as long as the buyer bought for value and in good faith.

5.   ASSIGNMENT (AND DELEGATION)

A contract for sale or a lease involves bilateral obligations to deliver and to pay and their converse rights to obtain delivery and payment. Generally an obligation may be delegated unless a contractual prohibition exists or to do so would have the effect of depriving the other party of the substantial benefit of the bargain. Sections 2–210(2)(a) and (d) and Section 9–407(b)(2) (if there is a provision making delegation of a material performance under the lease a default). Usually the latter prospect arises in contracts for personal services or which call for the exercise of skill or discretion. Output, requirement, and exclusive dealing contracts normally should no longer fall in this category due to the reasonably objective criteria supplied in Section 2–306 (see Empire Gas Corp. v. American Bakeries Co. (1988)), and the availability of Section 2–609, which remove most of the "personal discretion" element. Any delegation under Section 2–210(2)(c) affords ground to demand assurance under Section 2–609, and even though Section 2A–303, the comparable section in Article 2A to Section 2–210, is silent on this point, that also would be true in the case of a lease, as applicable, under Section 2A–401. See Official Comment 7 to Section 2A–303. Normally a delegating party remains bound and is not relieved of the obligation, and so is responsible for a failure to perform to the other party, unless otherwise agreed in a "novation." Sections 2–210(2)(a) and 2A–303(6).

Generally a right under a sale contract or a lease also may be assigned. Once the transfer of a right has occurred, the transferor's interest is ended and the right is the property of the transferee. Sections 2–210(1) and 2A–303(2) confirm this basic rule, but there are significant exceptions.

Before describing the exceptions, it may be noted that often the parties do not distinguish between obligations and rights, but assign "the contract" or "all rights under the contract." Sections 2–210(3) and 2A–303(5) provide in that case that both obligations and rights are assigned unless the language or circumstances (such as where the contract is assigned as collateral for a loan) indicate only an assignment of rights is intended. Section 2A–303 deals with both voluntary and involuntary assignments; Section 2–210 appears to deal only with voluntary assignments.

Both Section 2–210(1)(a) and 2A–303(2) allow a contrary agreement prohibiting an assignment or making an assignment a default to overcome the basic rule in favor of assignment. A limit on such an agreement is stated in Section 2–210(1)(a); a right to damages for breach of the whole contract or a right arising out of the assignor's due performance of its entire obligation can be assigned despite agreement otherwise. Thus a seller should be able to assign a right to receive the price even though the seller has warranted the goods. The rule in Section 2A–303(3) is the same. But see Official Comment 3 to Section 2A–303, drawing a distinction between operating and non-operating leases. Beyond this, and with the exception of a presumptive limitation in Section 2–210(4), restrictions on anti-assignment or default agreements mainly relate to security interests under Article 9 when the sale has produced a right to payment for goods sold. Thus, Section 2–210(1)(a) cross-references Section 9–406, and that provision provides (with three possible exceptions):

"(d)... a term in an agreement between an account debtor (the person obligated on an account, chattel paper or general intangible–Section 9–102(a)(3)) and an assignor, or in a promissory note, is ineffective to the extent that it:"

(1) prohibits, restricts or requires the consent of the account debtor or person obligated on the promissory note to the assignment or transfer of, or the creation, attachment, perfection, or enforcement of a security interest in, the account, chattel paper, payment intangible, or promissory note; or

(2) "provides that [these circumstances] may give rise to default, breach, [etc.] under the account, chattel paper, payment intangible or promissory note."

Section 2A–303(2) is much the same, except Section 2A–303(2) cross-references Section 9–407 and, because of the nature of a lease which may involve executory obligations on both sides so there is an interest in dealing with the original parties, Section 9–407(b)(1) validates agreements that make a voluntary transfer of the lessee's right of possession or use a default. Section 2A–303(7) requires any effective prohibition or default provision in a consumer lease to be in record form and to be specific and conspicuous.

Section 9–406(f) also overrides certain restrictions on designated assignments of accounts and chattel paper created by rule of law, statute or regulation. A number of states have provided non-uniform amendments to Article 9, however, that preserve restrictions on assignment of certain receivables, such as payments under a worker's compensation law or a structured settlement.

Where the sale or lease agreement is silent on the question of assignment, Section 2A–303(3) states, and Section 2–210(1) and through Section 9–406(f), infers that the transfer of a right to damages for default with respect to the whole contract or the transfer of a right to payment arising out of the transferor's due performance of the transferor's entire obligation is not a transfer that the law restricts because it materially impairs the prospect of obtaining return performance by, or that materially changes the duty of, or that materially increases the burden or risk imposed on, the other party, and thus this type of transfer does not afford a remedy under Section 2A–303(4) and Section 2–210(1)(b). In addition, Section 2–210(1)(b) further states that creating, perfecting, or enforcing a security interest in the seller's interest also is not subject to remedy until and then only to the extent enforcement results in an actual delegation of a material performance of the seller, in which case the security interest is effective but damages may be recovered. Section 2A–303(2), by cross-reference to Section 9–407(c), is the same as to a lessor's leasehold or residual interest.

Neither Section 2–210 nor Section 2A–303 contain all the law on assignment. Much of that law in this context is general contract law or is in Article 9, and, aside from the discussion above, is left to discussion in those places. Nor does the UCC deal explicitly with restrictions in other laws upon assignments, such as the federal Assignment of

Claims Act, although state law restrictions, as noted, may be overridden by Section 9–406(f).

6.   NEGOTIATION OF NEGOTIABLE DOCUMENTS OF TITLE

In some instances the transferee of a negotiable document of title (see Chapter 5) also will take better title to the document and to the goods represented by the document than the transferor had.

Suppose O stores in W's warehouse goods for which W issues a negotiable warehouse receipt to O calling for delivery of goods "to bearer." O's office is burglarized and the receipt is stolen. Later the receipt comes into the hands of P, who purchased it in good faith without knowledge of the theft and in the regular course of business or financing. P is the "holder" of the document. P has title to it and to the goods. W must hold and deliver the goods to or for P. Sections 7–501, 7–502.

Or suppose, in the same case, that W issued a warehouse receipt calling for delivery of the goods "to the order of O," and that before the receipt was stolen O had indorsed it in blank. P would be the "holder" and would be the owner of the document and the goods. Sections 7–501, 7–502.

The same principles would hold true in the above cases if the document involved were any negotiable document as defined in Section 1–201(b)(16) of the UCC.

CHAPTER 8

RISK OF LOSS

---

1. INTRODUCTION

Much sales litigation involves situations where the goods which form the subject matter of the contract are damaged, lost, or destroyed after the contract is made but before it has been fully performed. The question involved in these cases is, who bears the risk of loss, the seller or the buyer? As mentioned in an earlier chapter, at common law and under the Uniform Sales Act, risk of loss normally followed title. Risk of loss was recognized as one of the incidents of ownership, although this could be changed by the agreement of the parties, but in many instances an agreement will be silent because the parties do not focus on the issue. In leases, there is a much greater chance the agreement will address the issue because most leases involve a record signed by both parties.

Article 2, in cases where the parties have not agreed on the matter of risk of loss (see Section 2–509(4)), separates risk of loss from title and treats risk of loss primarily as a "contractual" problem rather than one dependent on who has the title or "property" in the goods. See Section 2–509. In this regard, the terms "F.O.B.," "F.A.S.," "C.I.F." or "C. & F." will have a bearing. Thus, inquiry into who has title is no longer relevant in risk of loss problems.

Of course who has title in the lease context is not an issue as the lessor retains title. Section 2A–219(1) then, in essence, treats risk of loss as one of the incidents of ownership and, absent agreement, risk of damage or destruction from other than acts of the lessee is retained by the lessor, except in the case of a finance lease (Section 2A–103(1)(l)). In a finance lease, the fact and substance of ownership diverge because, as discussed in Chapter 1, a finance lease is an alternative for a security interest in financing the acquisition of the use of goods, and the lessee is substantively treated as the owner for the purpose of risk of loss. Thus in a lease risk of loss passes to the lessee at the agreed time or otherwise in a finance lease in accordance with Section 2A–219. Section 2A–219 also controls the time of passage when risk of loss passes by agreement but the time is not agreed upon. As previously noted, Section 2A–219 does not deal with responsibility for loss caused by the wrongful act of either the lessor or the lessee, such as failure to repair. See Official Comment to Section 2A–219 and also Official Comment 3 to Section 2A–525 and Section 2A–218 on insurance.

Sections 2–509 and 2A–219 contain the rules for determining risk of loss and the time of its passage in most cases. These rules are constructed around three possible situations involving how delivery of the goods is to be made.

(1) The contract may require or authorize shipment of the goods. Such a contract may or may not require delivery of the goods at a particular destination. As discussed in Chapter 6, this means it may be either a shipment or a destination contract.

(2) The goods may be in the possession of a bailee and under the contract delivery is to be made without moving the goods.

(3) The situation may not fall into either category (1) or (2). The contract may call for the buyer or lessee to pick up the goods or for delivery by some means other than a carrier such as by the seller or lessor's truck.

The rules in Sections 2–509 and 2A–219 do not govern all risk of loss cases. Section 2–509(4) notes three exceptions:

(a) The rules in Sections 2–509 and 2A–219 are subject to a contrary agreement by the parties.

The parties are free to make their own rules which may be completely different from those in the UCC.

(b) Risk of loss in a sale on approval is governed by Section 2–327.

(c) When there is a breach of contract or default by either party any risk of loss problem is governed by Sections 2–510 and 2A–220.

What is the legal significance of bearing the risk of loss? Ordinarily, risk of loss problems involve either an action for the price or for the rent by the seller or the lessor, or an action by the buyer or the lessee for restitution of the price or the rent or some part thereof already paid. If risk of loss is on the seller or lessor, they cannot recover the price or the rent and, moreover, are still bound to deliver or respond in damages, unless some excuse can be found such as in Section 2–613 or Section 2A–221. If the buyer or lessee has already paid the price or rent, the seller or lessor must return it. On the other hand, if the risk rests on the buyer or lessee, it is liable for the price or the rent even though the buyer or lessee may not have received the goods or may have to procure other goods to meet the buyer or lessee's needs. Sections 2–709(1)(a) and 2A–529(1)(a).

2. RULES GOVERNING RISK OF LOSS IN THE ABSENCE OF BREACH

a. Goods Shipped by Carrier

Sections 2–509(1), and 2A–219(2)(a) if risk is to pass to the lessee, contain the first risk of loss rule: if the contract requires or authorizes the seller to ship the goods by carrier: (1) if the contract does not require the seller to deliver them at a particular destination, the risk of loss passes to the buyer when the goods are delivered to the carrier even if the shipment is under reservation under Section 2–505; and (2) it does require the seller to deliver the goods at a particular destination and the goods are there tendered while in possession of the carrier, the risk of loss passes to the buyer when the goods are there tendered so as to enable the buyer to take delivery. Section 2A–219(2), of course, uses the terms "lessor" and "lessee."

These provisions distinguish between shipment and destination contracts. In the shipment contract the buyer or lessee bears the risk of loss while the goods are in transit, whereas in a destination contract the risk remains on the seller or lessor during transit. This is consistent with the UCC sections dealing with the seller's tender obligations, see Sections 2–503 and 2–504, and with the implicit conclusions on that issue for leases that would be derived by analogy from the provisions of Article 2 and the nature of a lease as discussed in Chapter 6. Basically, this rule provides that risk of loss passes when tender obligations are fulfilled. If it is not clear which type of contract is intended, the preference in resolving the ambiguity is for the shipment contract. Pestana v. Karinol Corp. (1979) and see Official Comment 5 to Section 2–503.

The UCC does not define "carrier," making it somewhat uncertain what the term includes. It is generally agreed that it at least includes railroads, commercial air carriers, and trucking companies. See Nordstrom, The Law of Sales 396 (1970) and White and Summers, Uniform Commercial Code 3d 220 (1988). Does it include the seller's own truck? If not, cases calling for delivery by seller's truck would be governed by the residuary rule. The UCC does not provide a clear answer, but the better answer is the seller's truck is not included. See Nordstrom, supra, and 1 N.Y. State Law Revision Commission 1955 Report 488 (1955).

The risk of loss provisions reflect that business persons commonly use mercantile symbols and terms which are understood to have definite risk of loss consequences. These must be interpreted in light of applicable use of trade and any course of performance or course of dealing between the parties. In general, the following is a list of some terms commonly used with a general statement of their risk of loss consequences:

(1) "F.O.B. Philadelphia" (seller's or lessor's city), "F.O.B. seller's or lessor's plant," "F.O.B. seller's or lessor's place of business," are all shipment contracts. The risk of loss is on the buyer or lessee while the goods are in transit. Sections 2–

509(1)(a) and 2A–219(2)(a)(i). Risk of loss passes when conforming goods are delivered to the carrier.

(2) The same language as above, except that the term is F.O.B. buyer's or lessee's city, plant, or place of business, is a destination contract. The risk of loss remains on the seller or lessor until the goods are tendered at the place of destination. Sections 2–509(1)(b) and 2A–219(2)(a)(ii).

(3) The same language as in the first example above, except that the words "Ship to Chicago (buyer's or lessee's city)" or some other destination are added. It has been argued that these additional words change what would otherwise have been a shipment contract into a destination one. Existing case law rejects this position on the theory that the seller or lessor must know where to ship the goods in order to make a proper contract of carriage. See Eberhard Mfg. Co. v. Brown (1975). Thus the words are those of direction only and do not obligate the seller or lessor to deliver to that named destination. It is a shipment contract and risk of loss is on the buyer or lessee while the goods are in transit. This resolution seems consistent with the preference for a shipment contract described in Official Comment 5 to Section 2–503.

(4) The same language as in the first example above, except that the words, "freight allowed" or "seller is to pay the freight" are added. Assuming there is no contrary agreement, the term "F.O.B.

place of shipment" will place the obligation to pay the freight or cost of transportation on the buyer or lessee. Use of the words above shifts the obligation of transportation costs to the seller or the lessor. Is this tantamount to an agreement by the seller or lessor to deliver to a destination? Official Comment 5 to Section 2–503 says "no;" this would remain a shipment contract, the rule under the Uniform Sales Act (Section 19, Rule 5), which would have treated a contract in which the seller pays the freight as a destination contract, is intended to be rejected. But see National Heater Co., Inc. v. Corrigan Co. Mechanical Contractors, Inc. (1973), which illustrates the need to closely read the language used. Official Comment 5 explains that the shipment contract is the normal one and the destination contract is the variant kind. There is no destination contract unless the seller or lessor has "specifically" agreed to deliver at a named destination or the term used "contemplates such delivery."

In both shipment and destination contracts transfer of risk of loss from the seller or lessor to the buyer or lessee requires that the goods be delivered to the carrier (shipment contracts) and tendered at point of destination (destination contracts). The previous use of the word "duly" in Section 2–509 in connection with both shipment and destination contracts caused confusion in relation to Section 2–503, which details a seller's obligations for tender of delivery, and accordingly, is omitted. A similar omission is made in Section 2A–219. If a seller or lessor is in breach or default, Sections 2–510 or 2A–220 will apply. Thus, Official Comment 2 to Section 2–509 states that delivery to the carrier in shipment contracts requires adherence to the performance obligations of Section 2–504. These obligations are discussed in Chapter 6. Tender in destination contracts would require meeting the obligations imposed by Sections 2–503(1) and (3). The principles involved should be applicable in the case of leases as well.

b. Goods in Possession of Bailee

The goods to be delivered may be in the possession of a bailee, such as a warehouse, and the contract may provide that delivery of the goods is to be made without removing them from the physical possession of the bailee. Sections 2–509(2), and 2A–219(2)(b) if risk is to pass to the lessee, provide for this possibility in the following language (Section 2A–219(2)(b) only deals with acknowledgment by the bailee as reflecting current practice in lease transactions and, of course, uses "lessee" rather than "buyer"):

(2) If goods are held by a bailee to be delivered without being moved, the risk of loss passes to the buyer:

(a) on the buyer's receipt of a negotiable document of title covering the goods;

(b) on acknowledgment by the bailee to the buyer of the buyer's right to possession of the goods; or

(c) after the buyer's receipt of a non-negotiable document of title or other direction to deliver in a record, as provided in Section 2–503(4)(b).

In each of these three circumstances the buyer, or lessee as applicable, will have gained control over the goods, for the bailee will have become the bailee of the buyer or lessee instead of the bailee of the seller or lessor. Thus the underlying rationale of the rule is that the risk of loss should pass to the buyer or lessee when that party gains control of the goods.

Special mention should be made of the last case listed. A buyer is not required to accept tender of a non negotiable document of title or a direction in record form by the seller to the bailee to deliver to the buyer. The buyer may demand another type of tender such as a negotiable document or an acknowledgment. If, however, the buyer does accept the tender of a non negotiable document or a direction, risk of loss would not pass until the buyer has a reasonable time to present the non negotiable document or the direction to the bailee. Even then should the bailee refuse to honor the document or the direction the tender is defeated and risk of loss would not pass. Section 2–503(4). See also Commonwealth Propane Co. v. Petrosol Intern., Inc. (1987).

A seller or a lessor might argue in some cases that if they remain in possession of the goods after selling or leasing them, at that point they become a bailee and risk of loss may pass even though the seller or lessor is a merchant and has not yet delivered the goods. The leading pre-UCC case is Courtin v. Sharp (1960). In a case under the UCC, Caudle v. Sherrard Motor Co. (1975), S, a dealer, agreed to sell a house trailer to B. The trailer was not ready for delivery at the time of contracting. B had to leave the city for a few days on business and agreed to pick the trailer up on his return. Approximately three days after the purchase and before B returned, the trailer was stolen from S's place of business. S argued, among other things, that after the sale to B, he held the trailer as B's bailee. Therefore, under former Section 2–509(2)(b), risk of loss had passed to B. The court rejected this argument and held that former Section 2–509(3), discussed below, governed the risk of loss. As S was a merchant the court said that risk of loss would not pass to B until B took physical possession of the trailer.

c. Other Situations

Sections 2–509(3), and 2A–219(2)(c) where risk is to pass to the lessee, provide the rule for determining risk of loss in situations not covered by the other provisions. This provision states that in any case not otherwise covered, the risk of loss passes to the buyer or lessee on receipt of the goods. The usual situation which would come within these provisions is that in which the goods are left in the seller's or lessor's possession for delivery by the seller or lessor, or because the buyer or lessee is to pick them up. Thus the typical situation is found in the facts of the *Caudle* case discussed above.

" 'Receipt of goods' means taking physical possession of goods." Sections 2–103(1)(*l*) and 2A–103(3). This rule reflects the widespread use of insurance. A merchant seller in particular is quite likely to have insurance coverage on goods so long as they remain at the merchant's place of business and even though title to them may have passed, while in almost no case is the buyer or lessee likely to have effected insurance on goods not yet within that party's control. This is probably true even if the buyer or lessee also is a merchant. Thus the policy is to place the risk of loss on the party more likely to be covered by insurance.

Whether or not the buyer has taken possession of the goods sometimes can be a difficult question to answer. In Ellis v. Bell Aerospace Corp. (1970), B purchased a helicopter at S's factory. After the helicopter was assembled and ready for delivery, S stored it with a bailee because of lack of storage space. Later S took the helicopter from the bailee's possession and flew it back to S's factory where, according to the original agreement between the parties, B was to be instructed in its operation. During this instruction, the helicopter crashed. The court held that risk of loss was governed by former Section 2–509(3) and B had not received the goods. S had not, according to the court, relinquished dominion and control over the aircraft, and the court did not apply former Section 2–509(2) on goods held by a bailee to determine risk of loss, evidently because it believed that the helicopter remained under the practical control of S. Another interesting case is Ron Mead T.V. & Appliance v. Legendary Homes, Inc. (1987), where a seller delivered appliances to the buyer's unattended home construction site after hours and placed them in a garage which it then locked. Nonetheless, the appliances were stolen and the court determined the buyer had never actually received the goods to pass risk of loss.

Now suppose S agrees to sell a used refrigerator to B, and the latter is to pick up the refrigerator at S's home two weeks from the date the contract is made. If S has the refrigerator available for B at his home on the day agreed, there is proper tender of delivery, but risk of loss will not pass to B on that day under Section 2–509 unless B picks up the refrigerator. But see Section 2–510. Now assume the same facts, except that S is to make certain repairs to the refrigerator and B is to pick it up after these repairs have been made. Proper tender should require S, in addition to holding the goods available for B to pick up, to give B notice when the repairs have been made. Risk of loss should remain on S until a reasonable time after such notice and B picks up the refrigerator.

3. EFFECT OF BREACH ON RISK OF LOSS

a. Seller's or Lessor's Breach

As a general rule the provisions of the UCC place the risk of loss on the party who breaches or is in default on the contract, even though the breach or default may be unrelated to the loss and even though perhaps the risk would have fallen on the other party in the absence of a breach. Sections 2–510 and 2A–220.

Sections 2–510(1), and 2A–220(1)(a) if risk is to pass to the lessee, state:

(1) If a tender or delivery of goods so fails to conform to the contract as to give a right of rejection, the risk of their loss remains on the seller or with the lessor or, in the case of a finance lease, the supplier until cure or acceptance.

This provision envisages those situations in which the seller's or lessor's tender is so defective as to give the buyer or lessee the right to reject the goods. A defective tender does not necessarily give the buyer or lessee a right to reject. As to the right to reject, see Chapter 10. Assuming a non-conforming tender is such as to give a right to reject, the seller or lessor or supplier may nevertheless correct the non-conformity by effecting cure. Sections 2–508 and 2A–513. This is normally done by the seller or lessor or supplier notifying the buyer or lessee of an intention to cure and then making a conforming tender or delivery within the appropriate time. Risk of loss would pass upon completion of cure. Official Comment 2 to Section 2–510.

Suppose, for example, S contracts to sell and deliver to B under terms F.O.B.S' city 1000 bushels of No. 1 grade wheat on or before July 1. The wheat arrives by freight car on a railroad siding at B's warehouse on June 20. B inspects it and finds it is

filled with weevils and is not No. 1 grade. B immediately notifies S that B will not accept the wheat.
Risk of loss would remain on S, and in fact would
have been on S throughout transit even though this
was a shipment contract, because the goods when
delivered to the carrier were non-conforming, and
the non-conformity was such as to give B the right
to reject. S, by notifying B of the intention to cure,
would have until July 1 to make a conforming
tender but risk would not pass until that cure was
tendered.

In some instances a buyer or lessee may accept
non-conforming goods either because the buyer or
lessee does not know of the non-conformity or because the buyer or lessee reasonably assumes that
the non-conformity will be cured. See Sections 2–
608 and 2A–517. Once there is an acceptance, the
right of rejection is lost and risk of loss passes to
the buyer or lessee despite the non-conformity. Later, however, upon discovery of the non-conformity
or after the seller's or lessor's failure to cure, the
buyer or lessee may revoke acceptance. Sections 2–
608 and 2A–517. In that case, Sections 2–510(2) and
2A–220(1)(b) provide that if the buyer or lessee
rightfully revokes acceptance, the buyer or lessee, to
the extent of any deficiency in effective insurance
coverage may treat the risk of loss as having rested
on the seller or lessor from the beginning.

To illustrate, suppose S, pursuant to a contract
with B, delivers a given item of road-building equipment to B, who accepts the equipment and proceeds
to use it in B's business. Approximately two weeks

later a serious defect shows up in the equipment, making it totally unfit for use. B immediately notifies S and asks S to pick up the equipment. That same evening B's garage, where the machine is stored, is destroyed by fire and the machine is a total loss. To the extent that B's loss on the equipment is not covered by insurance and B had the risk of loss, B may recover payments made or refuse further payment.

In a finance lease, the lessee in most cases does not have a right to revoke acceptance against the lessor (but may have a claim against the supplier). Sections 2A–516(2), 2A–517 and 2A–209. Where the lessee under a finance lease may revoke acceptance, the lessee may not treat the risk of loss as having remained with the supplier from the beginning. Official Comment to Section 2A–220.

b. Buyer's or Lessee's Breach

Sections 2–510(3) and 2A–220(2) provide:

If the buyer, or lessee whether or not risk of loss is to pass to the lessee, as to conforming goods already identified to the contract repudiates or is otherwise in breach or default and this occurs when risk of loss is on the seller, or lessor or supplier, the seller or lessor or supplier may, to the extent of any deficiency in effective insurance coverage, may treat the risk of loss as resting on the buyer or lessee for a commercially reasonable time.

To illustrate, suppose B agrees to buy 300 bales of cotton goods from S for shipment to B on July 15. On July 13, S prepares 300 bales for shipment to B. On July 14, just as S is preparing to haul the goods to the carrier, B calls and repudiates the contract. On the night of July 15, while the cotton goods are still stored in S's warehouse, a fire destroys the goods. Risk of loss is on B to the extent the loss is not covered by insurance. Assuming this was a shipment contract, risk of loss would not have passed to B, if it was to pass, until the goods were tendered to the carrier. Sections 2–510(3) and 2A–220(2) in the case of a lease, are applicable to this fact situation because the goods were (1) conforming, (2) identified before the breach or default and loss occurred and (3) destroyed when risk of loss had not passed. Had the goods been non-conforming, these provisions literally would not apply and the entire loss, regardless of insurance coverage, would remain on seller or lessor. Evidently the slightest non-conformity in the goods would preclude the application of these provisions. The goods were identified by preparing them for shipment to B. This took place before the breach or default and loss occurred. If the goods destroyed in the warehouse had met the general contract description, but had not been particularized in any way as those intended for shipment B, these provisions also would not apply. Finally, risk of loss had not passed at the time of the fire. If it had, these provisions would not apply, and the entire loss would fall on B without regard to insurance coverage.

These provisions of the UCC do not require a causal connection between the seller's or lessor's or the buyer's or lessee's breach or default and the loss in order to place risk of uninsured loss on the other party. In similar cases at common law some courts had refused to place risk of loss on the breaching party, reasoning that where the loss is accidental the breach is not the "proximate cause of the loss." This approach was not followed in the process amending Articles 2 and 2A.

4. SALE ON APPROVAL AND SALE OR RETURN

The "sale on approval" and the "sale or return" have been discussed in Chapter 6 in relation to passage of title. In a number of cases involving these transactions, the goods have been lost, damaged, or destroyed either while in the buyer's possession or while being returned to the seller. The court was then faced with the problem of determining who bore the risk of loss.

If the transaction is a sale on approval, risk of loss remains on the seller until the buyer accepts the goods, unless the parties agree otherwise. Section 2–327(1)(a). If the buyer notifies the seller of an election to return the goods, the return is at the seller's risk and expense unless the parties agree otherwise. Section 2–327(1)(c).

If the transaction is a sale or return, however, risk of loss passes to the buyer under the same conditions as in a regular sale, again excepting an

agreement to the contrary. Should the buyer elect
to return the goods, the return is "at the buyer's
risk and expense unless otherwise agreed." Section
2–327(2)(b).

CHAPTER 9

WARRANTY OBLIGATIONS

1. INTRODUCTION

Discussion in this chapter largely focuses on warranty liability under the UCC. There is no attempt to deal with products liability in general. For a treatment of products liability in the Nutshell series, see Phillips, Products Liability 3rd ed. (1988). Given the development of products liability, however, warranties which go to the quality of the goods primarily are of importance where the defect makes the goods less valuable and where consequential damages other than personal injury are sustained. Those are situations where strict liability in tort may not apply. Where there is personal injury, or defective goods damage other property, at least in a non-commercial setting tort law is likely to play the predominant role, unless the often shorter statute of limitations for that theory has been allowed to expire and the UCC statute of limitations has not run so warranty is all that is left. See, generally, Mid Continent Aircraft Corp. v. Curry County Spraying Service, Inc. (1978), Morrow v. New Moon Homes, Inc. (1976), and Meadows, Garvin and Dessin, Sales (The Uniform Commercial Code Survey), 57 Bus. Law. 1669, at 1685–1687 ("Economic Loss Doctrine") (2002) (the economic loss doctrine provides that a party is limited to contract remedies when the damages suffered are merely economic in nature, that is, when there is no personal injury or property damage involved; discussing Alcan Aluminum Corp. v. BASF Corp. (2001), involving damages to panels from a foam insulation system supplied by BASF and holding damage to property other than the defective product itself can be basis for a tort recovery but damage to an assembled product as a whole from a defective component is not damage to other property based on either a forseeability analysis, or that the damage was not caused by a sudden or calamitous occurrence, and McLaughlin v. Denharco, Inc. (2001), a similar case). See also Robinson Helicopter Co., Inc. v. Dana Corp. (2003) (economic loss rule also applicable to intentional fraud cases where fraud committed in the performance as opposed to the inducement of the contract), and infra this chapter. But also see Teledyne Technologies Inc. v. Freedom Forge Corp. (2002) (crankshaft obtained by airplane manufacturer which caused damage to aircraft, engines, other components, and personal injuries involved other property and economic loss doctrine did not bar suit). The increasing impact of "products liability statutes" which limit one or more aspects of products liability actions, and which may apply to UCC warranty recoveries, also must be considered. See, e.g., Neb.Rev.St.Ann. § 25–21, 181 and NDCC 28–01.1–02. See Paracelsus Healthcare Corp. v. Philips Electronics North America (2001) (North Dakota Product Liability Act did not supplant warranty provisions of UCC as UCC warranty actions against a seller are not generally viewed as products liability actions). Discussion of these statutes, which exist in one form or another in about half the states, is beyond the scope of this chapter.

Within the context where warranty is significant, warranties are important in sales or lease transactions because they establish the seller's or lessor's duties with respect to the characteristics and utility of the goods. Under the UCC, warranties are divided into three categories: "express," "implied," and the warranty of title which is not classified as either an "express" or "implied" warranty but which, in fact, is an implied warranty. The comparable warranty against interference in Article 2A is treated as an implied warranty. In addition, Article 2 as amended includes, as a codification of better case law, express warranty like obligations and remedial promises.

2. EXPRESS WARRANTIES OR OBLIGATIONS; REMEDIAL PROMISES

Section 2–313 (2) and (3) provide:

(2) Express warranties by the seller to the immediate buyer are created as follows:

(a) Any affirmation of fact or promise made by the seller which relates to the goods and becomes part of the basis of the bargain creates an express warranty that the goods will conform to the affirmation or promise.

(b) Any description of the goods which is made part of the basis of the bargain creates an express warranty that the goods will conform to the description.

(c) Any sample or model that is made part of the basis of the bargain creates an express warranty that the whole of the goods will conform to the sample or model.

(3) It is not necessary to the creation of an express warranty that the seller use formal words such as "warrant" or "guarantee" or that the seller have a specific intention to make a warranty, but an affirmation merely of the value of the goods or a statement purporting to be merely the seller's opinion or commendation of the goods does not create a warranty.

This warranty extends only to an "immediate buyer;" that is, a buyer that enters into a contract with the seller. Section 2–313(1). This is because there only is a "bargain" between such parties. If such exists, it is not relevant what method is utilized to make the warranty to the buyer, whether in the sales contract, by a seller's ad, by a warranty by the seller with the product, or otherwise. Section 2A–210 is the same but there is no express limitation to a party that enters into a lease with the lessor as, given current distribution methods for goods, there is no need to distinguish this warranty from an obligation to a remote purchaser as there is under Article 2.

a. Affirmation of Fact or Promise

An express warranty is created by an affirmation of fact or a promise which relates to the goods and becomes part of the basis of the bargain. For example, S, in negotiations leading to the sale of an automobile to B, states that the automobile is new. In fact, it is used and has been driven approximately 1200 miles. S's statement is an affirmation of fact and an express warranty. It is not necessary that S have knowledge that the statement is false. In many cases the question of whether there is an express warranty is an easy one; an example is a printed warranty card delivered with the product. In other cases, the issue is not so easily resolved. To illustrate, suppose, as in Boud v. SDNCO (2002), there is a brochure from the seller showing a picture of a yacht captioned: "Offering the best performance and cruising accommodations in its class...." The court held the photograph and caption were not specific or objective enough to qualify as either a fact or a promise. In contrast, in Bobholz v. Banaszak (2002), a seller advertised on eBay that a skiboat was in "perfect" condition. There were cracks in the engine's manifold which allowed water to enter and irreparably damaged the engine. The court found the seller's statement about condition was an express warranty.

Now suppose S in the same negotiations promises to take care of any mechanical defects during the first six months. Under Section 2–313(4), this is a remedial promise, defined in Section 2–103(1)(n) as a promise by the seller to repair or replace goods or to refund all or part of the price of goods upon the happening of a specified event, and when made by a seller to an immediate buyer it creates an obligation that the promise will be performed upon the happening of the specified event. As such, it is like an express warranty, but avoids the issue of whether it is breached at the time of sale or only when it is not performed. Compare under prior law, Imperia v. Marvin Windows of New York, Inc. (2002). Between 1989 and 1992 homeowners purchased windows and doors with a speciality coating the salespeople had stated would be maintenance free for 10 years. Problems appeared between 1994 and 1997. The court concluded this could be a warranty as to future performance, a crucial determination under prior law in reference to the statute of limitations.

A statement made soon after the closing of the deal may become an express warranty through a modification of the bargain, which need not be supported by consideration but which may require a record in relation to the statute of frauds. See Sections 2–209 and 2A–208, Official Comment 9 to Section 2–313, Moldex, Inc. v. Ogden Engineering Corp. (1987) and Bigelow v. Agway, Inc. (1974). But see Terry v. Moore (1968). On the other hand, a statement that does not relate to the goods does not constitute an express warranty even if it might constitute an otherwise enforceable promise. See Royal Business Machines, Inc. v. Lorraine Corp. (1980) (statement that replacement parts were readily available is not a fact that relates to the goods sold as required by Section 2–313).

Originally cases in sales of goods for breach of warranty were brought in forms of action which would be regarded today as tort actions. Later, after the action of special assumpsit (contract) evolved and beginning with a case decided in 1778, breach of warranty was generally treated as a contract action. After the shift to the contract theory, some courts took the position that an affirmation of fact made by the seller did not constitute a warranty unless made with the intention of creating a warranty. Proof of such intent generally required a statement by the seller that the seller was warranting or guaranteeing the goods in some respect; in short, since warranty liability was contractual, the statement had to be one intended by the seller and understood by the buyer as constituting part of the contract. Thus if a court found that the seller did not intend the representation as a warranty and that it was made innocently (even if inaccurately), the buyer had no remedy. For example, in Seixas v. Woods (1804), the seller had advertised wood as brazilletto, which was very valuable. In addition the seller showed the buyer an invoice describing the wood as brazilletto, and when the buyer agreed to buy it the seller billed the buyer for this kind of wood. The wood was in fact peachum having little or no value. The court held that such a representation did not constitute an express warranty.

Later cases repudiated this idea and held that it was not essential that the word "warranty" be used. Further, it was not necessary that a representation be intended by the seller and understood by the buyer as a warranty. It will be noted that Section 2–313(3) expressly approves the modern principle. The same is true in Section 2A–210(2) for leases. In essence, then, an express warranty is a statement or promise to which the law, rather than the lessor or the seller, ascribes warranty status.

b. Opinion

Under pre-UCC law, a seller's or lessor's statement was considered an express warranty only if the buyer or lessee justifiably relied on it as an inducement to the purchase or lease of the goods. It is common knowledge that sellers and lessors tend to praise or "puff" their wares. Assertions praising goods may be so general or improbable that no person would be justified in relying on them. Statements that goods are "the best in the market," "unsurpassed and unsurpassable," "high class," or "will sell like hot cakes," have been held to be mere "seller's talk" or "puffing" and not warranties. Subject to some exceptions, any statement which a court finds to be an expression merely of opinion or value is held not to constitute a warranty.

The UCC adopts these basic pre-UCC principles by providing in Sections 2–313(3) and 2A–210(2) that "an affirmation merely of the value of the goods or a statement purporting to be merely opinion or commendation of the goods does not create a warranty." See Boud v. SDNCO (2002), discussed earlier.

Courts have experienced difficulty in determining whether a statement is mere puffing or a warranty and in some instances it is difficult to reconcile the decisions. In one case, Wat Henry Pontiac Co. v. Bradley (1949), the court held that a car salesman's statements that a used car was in "A–1 shape" and "mechanically perfect" constituted an express warranty. On the other hand, in Frederickson v. Hackney (1924), the court held that the seller's statements to the buyer, a farmer, that a bull calf being sold for breeding purposes would "put the buyer on the map" and help to "build up" his herd did not constitute an express warranty after the bull proved sterile. Compare also Crothers v. Cohen (1986) (car with accelerator that stuck breached warranty that car was a "good runner") and Bernstein v. Sherman (1986) (untrue statement that car frame was in "good condition" breached a warranty), with Foley v. Dayton Bank & Trust (1985) (statement that to best of knowledge used truck was in good condition did not constitute a warranty) and Boud v. SDNCO (2002) (statement that boat offered "the best performance . . . in its class.").

In reconciling such decisions, the reasonableness of the buyer's or lessee's reliance given the buyer's or lessee's knowledge and experience, particularly in relation to that of the seller or lessor, would seem to be the controlling factor. Statements that a ladder is "strong," "will never break," and "will last a lifetime" are so clearly improbable that no buyer or lessee should rely on them. The context within which a statement is made also may be relevant in determining the reasonableness of the buyer's or lessee's reliance. Thus, if a statement is made in writing, there is probably more likelihood of a finding of reasonable reliance than if the statement were made orally. Compare Collins v. Uniroyal, Inc. (1974) (shown reliance) with Cuthbertson v. Clark Equipment Co. (1982) (no evidence that manual read and no express warranty). See generally Interco Inc. v. Randustrial Corp. (1976). Keith v. Buchanan (1985) perhaps is consistent with these cases even though the buyer did not show any reliance on affirmations made in an advertising brochure; the court stated the seller could show that the representations formed no part of the bargain. See the discussion of the "basis of the bargain" and Section 2–313B, infra, in this chapter.

c. Express Warranty by Description

An express warranty may arise from a description of the goods. Sections 2–313(2)(b) and 2A–210(1)(b) provide that any description of the goods which is made a part of the basis of the bargain constitutes an express warranty that the goods conform to the description. For example, a description in a contract that a television set is a "Zenith, Model 1990 C4, Color T.V." would be an express warranty that the set delivered will conform to that description.

Under the Uniform Sales Act warranties of description were classified as "implied" rather than "express." The UCC classification seems more realistic. Any description which is made a part of the basis of the bargain constitutes an affirmation of fact or a promise that the goods conform to the description. The importance of this UCC classification is that a disclaimer of implied warranties (dis-

claimer clauses are discussed later in this chapter)
will have no effect on description warranties. Suppose, however, a description is sufficient to create
an express warranty but there is a clause disclaim-
ing both implied *and express* warranties. How is
this conflict to be resolved? That problem is discussed below.

Does a description of the goods as a "haybaler"
create an express warranty that the machine will
bale hay? In short, does the express warranty of
description encompass quality? If the implied warranty of merchantability accompanies the transaction, the question is academic as the baler would
have to bale hay in order to meet the standard of
merchantability. Suppose, however, the implied
warranty is validly disclaimed. The UCC does not
give a specific answer. Official Comment 6 to Section 2–313 seems to indicate a positive answer. If
this is correct, goods described by a generic title
such as, "automobile," "television set," or "haybaler," always will carry a warranty that they are to a
degree suitable for the purpose for which such
goods are used. Carrying this thought too far, however, would render the implied warranty of merchantability without function. In short, generally
the warranty of description should require delivery
of a car rather than a truck; the warranty of merchantability should determine whether there is liability if the car is not suitable for its ordinary
purpose of driving. Somewhere, there is a line;
perhaps an engineless shell is not a "car."

d. Warranty by Sample or Model

The last method by which an express warranty may be created is when the sale or lease is by sample or model. Sections 2–313(2)(c) and 2A–210(1)(c) provide that when any sample or model is a part of the basis of the bargain the seller or lessor expressly warrants that the whole of the goods will conform to the sample or model. As in the case of a warranty by description, this warranty previously was classified as "implied" under the Uniform Sales Act.

The UCC distinguishes between a sample and a model. Official Comment 8 to Section 2–313 explains that a "sample" is drawn from the bulk of the goods. For example, S and B are negotiating for the sale of 2,000 bushels of wheat. S shows B a bin which contains a large quantity of wheat from which S informs B the wheat being sold will be taken. S takes a small quantity of grain from the bin for B's examination. The quantity drawn from the bulk would be a sample. A model is a facsimile of the goods. It is not drawn from the bulk, and may be larger or smaller than the goods contracted for. A typical example would be a small operating model of a storm window or door.

An express warranty is created only if the sample or model is made a part of the basis of the bargain. A seller or a lessor may argue that in some cases the item exhibited constituted only a guide or suggestion and was not a representation of what the bulk of the goods would be like. Official Comment 8 to Section 2–313 recognizes that it is not always clear from the facts if the item shown is merely illustrative or "a straight sample." For example, in Sylvia Coal Co. v. Mercury Coal and Coke Co. (1967), S exhibited a small quantity of coal but made it clear that the coal actually being sold was of inferior quality. The court held that there was no warranty that the coal to be delivered would conform in quality to that exhibited. Evidently, the burden of proving that an item exhibited is not intended to become a part of the basis of the bargain rests on the seller or lessor. Official Comment 8 to Section 2–313. The same comment states that this presumption of inclusion in the bargain is stronger in the case of a "sample" than a "model." This is because a sample is drawn from the bulk and would generally carry with it a strong presumption that the sample describes the characteristics of the whole unless clearly indicated otherwise.

e.   Basis of the Bargain

In order for a promise, affirmation of fact, description, sample, or model to constitute an express warranty it must be a "part of the basis of the bargain." At common law and under the Uniform Sales Act there had to be "reliance" by the buyer, and presumably the lessee, on a promise or affirmation of fact. The UCC does not explicitly require "reliance," and the extent to which the "basis of the bargain" test in the UCC substitutes for "reliance" test is not explicit either.

However, some general observations as to the meaning of the "basis of the bargain" requirement can be made on the basis of the comments to Section 2–313. Official Comments 5 and 9 make it clear that the promise, affirmation of fact, description, or exhibition of a sample or model may occur in the negotiations leading up to the closing of the transaction. It does not have to occur or be repeated at the time the transaction is closed. This is in accord with pre-UCC law. Official Comment 8 also states that it is not necessary for the buyer (or the lessee) to show particular reliance on any statement made during negotiations because such a statement is regarded as a part of the description of the goods. Rather the comment states that any fact which is to take such affirmations, once made, out of the agreement requires clear affirmative proof. Thus, a statement or promise, description, or sample or model, made or furnished by the seller or lessor about the goods during discussion leading to a sale is presumed to become a part of the resulting bargain, and the burden of proving that it did not rests on the seller or lessor. One way to meet the burden is to show a statement constituted opinion or puffing because a buyer or lessee would not rely on opinion or puffing as an inducement, that is, as part of the bargain, to purchase the goods. Another way is to show the asserted sample was merely understood to suggest the nature of the goods rather than to "be" the goods. See Official Comment 8 to Section 2–313. Yet, another way is to show that the buyer or lessee did not rely on a statement even though they could have. For example, in Hellman v. Kirschner (1921), the buyer purchased a used car described as a "model 57–V." When the buyer sued the seller for breach of warranty because the car was a model 57–J, the seller on appeal was able to obtain a reversal based on showing that the buyer had inspected the car before the purchase so that the buyer received what the buyer had accepted after inspection. See also Frisch and Wladis, General Provisions, Sales, Bulk Transfers, and Documents of Title, 44 Bus. Law. 1445, at 1455–56 (1989). But some courts miss the point. See, e.g., Hawkins Const. Co. v. Matthews Co. Inc. (1973) (express warranty found even though buyer did not rely on brochure statements).

f. Express Obligations

Modern distribution schemes for goods involve sales by manufacturers to wholesalers to retailers before the ultimate retail customer is reached, who may be either a buyer or a lessee of the goods. In some situations, the retailer may disclaim warranties in the sale or lease to the customer because the manufacturer provides an express obligation and a "remedial promise" for that party along with the product. In other cases, the retail purchaser may be induced to acquire the product through advertising by the manufacturer. These obligations and ads are not easily classified as express warranties (or remedial promises) because the "bargain" is with the retailer and not the manufacturer, even though under prior law many decisions so classified them.

See, e.g., Hill v. BASF Wyandotte Corp. (1982) (warranty with product) and Randy Knitwear, Inc. v. American Cyanamid Co. (1962) (advertising warranty).

Section 2–313A follows case law and practice in extending an express obligation undertaken by a seller with respect to new goods or goods merchandised as new goods (such as a car that has been test driven), that are acquired in a transaction of purchase in the normal chain of distribution, by a remote purchaser (a person that buys or leases goods from a buyer that has a contract with the seller) if the obligation is in a record packaged with or accompanying the goods which the seller reasonably expects to be and is furnished to the remote purchaser. Section 2–313A(1), (2) and (3) and Official Comments 1, 2, 3, 4, 5 and 8 to Section 2–313A .. The express obligation is defined in much the same way as an express warranty and remedial obligation, including the exclusion of mere commendation and opinion, but the basis of the bargain concept is replaced by a requirement that a reasonable person must believe that an obligation is created. Official Comments 1 and 5 to Section 2–313A.

Section 2–313A(5) then answers several questions that may arise in this context, but the answers to which are unclear under prior law. Can the seller limit or modify remedies available under the statute if the obligation is breached? Under Section 2–313A(5)(a), the seller may do so if the limitation or modification is furnished to the remote purchaser no later than the time of purchase or is contained in the record that creates the obligation. What is the seller's liability for damages for breach? Under Section 2–313A(5)(b), absent modification or limitation, it is the same as a seller has to an immediate purchaser, except for lost profits (which probably would not be forseeable under Section 2–715 in most cases anyway). It would not appear the remote purchaser could revoke acceptance as the transaction is not with the party having the obligation or making the remedial promise. The remote purchaser should be able to recover the difference in value between the retail valued the goods as warranted and their actual value. See Section 2–313A(5)(c). See Official Comments 7 and 9 to Section 2–313A.

Section 2–313B deals with an express obligation of a seller arising from an ad or similar communication to the public that a remote purchaser enters into a transaction of purchase with knowledge of and with the expectation that the goods will conform or that the remedial promise will be performed. If an immediate buyer from the seller relies on the seller's ad, the applicable section is Section 2–313 on express warranty. Official Comment 1 to Section 2–313B.

As in the case of an obligation under Section 2–313A, the scope is limited to new goods or goods sold or leased as new goods in a transaction of purchase in the normal chain of distribution, a reasonable person must believe an obligation was created (note the actual purchaser also must have the subjective expectation the goods will conform to the representations in the ad), and mere opinion or commendation of the goods does not create an obligation. Section 2–313B(1), (2), (3) and (4). The remote purchaser must know of the ad; a purchaser that does not may not recover even if one who did know may. However, as in the case of an express warranty reliance is assumed unless the seller can show otherwise, as previously discussed. See Official Comments 2 and 3 to Section 2–313B. Also the ability to modify or limit remedies is the same, as is the remedy structure. Official Comment 6 to Section 2–313B. One issue in this context not explicitly addressed is the age of the ad, which can be relevant if the product is subsequently changed. Official Comment 4 to Section 2–313B, however, suggests in this circumstance it is unlikely the ad will have created a reasonable or even a subjective expectation about the goods and if a known corrective press release has occurred, it must be taken into account.

3. WARRANTY OF TITLE OR AGAINST INTERFERENCE AND WARRANTY AGAINST INFRINGEMENT

a. Warranty of Title or Against Interference

Sections 2–312(1) and 2A–211(1) provide that there is in a contract for sale or lease a warranty by the seller or lessor that:

(a) in the case of a sale, the title conveyed shall be good, its transfer rightful, the buyer will not be unreasonably exposed to litigation because of a colorable claim to or interest in the goods, and the goods will be delivered free from any security interest or other lien or encumbrance of which the buyer at the time of contracting has no knowledge, and

(b) in the case of a lease, other than a finance lease, that for the lease term no person holds a claim to or interest in the goods not attributable to the lessee's own act or omission, other than a claim by way of infringement, which will interfere with the lessee's enjoyment of its leasehold interest or which will unreasonably expose the lessee to litigation from a colorable claim to or interest in the goods.

Section 2–312(1) makes several changes in prior law. First, the prior law treated the warranty of title as "implied," whereas under the UCC today it is neither an "express" or "implied warranty." This change is significant in connection with disclaimer clauses. Section 2–316(5) provides that all implied warranties may be disclaimed, assuming specified requirements are met. A disclaimer of implied warranties meeting all requirements of Section 2–316(5) will not be sufficient to exclude the warranty of title or against interference. To illustrate, assume the following language is placed in conspicuous print in a contract between S and B: "Seller makes no warranties, express or implied, and it is understood that these goods are sold 'as is' ". This clause is not sufficient to exclude the title warranty as it is not specific. This does not mean that the title warranty or the warranty against interference cannot be disclaimed or modified; the means by which this may be done is discussed later in this chapter. For other purposes, however, the warranty of title or against interference may be treated as an implied warranty. See Sections 2–312(3) and 2A–211(4); this could be important, in relation to a demand for examination, limitation of remedy, and perhaps even for the impact of course of dealing or performance and usage of trade. See Sections 2–316(6), (7) and (8) and 2A–214(3)(b) and (c) and (4).

A second change from prior law made by Section 2–312(1) but not Section 2A–211(1) is abolition of the warranty of quiet possession. The Uniform Sales Act provided that the seller warranted "that the buyer shall have and enjoy quiet possession of the goods". The UCC does not include such language. However, even though the disturbance of quiet possession is not mentioned specifically, it is one way in which the breach of the warranty of title may be established. Of course, non-interference with the enjoyment by the lessee of its leasehold interest is the essence of the comparable Article 2A warranty. Official Comment 1 to Section 2A–211.

The Article 2 change is significant because of the effect on the running of the statute of limitations. Under pre-UCC law, a cause of action for breach of the warranty of quiet possession did not arise until the buyer's possession was actually disturbed. This meant that even where the statute of limitations had run so as to bar the buyer's right to sue for breach of the implied warranty of title, it might not have run so as to bar an action for breach of the distinct warranty of quiet possession. For example,

A steals a watch from O and sells it to S. B in turn purchases the watch from S, without knowledge of the circumstances, on July 1, 1963. Under the Uniform Sales Act, B had an immediate cause of action for breach of the implied warranty of title, and the statute of limitations on an action for breach of this warranty began to run from that time. Suppose, however, that O did not recover the watch from B until more than five years later (August 1, 1968). Assuming that the state's statute of limitations for actions for breach of warranty was four years, B could not sue for breach of the implied warranty of title, but remained free to sue for breach of the implied warranty of quiet possession until July 31, 1972.

Under Article 2, the basic statute of limitations for breach of a sales contract is four years. Section 2–725(1). Furthermore, a cause of action for breach of a sales contract arises as soon as the breach occurs regardless of the aggrieved party's lack of knowledge of the breach. In the case of warranties, breach usually occurs when tender of delivery is made. Section 2–725(3)(a). Under these rules, in the watch case B would be barred under Article 2 from suing for breach of warranty after four years from the time the watch was delivered by S even though B was not deprived of possession until August 1, 1968. To address that problem, Section 2–725(3)(d) provides that a right of action for breach of warranty arising under Section 2–312 accrues when the aggrieved party discovers or should have discovered the breach.

Under Article 2A, the limitations period also is four years and the cause of action accrues when the act or omission on which the default or breach of warranty is based is or should have been discovered or when the default occurs, whichever is later. Section 2A–506(1) and (2). Under Section 2A–211, like under Article 2, disturbance of possession is not a condition precedent to maintaining an action. Thus the hypothetical would not produce a different result if B leased the watch and the warranty against interference is breached.

A buyer can show a breach of the warranty of title, and similarly a lessee other than a finance lessee a breach of the warranty against interference, by proving essentially any one of three things: (1) the title conveyed is not good, (2) the transfer is not rightful or (3) the goods are subject to a security interest, lien, or encumbrance which the acquiring party had no knowledge at the time of contracting. The following examples will illustrate each of these three circumstances.

T steals O's watch and sells it to S who buys it in good faith. S, in turn, sells or leases the watch to B, who also purchases in good faith. S has not conveyed good title; hence, S has breached the warranty.

O entrusts his watch to S, a jeweler who both repairs and sells new and used watches. S repairs O's watch but, without O's permission or knowledge, sells or leases the watch to B, a person who is a buyer in ordinary course of business. Under Section 2–403(2), B receives good title as against O. As to B as lessee, see Official Comment 3 to Section 2A–304 and Section 2A–307(2). Nevertheless, S's transfer was wrongful, and S could be liable to B for breach of the warranty if the facts were such that O had more than a colorable claim to the watch even if B ultimately wins in the litigation brought by O against him. See Sumner v. Fel–Air, Inc. (1984) and Saber v. Dan Angelone Chevrolet, Inc. (2002). Both Section 2–312(1)(a) and 2A–211(1)(b) now expressly state that unreasonable exposure to litigation because of any colorable claim to or interest in the goods breaches the warranty. As to what is colorable, see C.F. Sales, Inc. v. Amfert (1983). An entrusting rule similar to that of Section 2–403(2) also exists in Sections 2A–304(2) in favor of a subsequent lessee in ordinary course of business (Section 2A–103(1)(n)) and in Section 2A–305 in favor of a buyer in ordinary course of business and a sublessee in ordinary course of business.

S grants C a security interest under Article 9 of the UCC in a piece of equipment, which security interest is perfected. S sells and delivers the equipment to B, who buys without knowledge of C's security interest. S has breached the warranty of title because C's interest remains good against B under Sections 9–201(a) and 9–317(b). The rule under Section 2A–307(3) is similar to that in Article 9 if B had leased the equipment instead of buying it; however, because a lease is a limited interest the mere presence of a security interest would not necessarily constitute a breach of the warranty as it may not interfere with a lessee's use of the goods. "Knowledge" under Section 2–312(1)(b) means actual knowledge. Section 1–202. Thus public or constructive notice by the filing of a financing statement would not be sufficient to give B "knowledge". It should be noted that in some instances security interests, even though perfected, are terminated upon a sale or a lease to a buyer or a lessee. For example, under Section 9–320(a) a buyer, and under 9–321(c) a lessee, in ordinary course of business takes free of a security interest created by the seller or lessor even though the buyer or lessee has knowledge of the security interest. Under such circumstances, there would not be a breach of the warranty.

There are several particularities involving leases related to the above situations. The entrustment example above would come out the same if O leased and entrusted the watch to S who re-leased it or sold it to B. Sections 2A–305(2) and 2A–211(1). But whether B would prevail against S if B leased stolen goods under a finance lease is a more difficult question, as under Section 2A–211(2) a finance lessor only warrants that no person holds a claim or interest in the goods that arose from an act or omission of the lessor which will interfere with the lessee's enjoyment of its leasehold interest. Is S's failure to obtain good title "an act or omission of the lessor"? That seems doubtful. This analysis suggests a lessee should bargain for an express warranty against claims or interests of parties that arose prior to the lessor acquiring its interest in the goods as well as make a careful check for such claims or interests. See Bank of Nova Scotia v. Equitable Financial Management, Inc. (1989) (finance lessor did not warrant against prior security interest). Also in Section 2A–211(1)(a), an adverse claim attributable to the lessee's own act or omission, such as impoundment of a leased car due to an unpaid traffic ticket, will not breach the warranty.

The same is true for the warranty of title. Thus, Section 2–312(1)(a) makes provision that the buyer will receive a good, clean title transferred in a rightful manner. This means the buyer will not be exposed to a lawsuit in order to protect it. See American Container Corp. v. Hanley Trucking Corp. (1970). See also Jeanneret v. Vichey (1982), where the court had to struggle over the effect of the claim of the Italian government to a painting which apparently could not be enforced unless the painting was transported to Italy, but which made it difficult to sell the painting to a reputable American dealer. Even more to the point, it arguably misled the court in Wright v. Vickaryous (1980), to afford relief when the security interests in fact had been released even though the filings still were of record; the buyer easily could have paid both the seller and the secured parties so the warranty should not have been breached. The fact the market for the goods had dropped sharply suggests the reason for the litigation.

b. Warranty Against Infringement

A problem arises when the buyer's or lessee's use of goods constitutes an infringement of a patent or trademark owned by a third party, for which infringement even an innocent buyer or lessee is liable to the third party. Sections 2–312(2) and 2A–211(3) of the UCC deal with the problem specifically:

> A seller or lessor (except a finance lessor) that is a merchant regularly dealing in goods of the kind warrants that the goods will be delivered free of the rightful claim of any third person by way of infringement or the like, but a buyer or lessee that furnishes specifications to the seller or the lessor (or a supplier) holds that person harmless against any such claim which arises out of compliance with the specifications.

Note that under these provisions the warranty is implied only when the seller or a lessor other than a finance lessor is a merchant and the goods sold or leased are a part of normal stock sold or leased in the normal course of business. A sale or lease by a non-merchant does not, in the absence of an agreement to the contrary, carry with it such an implied warranty. Moreover, even if the seller or lessor is a merchant dealing in goods of the kind, there is no implied warranty against infringement where the goods are manufactured by a seller or lessor (or supplier) according to specifications furnished by the buyer or lessee. In fact, under these latter circumstances it is possible that manufacture in compliance with the buyer's or lessee's specifications will itself constitute an infringement, making the manufacturing party liable to the patent or trademark owner. In such a case the UCC requires the buyer or lessee to indemnify the liable party against loss.

4. IMPLIED WARRANTIES

a. Generally

In many transactions the seller or lessor makes no express warranties other than one of description and the parties do not mention the question of warranties in their negotiations. In such cases, the law initially comes to the aid of the buyer or lessee and gives the buyer or lessee the benefit of one or more implied warranties, which are in so many words annexed to the agreement and become part of the contract by operation of law. See Sections 1–201(b)(3) and (12). Even if the seller or lessor makes one or more express warranties, implied warranties still arise and, in the case of the implied warranty of fitness, even if inconsistent with the express warranty. Sections 2–317 and 2A–215. As one court explained it, the implied warranty is not one of the essential elements to be stated in the contract nor does its application or effective existence rest or depend upon the affirmative intention of the parties; it is a child of the law.

It, because of the acts of the parties, is imposed by the law. It arises independently and outside the contract [agreement]. The law annexes it to the contract [agreement]. It writes it, by implication, into the contract [agreement] which the parties have made. Its origin and use are to promote high standards in business and to discourage sharp dealings. It rests upon the principle that "honesty is the best policy," and it contemplates business transactions in which both parties may profit. Bekkevold v. Potts (1927).

That the warranty of title and the warranty arising in sales by description and by sample were classified as implied under the Uniform Sales Act and are treated differently under the UCC has already been mentioned. However, the warranty of title and against interference or infringement essentially still is implied as it too arises by imposition of law. The UCC provides specifically for two implied warranties of quality: the implied warranty of merchantability, Sections 2–314 and 2A–212, and the implied warranty of fitness for a particular purpose, Sections 2–315 and 2A–213. The lessor in a finance lease does not make these warranties; rather the recourse, if any, of the lessee is against the supplier under the supply contract of which, to the extent of the leasehold interest, the lessee is made a beneficiary. See Sections 2A–212(1), 2A–213, 2A–103(1)(*l*), (t) and (v), and 2A–209. The UCC also recognizes that other implied warranties may arise from course of dealing or usage of trade. Sections 2–314(3) and 2A–212(3).

b. Warranty of Merchantability

Sections 2–314 and 2A–212 provide:

A warranty that the goods will be merchantable is implied in a contract for their sale or lease (except a finance lease) if the seller or lessor is a merchant with respect to goods of that kind. In a sale, the serving for value of food or drink to be consumed either on the premises or elsewhere is a sale.

Goods to be merchantable must be at least such as to pass without objection in the trade under the contract description; in the case of fungible goods, to be of fair average quality within the description; to be fit for the ordinary purposes for which goods of that description are used; to run, within the variations permitted by the agreement, of even kind, quality and quantity within each unit and among all units involved; to be adequately contained, packaged, and labeled as the agreement requires; and to conform to any promises or affirmations of fact made on the container or label.

In determining when goods are "unmerchantable," pre-UCC case law may still be relevant, although the language used by some courts in attempting to define standards of merchantability was somewhat vague. Thus in Mathieu v. George A. Moore & Co. (1925), S agreed to sell B 200 tons of Indo–Chinese sugar described as "native brown sugar." B produced evidence that the sugar delivered was of poor quality with average polarization of only about 75 compared with 82 for the poorest

Philippine sugar; however, other evidence showed that the contract price was lower than the prevailing market price for Philippine sugar. In holding that the evidence did not show the sugar was unmerchantable, the court said the seller need only deliver sugar of "fair average quality" of the season, and the kind ordinarily exported from Indo–China. The court added that the law does not require the best goods in the market, nor necessarily the second best, but it does require better than the worst; the goods must at least be of "medium quality goodness." Another court in Keenan v. Cherry & Webb (1925), stated that merchantability means "that the article sold shall be of the general kind described and reasonably fit for the general purpose for which it shall have been sold." In a final case, Wallace v. L. D. Clark & Son (1918), the court stated that to be merchantable goods had to be "salable and fit for the market."

The UCC attempts to deal with this issue by setting out a number of minimum ("at least such") standards to which goods must conform to be merchantable. This listing is not intended to be exhaustive. Thus, other requirements of merchantability may arise through case law. Moreover, as trade and consumer expectations increase, or as standards for safety and the like evolve, the definition of "merchantability" is flexible enough to incorporate them. See T. J. Stevenson & Co. v. 81,193 Bags of Flour (1980). Thus, attributes of merchantability may be established by course of dealing and usage of trade.

In order to pass muster as "merchantable," goods must meet all the standards, as applicable, specified in Sections 2–314(2) and 2A–212(2). A good may be adequately contained, packaged, and labeled, but may be unmerchantable because it is not fit for the ordinary purpose for which such goods are used. Conversely, goods may meet all the other standards but may be found unmerchantable for failure to be contained, packaged and labeled as the agreement, including course of dealing or usage of trade, requires.

Perhaps the most significant standards commonly involved from the lists under Sections 2–314(2) and 2A–212(2) are that the goods must pass without objection in the trade under their description (with defects known) and must be fit for the ordinary purpose for which such goods are used. Thus a bottled drink with loose glass inside, a new automobile with a defective steering column, or a race horse with a broken leg bone would fail to meet either of these standards and would not be merchantable. However, there is a difference between unmerchantable and unmarketable goods. See Pleasurecraft Marine Engine Co. v. Thermo Power Corp. (2001) (obsolete marine engines were not unmerchantable). Moreover, in most jurisdictions the courts recognize that unless a product actually manifests the alleged defect, a cause of action for breach of warranty is legally insufficient; in other states only a breach is required. Grant v. Bridgestone/Firestone, Inc. (2002).

There are products which may pass without objection in the trade and that are employed for the ordinary purpose for which such goods are acquired, but which may be harmful, especially with overuse. Examples are cigarettes which may cause cancer, butter which contains cholesterol which may cause heart disease, and whiskey which may cause drunkenness. A case involving such a problem is Green v. American Tobacco Co. (1969) construing Florida law. There the plaintiff contended that there was a breach of implied warranty as Mr. Green's death by lung cancer was caused by smoking defendant's cigarettes. A jury found that although Mr. Green's lung cancer resulted from smoking defendant's cigarettes, the cigarettes "were reasonably fit and wholesome for human use." The Fifth Circuit Court of Appeals in banc reversed a decision by the Court of Appeals directing a verdict for the plaintiff. The in banc court adopted the dissenting opinion of the Court of Appeals as its majority opinion. The following statement from that opinion shows the court's reasoning:

We are not dealing with an obvious harmful, foreign body in a product. Neither do we have an exploding or breaking bottle case wherein the defect is so obvious that it warrants no discussion. Instead we have a product (cigarettes) that is in no way defective. They are exactly like all others of the particular brand and virtually the same as all other brands on the market.

Another set of cases illustrating a similar point are the food cases involving bones in fish, cherry pits in pie or ice cream, and even the mixed blessing of a pearl in oysters. Most courts today do not use a "foreign/natural" test, but rather a "reasonable expectation" test. Thus in Morrison's Cafeteria of Montgomery, Inc. v. Haddox (1983), a fish bone in fish that caused injury under the facts was not enough to destroy merchantability, but in Carreiro v. 99 West, Inc. (2002), the court surmised that a fact finder could conclude that a patron of a baked scrod fish dinner at a restaurant should not have reasonably expected to find a bone fragment in the shape and size of half a pea when the usual bones found were very thin, flexible, wiry type. See also O'Dell v. DeJean's Packing Co., Inc. (1978), where a pearl in a can of oysters was held to produce unmerchantability.

This reasoning is in line with that of the Restatement of the Law Torts: Product Liability. Section 2 of that Restatement states that a product is defective when, at the time of sale or distribution, it contains a manufacturing defect, is defective in design, or is defective because of inadequate instructions or warnings. Comment h to this section indicates that whether a fish bone in commercially distributed fish chowder constitutes a manufacturing defect is best determined by focusing on reasonable consumer expectations. See also Section 7. The Reporter's Note Comment d to the section also indicates Pennsylvania law and the law of other states supports the position taken in the section and cites cases to the effect that tobacco is not per se a defective product merely because it caused or increased the risk of lung cancer and other life threatening diseases. See also Reporters' Note to Comment a to the section concerning harm from a sharp knife. Finally, the Reporters' Note to Comment j to the section states that the position of this Restatement is consistent with a comment to Restatement, Second, § 402A, which stated that a seller is not required to warn with respect to products or ingredients in them which are dangerous or potentially so when consumed in excessive quantity or over a long period of time when the danger or potentiality of danger is generally known and recognized as in the case of alcoholic beverages or foods containing such substances as saturated fats.

c. Establishing Liability

A seller's or lessor's liability for breach of the implied warranty of merchantability requires proof by the buyer or lessee not only that the goods were not merchantable when they left the control of the seller or lessor (see Official Comment 15 to Section 2–314), but also that (1) the seller or lessor was a "merchant" with respect to goods of that kind (thus this warranty is not made by a casual seller, such as a person selling one's car), (2) the seller or lessor "sold or leased goods", (3) the injury or damage proximately resulted from the defect in the goods (Official Comment 15 to Section 2–314), and (4) notice was given to the seller or lessor and supplier, if any, of the breach of warranty. On the latter, see Sections 2–607(3)(a) and 2A–516(3)(a). The meaning of "merchant" and "goods," the problem of damages, and the notice requirement are all discussed elsewhere. Discussion here is limited to a few problems primarily involving the question of whether a transaction is one for the sale or lease of goods. This part of the discussion is also relevant to the implied warranty of fitness.

As indicated above, the application of Sections 2–314 and 2A–212 (as well as Sections 2–315 and 2A–213) is limited expressly to a sale or lease of goods. It is not relevant whether the goods are new or used (except as to the standard for merchantability), and whether they are acquired for use or for disposition. Official Comments 4 and 10 to Section 2–314. Some transactions which involve both goods and services have posed a problem for the courts. Although there was authority to the contrary, some courts under pre-UCC law held that the serving of food to be consumed on the premises was not a sale of goods but was instead a sale of services, and, therefore, not subject to the implied warranty of merchantability. The injured party's recourse was only in tort based on negligence. Of course, this was nonsense as pointed out in Broyles v. Brown Engineering Co. (1963), where the court held that a contract for engineering services to develop plans for the drainage of a tract of land could carry a warranty the plans would reasonably accomplish the purpose when the project did not involve uncontrollable elements for success that would indicate the parties did not contemplate such a standard. Under the UCC, Section 2–314(1) states: "The serving for value of food or drink to be consumed either on the premises or elsewhere is a sale under this section."

Another problem area has been the blood transfusion cases. The landmark case is Perlmutter v. Beth David Hosp. (1954). There the plaintiff received a blood transfusion and contracted hepatitis from contaminated blood. Plaintiff brought suit alleging breach of the implied warranties of merchantability and fitness. The court denied liability on the theory that the implied warranties did not apply as the supplying of blood to a patient was not a sale but a service. This distinction has been rejected by several courts which have focused on the aspect that caused the trouble, the sale of the blood as goods. Other courts have held that even though supplying blood is a service, warranty liability should be extended to cover the transaction. See Hoffman v. Misericordia Hosp. of Philadelphia (1970). Another approach has been to impose liability on the basis of strict liability in tort. See Cunningham v. MacNeal Memorial Hosp. (1970). On the other hand, one can conclude that the courts who do not find liability have refused for policy reasons to impose liability on noncommercial suppliers of blood (hospitals and blood banks) in the absence of negligence. Many states now have statutes attempting to limit the liability of non-commercial blood suppliers. Most provide that the supplying of blood is a service, not a sale, and not covered by the implied warranties of merchantability and fitness. Statutes worded in this way leave unresolved the question of warranty liability in service transactions and strict liability in tort. However, as to the latter see the Reporter's Note to Comment d to Section 20 of the Restatement of the Law Torts: Products Liability. Courts may very well construe these statutes as also precluding such liability. It is, of course, possible for a statute expressly to restrict liability to "instances of negligence or willful misconduct." See Ill.—S.H.A. ch. 91, § 181.

Warranty liability has been extended to non-sales or lease transactions even though this is beyond the UCC. Traditionally liability in other areas has been imposed only upon proof of negligence, fraud, misrepresentation, or the like. It was mentioned above that some courts that have imposed liability on the supplier of blood for breach of warranty even though such could be considered the supplying of a service. Courts have reached similar results in other service cases. See in addition to the *Broyles* case, supra, Vitromar Piece Dye Works, Inc. v. Lawrence of London, Ltd. (1969). Other transactions to which liability in the nature of implied warranty has been extended include leases of goods (prior to Article 2A), and transactions involving real estate. See Cintrone v. Hertz Truck Leasing & Rental Service (1965); Sawyer v. Pioneer Leasing Corp. (1968); J.L. Teel Co. v. Houston United Sales, Inc., 491 So.2d 851 (1986); Javins v. First Nat. Realty Corp. (1970); and Schipper v. Levitt & Sons, Inc. (1965), where the Supreme Court of New Jersey held there was an implied warranty in the sale of a home where the seller was a mass producer and seller of homes. As to strict liability in tort, see Sections 19 and 20 of the Restatement of the Law of Torts: Products Liability.

d. Implied Warranty of Fitness

This warranty is found in Sections 2–315 and 2A–213, which provide:

Where the seller or lessor (except in a finance lease) at the time of contracting has reason to know any particular purpose for which the goods are required and that the buyer or lessee is relying on the seller's or lessor's skill or judgment to select or furnish suitable goods, there is unless excluded or modified an implied warranty that the goods will be fit for that purpose.

Goods may be merchantable within that standard and yet not be suitable for some special purpose. The standard of merchantability only is that the goods must at least be "fit for the ordinary purposes for which goods of that description are used," and thus the warranty of merchantability obligates the seller or lessor to see that the goods are fit for the general purposes appropriate to such goods. Sections 2–315 and 2A–213 impose a warranty on the seller or lessor who has reason to know of a particular purpose and thus is a warranty of performance. See Ingram River Equipment, Inc. v. Pott Industries, Inc. (1987) and Official Comment 2 to Section 2–315. For example, common interior housepaint may be unsuitable for use in rooms where temperatures often reach 180° F. but perfectly suitable where normal temperatures are maintained. Lewis v. Mobil Oil Corp. (1971) illustrates this distinction. There B purchased hydraulic equipment to operate his sawmill. He requested a local dealer in S's products to supply the proper hydraulic fluid to operate the equipment. The dealer, after consulting S's representative, supplied one of S's products which proved unsuitable and resulted in frequent breakdowns of B's equipment. The court found there was a breach of the implied warranty of fitness. There was no evidence the fluid furnished was not fit for general purposes. It probably met all criteria specified in Section 2–314, yet it was not suitable for B's particular needs. Another case is Solarz v. DaimlerChrysler Corp. (2002), which involved a minivan without a park-lock feature and where there was no modification to install a park-brake interlock. The court stated that safe and reliable family transportation was not a particular purpose of a minivan but rather the ordinary purpose. A final interesting case is Lithuanian Commerce Corp., Ltd. v. Sara Lee Hosiery (2002), where the court decided that if pantyhose purchased by the buyer for the Lithuanian market failed to allow Lithuanian women to engage in normal activities without having the hose fall down, wear out, or bleed color, these were failings that were encompassed by the implied warranty of merchantability.

The proof required to establish a seller's or lessor's liability for breach of an implied warranty of fitness differs in two important respects from that required in the case of the warranty of merchantability. First, it is not necessary to show that the seller or lessor was a merchant. It will be recalled that a non-merchant does not make an implied warranty of merchantability. Second, the buyer or lessee must show that the seller or lessor had reason to know the particular use for which the goods were required and reliance on the seller's or lessor's skill or judgment to select or furnish suitable goods. Such knowledge by the seller or lessor and reliance by the buyer or lessee are not required in an express sense with respect to the warranty of merchantability.

Under pre-UCC law there was no implied warranty of fitness when a good was purchased under its patent or other trade name. The reason for this was the theory that if a buyer asks for a good by its trade or patent name, the buyer is making its own choice and not relying on the skill and judgment of the seller. There was difficulty and confusion in applying this exception. Sections 2–315 and 2A–213 omit the "patent or other trade name" exception. The question whether the buyer or lessee relied on the seller's or lessor's skill and judgment must be determined from the facts of each case, and the designation of the goods in question by their patent or trade name is only one of the facts to be considered in determining whether there was reliance. Official Comment 5 to Section 2–315.

A number of courts have failed to recognize the distinction discussed in the previous cases between the implied warranties of fitness and merchantability. These decisions have permitted recovery for breach of both warranties merely on evidence that the goods were not suitable for the general and ordinary purpose for which such goods are used. See Tennessee Carolina Transp., Inc. v. Strick Corp. (1973) and Frisch and Wladis, General Provisions, Sales, Bulk Transfers, and Documents of Title, 44 Bus. Law. 1445, at 1458–59 (1989). While it is true that a defect may render a product both unfit for a particular purpose as well as unmerchantable, these two warranties are not interchangeable.

e. The Duty to Examine the Goods

What is the effect of the buyer's or lessee's examination or nonexamination of the goods on the right to claim the benefit of the implied warranties of quality (merchantability and fitness; it is submitted that while theoretically this concept could also be applicable in reference to the warranty of title or against interference, its application in that context neither is explicitly provided for or usual). There are two main problems: (1) if buyer or lessee examined the goods, should the defect have been discovered? (2) if the goods could have been examined but were not, may the buyer or lessee claim breach of warranty with reference to defects which an examination probably would have revealed?

The UCC contains this provision:

When the buyer or lessee before entering into the contract has examined the goods or the sample or model as fully as desired or has refused to examine the goods after a demand by the seller or lessor, there is no implied warranty with regard to defects that an examination ought in the circumstances to have revealed to the buyer or lessee.

Sections 2–316(6) and 2A–214(3)(b).

It should be noted that a similar concept applies with a similar result in regard to inspection after delivery. See Official Comment 6 to Section 2–316, Official Comment 15 to Section 2–314, and Official Comment 5 to Section 2–715. Official Comment 6 to Section 2–316 also explains that under the UCC "inspection" does not occur until after the contract has been made, while "examination" occurs before the contract is made.

Under Sections 2–316(6) and 2A–214(3)(b), if the buyer or lessee examines the goods, they are responsible for discovering defects which under the circumstances they ought to have discovered. Whether a defect is one which should have been discovered depends on the buyer's or lessee's skill and the normal method of examining such goods. Official Comment 6 to Section 2–316. If the buyer or lessee is a professional examining products in that person's field, the buyer or lessee will be expected to discover more than if that person is a nonprofessional.

These provisions also exclude all implied warranties with reference to defects which the nonexamining buyer or lessee should have discovered had they examined the goods. Official Comment 6 to Section 2–316 explains that in order for the buyer (or lessee) to be regarded as having refused to examine, it is not sufficient merely to show that the goods were available for examination and that the buyer or lessee failed to avail itself of the opportunity of examination. In addition, it must be shown that the seller or lessor made a demand that the buyer or lessee examine the goods fully. The demand is necessary in order to put "the buyer (or lessee) on notice that he is assuming the risk of defects which the examination ought to reveal." It should be emphasized, however, that by refusing to inspect, the buyer or lessee does not assume the risk of all defects, but only of those defects which an examination should have revealed.

5. EXCLUSION OR MODIFICATION OF WARRANTIES

This is an age of form contracts. Many sales contracts and even more leases are written on contract forms prepared by one of the parties, usually the seller or the lessor, and sometimes the form used follows a draft prepared by a trade association. This is a far cry from the genuinely negotiated contract in which the parties arrive at the terms by a process of mutual "give and take." If a form contract is used, its terms normally will be advantageous to the party drafting it. Often the contract is long, involved, and technical, with much fine print. Even if the buyer or lessee reads it, they may not understand the legal significance of many of the terms. The problems posed by the use of such contracts are among the most difficult with which the drafters of statutes and the courts must grapple.

One of the most frequent clauses placed in form contracts by a seller or lessor is a clause seeking to exclude or limit express and implied warranties. As a seller or lessor need not intend to warrant, these warranties may be viewed as ones imposed by law. As such, a seller or lessor may not wish that liability, and unless precluded by a non-uniform amendment to the UCC or independent law, a contractual provision excluding or limiting that liability is not precluded by the UCC. However, if literal effect were given to the obscure language: "no warranties, express or implied, attach to this sale or lease," the seller or lessor could cast on an unknowing buyer or lessee almost the entire risk of defects in the goods. The UCC is sensitive to this problem and includes a number of provisions in an attempt to deal with it.

a. Express Warranties

A problem arises when a seller or lessor uses words attempting to negate or limit an express warranty that the seller or lessor has made in the transaction. A typical case involving this problem is Lumbrazo v. Woodruff (1931), in which the buyer, an onion grower, purchased 300 bushels of onion seed from the seller who was a seed dealer. The printed form contract furnished by the seller contained the following provision:

> We give no warranty, express or implied, as to description, quality, productiveness, or any other

matter, of any seeds sent out and will be in no way responsible for the crop and the purchaser hereby waives the right of refusal and return of goods which is usually connected with the non-warranty.

The seller had written on the contract in pencil: "300 Bus.Jap.O. Sets—3.50", meaning 300 bushels Japanese onion sets at $3.50 per bushel. The buyer planted the onion sets, but they proved not to be Japanese onions. He suffered considerable financial loss as a result and sued the seller for breach of warranty.

To deal with problems of this sort, Sections 2–316(1) and 2A–214(1) provide:

Words or conduct relevant to the creation of an express warranty and words or conduct tending to negate or limit a warranty must be construed wherever reasonable as consistent with each other. However, subject to Section 2–202, negation or limitation is inoperative to the extent that such construction is unreasonable.

In the *Lumbrazo* case, the handwritten provision: "300 Bus.Jap.O. Sets—3.50" standing alone would constitute an express warranty of description under Section 2–313(2)(b) of the UCC; however, the quoted printed provision attempted to negate all express warranties and, if it were effective, would allow delivery of something entirely different than the subject matter of the contract without breach; in the case it could have been as easily turnip seed rather than onion seed. Under Section 2–316(1), a court attempting to resolve this problem should endeavor to construe the printed words, if reasonably possible, in such a way as to make them consistent with the handwritten words. If the two provisions cannot be reasonably construed to be consistent with each other, Section 2–316(1) then would require the court to hold the disclaimer inoperative. Thus in the *Lumbrazo* case, under the UCC, a court should hold, if it found the two provisions in conflict, that the printed provision attempting to negate express warranties is not sufficient to do so. It is this rule, of course, that prevents a seller or lessor from avoiding delivery of the exact thing agreed upon. Section 2A–214(1) is the same. Of course, the rule also prevents buyer or lessee disappointment in reference to product quality as well. In Bell Sports, Inc. v. Yarusso (2000), the motorcycle helmet manual stated the primary function of the helmet was to reduce the harmful effects of a blow to the head. The court determined this was an express warranty upon which the buyer was entitled to rely and thus the effort to disclaim any express warranties in the manual was ineffective.

A seller or lessor is protected against false allegations of oral express warranties, however, by the provisions on parol and extrinsic evidence, and against unauthorized representations by the customary "lack of authority" clauses. Thus whether or not language of disclaimer satisfies the requirements of the sections on disclaimer, the language used may be relevant under the sections on parol evidence to question whether the warranty was ever in fact created. See Western Intermodal Services, Ltd. v. Singamas Container Industry Co., Ltd. (2000) (section of lease which expressly disclaimed all express and implied warranties as to design or condition of goods leased precluded showing alleged oral agreement of lessor to procure flatracks capable of transporting steel coils). Moreover, oral language of disclaimer may raise issues of fact as to whether reliance by the buyer occurred and whether the seller or lessor had reason to know under the provisions on implied warranty of fitness for a particular purpose.

b. Warranty of Title or Against Interference

Sections 2–312(3) and 2A–211(4) allow disclaimer or modification of the title or interference warranty either by the use of "specific language", which in the case of a lease must be conspicuous and in a record, or by circumstances which give the buyer or lessee reason to know that the person selling or leasing does not claim title, is purporting to sell or lease only such right, interest, or title as that person or a third person may have, or is transferring the goods subject to any claims of infringement or the like. "Seller does not warrant title to the goods" or "the goods are being leased subject to any claim or interest of a person other than lessor" should be language sufficiently specific as a general proposition to exclude the warranty. For what is not sufficient, see Brokke v. Williams (1989) ("as is"). If in a sale the exclusion or modification is put in a record, Section 2–312(3) does not indicate that it must meet the standard of "conspicuousness," but that would seem a wise precaution.

Exclusion under "other circumstances" would occur in the case of sales by parties such as sheriffs and executors who are not selling in the ordinary commercial setting but should be understood as purporting to sell only "an unknown or limited right." See Official Comment 6 to Section 2–312. For example, C obtains a judgment against D and has S, the sheriff, levy on a tractor supposedly belonging to D. S sells the tractor to B at the execution sale. The tractor is subject to a conflicting claim of ownership by X. S does not make the warranty of title to B and would not be liable for damages. For a case involving a lease, see Bank of Nova Scotia v. Equitable Financial Management, Inc. (1989). However, foreclosure sales under UCC Article 9 are another matter; Section 9–610 provides that a disposition under that section includes warranties imposed by these sections unless properly excluded.

c. Other Implied Warranties

The provisions concerning modifications and exclusion of implied warranties of quality are found in Sections 2–316 and 2A–214. Section 2A–214(2) and (3) provide in pertinent part:

(2) Subject to subsection (3), to exclude or modify the implied warranty of merchantability

or any part of it the language must be in a record and be conspicuous. In a consumer lease the language must state "The lessor undertakes no responsibility for the quality of the goods except as otherwise provided in this contract," and in any other contract the language must mention merchantability. Subject to subsection (3), to exclude or modify any implied warranty of fitness the exclusion must be in a record and be conspicuous. Language to exclude all implied warranties of fitness in a consumer lease must state "The lessor assumes no responsibility that the goods will be fit for any particular purpose for which you may be leasing these goods, except as otherwise provided in the contract," and in any other contract the language is sufficient if it states, for example, that "There are no warranties which extend beyond the description on the face hereof." Language that satisfies the requirements of this subsection for a consumer lease also satisfies its requirements for any other contract.

(3) Notwithstanding subsection (2):

(3) unless the circumstances indicate otherwise, all implied warranties are excluded by expressions like "as is," "with all faults," or other language which in common understanding calls the lessee's attention to the exclusion of warranties and makes plain that there is no implied warranty if in a record and conspicuous.

Section 2–316(2) through (5) is essentially the same, except a record is not required to disclaim the implied warranty of merchantability in a non-consumer contract nor to disclaim all implied warranties (but if a consumer contract is evidenced by a record, the disclaimer must be set forth conspicuously). The difference is explained by leasing practice, which is more formal than sales practice, and thus requiring a record disclaimer is feasible. As noted earlier, an implied warranty can be excluded or modified by course of dealing or course of performance or usage of trade, and examination or the failure to do so after demand may preclude warranty recovery.

The provisions of Sections 2–316 and 2A–214 should not be confused with those of Sections 2–719 and 2A–503, which permit the exclusion or limitation of remedies. The distinction and relationship between these provisions is discussed in Chapter 12 but is essentially that a disclaimer removes all basis for remedy while a limitation or exclusion of remedy leaves some form of remedy.

As the statutes state, all implied warranties can be disclaimed if it is agreed that the goods are sold "as is", or "with all faults", or other similar language which in common understanding calls attention to the exclusion of warranties and makes plain that there is no implied warranty. Exactly what language is the equivalent of "as is" or "with all faults" is not clear. For example there are conflicting opinions as to whether a statement that a buyer of a used car accepts the car "in its present condition" is the equivalent of an "as is" clause. See First Nat. Bank of Elgin v. Husted (1965) and Hull–

Dobbs, Inc. v. Mallicoat (1966). See also Insurance Co. of North America v. Automatic Sprinkler Corp. (1981) ("this warranty is in lieu of all other warranties" not sufficient). There also is a division of authority under prior law whether the language must be conspicuous in a record in a sale. Section 2A–214(3)(a) resolves this issue for leases, and the requirement that the disclaimer in a consumer contract in a record must be conspicuous should settle the matter for both consumer and commercial sales under amended Section 2–316(6). Finally the Federal Trade Commission "Used Car Rule" is relevant here. See 16 CFR Pt. 455. For a brief discussion, see Butler and Kaswell, Federal Trade Commission Rulemaking in 1984, 40 Bus.Law. 1119, 1122–24 (1985). So too may be the Magnuson–Moss Act at 15 U.S.C. § 2308.

It will be noted that even when an "as is" clause is used, the buyer or lessee is allowed to show that the circumstances indicate that it should not be effective as a disclaimer. In Gindy Mfg. Corp. v. Cardinale Trucking Corp. (1970), the seller used a form contract containing an "as is" clause in the sale of new and used vehicles. The court held that the clause was not effective as a disclaimer. It gave as one reason that under the custom of the trade, while "as is" clauses may be expected in contracts for the sale of used vehicles, they are not in the sale of new ones. Compare Nick Mikalacki Construction Co. v. M.J.L. Truck Sales, Inc. (1986), where the truck was used and the buyer was aware of the "as is" clause but tried to argue it understood the clause to mean only that it was accepting only the defects of which it had actual knowledge.

A second way by which an implied warranty can be negated or modified is by course of dealing or course of performance or usage of trade. The meaning of these three terms is discussed in Chapter 4. Official Comment 5 to Section 2–316 explains that expressions like "as is" or "with all faults" are actually expressions which by usage of trade are understood as placing the entire risk of the quality of the goods on the acquiring party.

Sections 2–316(2) and (3) and Section 2A–214(2) are to be distinguished; they provide a method by which the implied warranties of merchantability and fitness may be specifically excluded or modified. Essentially the language used must focus on merchantability or fitness and general language such as "no implied warranties are made" would not be sufficient. Language couched in understandable terms to a consumer also must be used, and can be used in a commercial transaction. In leases, the language must be in a record and always must be conspicuous. In a consumer sale the rule is the same, except for a disclaimer of merchantability in a commercial sale where a record is not required. To meet the test of conspicuousness, a term must be "so written, displayed, or presented that a reasonable person against which it is to operate should have noticed it." Section 2–103(1)(b) (or Section 1–201(a)(10)) if revised Article 1 has been enacted. Same for Section 2A–103(1)(d). The definition further elaborates with respect to electronic agents and persons and with respect to the latter between an electronic environment and a writing. The purpose here is to prevent the buyer or lessee from being taken by surprise. Whether a term is "conspicuous" or not is for decision by the court, but the UCC sets out some specific standards: a heading in capitals equal to or greater in size than the surrounding text, or in contrasting type, font, or color to the surrounding text of the same or lesser size; language in the body of a record or display in larger type than the surrounding text, or in contrasting type, font, or color to the surrounding text of the same size or set off from surrounding text of the same size by symbols or other marks that call attention to the language; or a term that is so placed that one cannot proceed without taking action with respect to that term.

Many courts have considered the problem of conspicuousness. The cases reveal a general hostility of courts to disclaimer clauses, especially when a consumer is involved. In the following situations in sale transactions under former law, and in some lease transactions before Article 2A, disclaimer clauses have been held not to be conspicuous:

1. A disclaimer in smaller print than the rest of a purchase order,

2. Type of the same color and size as the type used for the other provisions,

3. A disclaimer in italics but in smaller and lighter type than much of the rest of a printed form,

4. A disclaimer in the same size type as the rest of the provisions but underscored,

5. Disclaimer language in bold face type on the back of the form contract not referred to adequately on the front page.

Consider, as an illustration, Stauffer Chemical Co. v. Curry (1989). There the disclaimer appeared on a 50 pound bag of insecticide in type about one half the size of the type used to convey other information on the bag and was located so it would be difficult to see if the bag was standing upright. The court determined the disclaimer was not sufficiently conspicuous.

What if the disclaimer does not meet the statutory test but the buyer or lessee admits it was noticed and that its import was understood? Cases like Smith v. Sharpensteen (1974), hold the disclaimer is effective since the goal of the statute is met. However, this view, by injecting a subjective test, reduces the certainty the disclaimer provisions also seek to promote.

6. PRIVITY IN REGARD TO WARRANTY

It is a general principle of contract law that in order for one party successfully to sue another for breach of contract the two parties must be in privity of contract. Basically, the principle recognizes that one should not be liable for breach of a legally enforceable promise (a contract) except to the party to whom the promise was made. If, for example S contracts to sell goods to B and then refuses without legal reason to perform, S should not be liable to X with whom S has no contract.

There are exceptions to this principle. B may have assigned B's rights to X, thereby giving X as the assignee of B the right to sue S. Or, at the time S and B contracted, they may have contracted for the direct benefit of X; in which case X could sue S as the third-party beneficiary of the contract between S and B.

This basic contract principle of privity has caused difficulty in actions for breach of warranty. Warranty often is considered a contract theory, although under the UCC it must be remembered "contract" (Section 1–201(b)(12)) has a broader meaning than "agreement" (Section 1–201(b)(3)). It is more appropriate to consider warranty as an obligation imposed by law, since many rules (for example, Sections 2–316(1) and 2A–214(1), 2–317(3) and 2A–215(3), 2–318 and 2A–216) appear inconsistent with an analysis of warranty as part of the agreement. But the concept of privity is a convenient theory to control liability exposure which cannot be easily measured in a society where goods distribution no longer is a face to face matter from manufacturer to user. In our society distribution of goods to the ultimate user can be a very involved process. The components of a manufactured article may be bought from a number of other manufacturers. The manufacturer (or packager) may then sell the finished product to a wholesale dealer, who in turn sells to a retail dealer who then sells or leases to the user. The product may even pass through the hands of other intermediaries before it reaches the hands of the retail dealer. In short, the marketing process in most instances involves a series of transactions rather than a single transaction. Further, the party who suffers injury may not have acquired the goods from anyone. That person may be an employee, a guest, a member of the family, or even a mere bystander. Articles 2 and 2A deal alternatively with the rules on liability in such a distributive situation, and Sections 2–313A and 2–313B also are a step forward.

The courts have sometimes referred to the situation where the buyer or lessee sues the component supplier, manufacturer, or distributor as a "vertical" privity problem. To illustrate: M manufactures and sells a good to R who in turn sells to B. B is injured by a defect in the good. The question of M's liability to B for breach of implied warranty presents a vertical privity problem. B purchased from R, not M, and is not in privity with M. Courts have denied recovery to B on that basis. In more recent years an increasing number of courts have allowed B to recover. Various theories have been used to rationalize this result. Especially in food cases, it has been common for the courts to reason that when the action is based on implied warranty the obligation is not merely an implied term in the agreement but is an obligation imposed as a matter of public policy to discourage the sale of unwholesome food. This view can find support in various UCC provisions. Some courts have also recognized that historically the principle of privity grew out of special assumpsit, whereas warranty liability has its origin in tort and is a century older than the action of special assumpsit; therefore the privity concept is inapplicable to warranty actions. Of course, to the extent warranty under the UCC is neither contract (agreement) nor tort, this analysis is unnecessary. Still other theories that have been used in appropriate fact situations are agency and third party beneficiary.

Assume the same example as above except that it is B's employee, E, not B who is injured by the defect. This presents what is termed a horizontal privity problem as well as a vertical one. Even if B is allowed to recover from M, should E, who entered into no contract of purchase, be allowed to recover from either M or R?

Neither Article 2 nor Article 2A as such require privity. Rather the UCC rules apply to the extent a privity requirement otherwise is determined to exist. Article 2 originally dealt with the privity question at a time when the law still was developing and so postulated three alternatives, and Article 2A followed that pattern as well in Section 2A–216. Section 2–318 also deals with the issue of privity in connection with remedial promises and the obligations under Sections 2–313A and 2–313B. Alternative A of Section 2–318 states:

A seller's warranty to an immediate buyer, whether express or implied, a seller's remedial promise to an immediate buyer, and a seller's obligation to a remote purchaser under Section 2–313A or 2–313B extends to any individual who is in the family or household of the immediate buyer or the remote purchaser or who is a guest in the home if it is reasonable to expect that the individual may use, consume or be affected by the goods and who is personally injured by breach of the warranty, remedial promise, or obligation. A seller may not exclude or limit the operation of this section.

Section 2A–216 Alternative A is basically the same, except Article 2A does not deal with remedial promises or include sections like Sections 2–313A or 2–313B because products are not leased until the retail level. Section 2A–216 also indicates its provisions do not displace products liability law, as is the case in some states like Delaware in sales, and explicitly states that a disclaimer or limitation of remedy good against a lessee is good against one not in privity, a matter the courts are divided on in sales.

Under the literal wording of this section, warranties would not extend to E as not a member of the family or household or a guest in the home.

Alternative B of Section 2–318 provides:

A seller's warranty to an immediate buyer, whether express or implied, a seller's remedial promise to an immediate buyer, or a seller's obligation to a remote purchaser under Section 2–313A or 2–313B extends to any individual who may reasonably be expected to use, consume or be affected by the goods and who is personally injured by breach of the warranty, remedial promise, or obligation. A seller may not exclude or limit the operation of this section.

Section 2A–216 Alternative B is the same with the qualifications noted above.

Alternative C of Section 2–318 provides:

A seller's warranty to an immediate buyer, whether express or implied, a seller's remedial promise to an immediate buyer, or a seller's obligation to a remote purchaser under Section 2–313A or 2–313B extends to any person that may reasonably be expected to use, consume, or be affected by the goods and that is injured by breach of the warranty, remedial promise, or obligation. A seller may not exclude or limit the operation of this section with respect to injury to the person of an individual to whom the warranty extends, remedial promise, or obligation extends.

Section 2A–216 is the same with the qualifications noted above.

Under either of the two latter alternatives any warranty by M or R would extend to E and M's warranty would extend to B. Under Alternative C, damages beyond those for personal injury and property damage, such as loss of bargain and perhaps even consequential damages, if foreseeable and unavoidable, might be recoverable. See Stoney v. Franklin (2001) (under statute patterned after Alternative C homeowners' claims against manufacturers of exterior insulation and window components were foreseeable as from persons who might reasonably have been expected to be affected by the product). While this may seem harsh, Official Comment 2 to Section 2–318, and the Official Comments to Sections 2–313A and 2–313B, as well as the text of Section 2A–216 itself, provide that a seller or lessor may disclaim warranty or limit remedy, and a disclaimer or limitation good against that seller's or lessor's buyer or lessee also is equally operative against beneficiaries of warranties under the section. See Morrow v. New Moon Homes, Inc. (1976) and Theos & Sons, Inc. v. Mack Trucks, Inc. (2000) (implied warranty disclaimer effective against original corporate purchaser equally effective against buyer from that corporation notwithstanding that disclaimer not brought to the attention of second purchaser). See also Moore v. Coachmen Industries, Inc. (1998) (a supplier of component part integrated into a finished product is protected by any warranty limitations provided by the product's maker; a buyer ordinarily looks only to the product maker for a complete and functional product). Some courts, however, have improperly (one justification for privity abrogation is a seller/manufacturer can still limit warranty coverage) ignored this guidance in the Article 2 comment. For example, see Spagnol Enterprises, Inc. v. Digital Equip. Corp. (1990). The last sentence of the two latter alternatives does not relate to disclaimers or limitations of remedy, but rather forbids exclusion of liability to the persons to whom the warranties, obligations, and promises extend. But in Haas v. DaimlerChrysler Corp. (2000), the court held that an automobile manufacturer's clearly stated warranty limitation requiring the second purchaser of the vehicle to pay a fee to transfer remaining warranty coverage violated neither the UCC or the Magnuson–Moss Warranty Act.

Most states adopted Section 2–318, Alternative A, and thus most states adopted the same alternative under Article 2A. However, even in those states which have adopted Alternative A, Official Comment 3 to former Section 2–318 explains that Section 2–318, and Section 2A–216 itself states, that it is not intended to preclude courts from extending warranties to other parties in the distributive chain. Some courts have accepted that invitation, particularly to the extent they would permit a recovery in strict liability in tort, or where the extension is believed to be sound policy. See Morrow v. New Moon Homes, Inc. (1976) and Old Albany Estates, Ltd. v. Highland Carpet Mills, Inc. (1979). Other courts have not gone beyond the legislative enactment. Gowen v. Cady (1988). United Technologies Corp. v. Saren Engineering, Inc. (2002) (unpublished), and Paramount Aviation Corp. v. Gruppo Agusta (2002) (provider of services to owner of goods who suffered economic injury due to defect in the goods is not entitled to recover from manufacturer). The division is especially sharp with respect to the implied warranty of title. See Crook Motor Co. v. Goolsby (1988) and Mitchell v. Webb (1979). On the other hand, a party not in privity may acquire standing by an assignment of rights (see Collins Co., Ltd. v. Carboline Co. (1988)), agency principles (see Costa v. Volkswagen of Am. (1988)),

or law (under Section 2A–209(1), the benefits of a
supplier's promises to the finance lessor under a
supply contract and of all warranties extend to the
finance lessee to the extent of the leasehold interest). See also Szajna v. General Motors Corp. (1986)
(interpreting Magnuson–Moss to allow a non-privity
plaintiff to recover for economic loss notwithstanding contrary state law).

7. MAGNUSON–MOSS

In 1975 Congress enacted the Magnuson–Moss
Warranty Federal Trade Commission Improvement
Act, 15 U.S.C.A. § 2301 et seq. Title 1 of this Act,
"Consumer Product Warranties" (effective July 4,
1975) contains provisions governing written and
implied warranties in sales to consumers. The application of Magnuson–Moss to leases is less clear,
particularly where the issue involves a written warranty or the enforcement of an implied warranty,
since those terms are defined as involving a sale.
Nonetheless, some authority has found that consumer lease transactions are within the scope of the
Act. See Freeman v. Hubco Leasing, Inc. (1985) and
Henderson v. Benson–Hartman Motors, Inc. (1983).
Administration of the Act is placed under the jurisdiction of the Federal Trade Commission, which has
issued various regulations under the Act (16 CFR
Pts. 700–703). Essentially the Act does three things:
(1) it requires disclosure of written consumer product warranty terms and conditions, (2) it provides
substantive rules that prevent disclaimers, require

"full" warranties to provide minimum remedy standards (although not "limited" warranties), and that prevent other deceptive practices in connection with warranties, and (3) it regulates informal dispute settlement procedures. Space limits discussion to a few of the most important provisions of Title I.

The Act requires any warrantor of a consumer product distributed in interstate commerce warranting the product by a written warranty to indicate clearly and conspicuously whether the warranty is a "full" (with statement of duration) or a "limited" warranty. There is no obligation under the Act, however, to give any written warranty. In order to be a "full" warranty, the warranty must meet certain minimum standards set out in the Act. 15 U.S.C.A. §§ 2303, 2304. Chief among these standards is the requirement that if the product contains a defect or malfunction which cannot be remedied after a reasonable number of efforts the consumer may elect either a refund of the purchase price or a replacement of the product without charge. If the product can be repaired this must be done, including replacing any component parts, without charge.

A warrantor giving a "full" warranty may not provide for a limitation on the duration of an implied warranty, but may in conspicuous and simple and readily understood language appearing on the face of the warranty limit or exclude liability for consequential damages unless precluded by state law. 15 U.S.C.A. §§ 2304, 2311. As pointed out below, any provision limiting or excluding liability for consequential damages would be subject to the provisions of Section 2–719 of the UCC, and Section 2A–503 if a lease were involved.

Magnuson–Moss contains some important provisions regarding implied warranties given under state law (Sections 2–314 and 2–315 of the UCC; Sections 2A–212 and 2A–213 if a lease were involved). A written warranty (full or limited) under the Act may not disclaim or modify (except as to time as noted below) any implied warranty. 15 U.S.C.A. § 2308. To the extent that the Act applies to a sale or a lease of goods, this would preclude a disclaimer under Section 2–316 or Section 2A–214. If the written warranty is a limited one, the duration of an implied warranty may be limited to the same duration as the written warranty, assuming the duration is reasonable and the limitation is set forth in clear and unmistakable language and prominently displayed on the face of the warranty. 15 U.S.C.A. § 2308. As noted, however, under a full warranty there can be no limitation on the duration of an implied warranty.

The Act is not intended to invalidate or restrict any right or remedy which is given to a consumer under state law or any other Federal law. 15 U.S.C.A. § 2311. The Act specifically provides that it does not supersede any state law regarding consequential damages for injury to the person or property. For example, M, an automobile manufacturer gives a written warranty (limited or full) under Magnuson–Moss, but inserts a provision limiting liability to replacement of defective parts. B, a con-

sumer purchaser of the automobile is severely injured in an accident caused by a defect in the
steering mechanism. M's liability for B's personal
injuries (consequential damages) would be governed
by Section 2–719(3) of the UCC, which makes such
a limitation prima facie unconscionable. M also may
be responsible in strict liability in tort, if that
theory has been adopted by the courts of B's state
and is not considered displaced by the UCC. See
Section 1–103(b) and Official Comment 4 to Section
2–318 and Official Comment to Section 2A–216.

8. OTHER THEORIES OF LIABILITY

There are other theories which often may be used
by a buyer or lessee or other party to recover
damages suffered as a result of defective goods. As
explained earlier, space limitations allow only a
mention of these theories. It should be pointed out
that these theories, including implied warranty, are
not necessarily mutually exclusive, nor are they
normally considered to be displaced by the UCC.
For example, a plaintiff may include in a complaint
a count alleging breach of warranty and also counts
alleging, as applicable, public misrepresentation,
negligent tort, and strict liability in tort. But see
Cline v. Prowler Industries of Maryland, Inc.
(1980), which discusses UCC displacement of some
theories. Given the clear expression to the contrary
in Section 2A–216 and Official Comment 4 to Section 2–318, no general displacement should be
found. However, where a court allows a count in

warranty and one in strict liability, there seldom is a persuasive explanation of the relationship between the theories. See Mid Continent Aircraft Corp. v. Curry County Spraying Service, Inc. (1978) and Morrow v. New Moon Homes, Inc. (1976). For this reason, the Restatement of the Law Torts: Products Liability and Official Comment 7 to Section 2–314 speak to this issue, as discussed below.

a. Public Misrepresentation

There are many cases in which a plaintiff has proceeded against a seller (especially the manufacturer) on the basis of the seller's advertising or labels attached to the product. The theory of recovery in such cases has not always been clear. Many courts have allowed recovery on an express warranty theory; essentially this theory is now clarified and codified in Section 2–313B. Other cases have been litigated on the theory of misrepresentation under Restatement of the Law Torts: Products Liability Section 9 (or its predecessor, § 402B of the Restatement (Second) of Torts and related sections).

The landmark case is Baxter v. Ford Motor Co. (1932). There the plaintiff purchased a Model A Ford from St. John Motors, a Ford dealer, who had acquired it from the Ford Motor Company. A pebble from a passing car struck the windshield, causing small pieces of glass to fly into one of the plaintiff's eyes. He lost the sight of that eye and sustained some loss of sight in the other, for which he sued both the dealer and Ford Motor Company. The plaintiff contended that the following advertising matter printed by Ford Motor Company and furnished by it to the dealer to be distributed for sale assistance constituted an express warranty that the glass in the windshield would not break, fly, or shatter. The advertisement read:

> Triplex Shatter–Proof Glass Windshield. All of the new Ford cars have a Triplex shatter-proof windshield—so made that it will not fly or shatter under the hardiest impact. This is an important safety factor because it eliminates the dangers of flying glass—the cause of most of the injuries in automobile accidents. In these days of crowded, heavy traffic the use of this Triplex glass is an absolute necessity. Its extra margin of safety is something that every motorist should look for in the purchase of a car—especially where there are women and children.

The trial court had refused to admit this advertising matter as evidence, thereby precluding the plaintiff from recovering from the Ford Motor Company on the theory of express warranty. The Supreme Court of Washington reversed the trial court, holding that the evidence should have been admitted. In its opinion the court stated:

> Since the rule caveat emptor was first formulated, vast changes have taken place in the economic structures of the English speaking peoples. Methods of doing business have undergone a great transition. Radio, billboards, and the prod-

ucts of the printing press have become the means of creating a large part of the demand that causes goods to depart from factories to the ultimate consumer. It would be unjust to recognize a rule that would permit manufacturers of goods to create a demand for their products by representing that they possess qualities which they, in fact, do not possess, and then because there is no privity of contract existing between the consumer and the manufacturer, deny the consumer the right to recover if damages result from the absence of these qualities, when such absence is not readily noticeable.

It should be noted that the court did not require that Baxter be in privity of contract with Ford Motor Company. This has been the position of most courts which have dealt with the problem.

A theory of liability based on advertisements and labels is now embraced in Section 9 of the Restatement of the Law Torts: Products Liability which provides:

> One engaged in the business of selling or otherwise distributing products who, in connection with the sale of a product, makes a fraudulent, negligent, or innocent misrepresentation concerning the product is subject to liability for harm to persons or property caused by the misrepresentation.

This section imposes strict liability; that is, it does not require proof that the misrepresentation was made fraudulently or negligently. Further it does not require privity of contract. A Comment to the Section explains that case law has not resolved whether an innocent misrepresentation may in the absence of product defect be a basis for liability to one who is not a "consumer" of the product. An employee or the wife of the purchaser could qualify.

Of course, any requirement of privity also may be abrogated in relation to warranty under Sections 2–318 and 2A–216. As a result, recovery in warranty in connection with advertising may be allowed in an appropriate case. Compare Thomas v. Amway Corp. (1985) with Collins v. Uniroyal, Inc. (1974), and now see Section 2–313B. Comment e to Restatement Section 9 indicates breach of express warranty is an independent basis of liability.

b. Negligence

A common law theory upon which a plaintiff may proceed against parties in the distributive chain is negligence. Whereas liability for breach of warranty or public misrepresentation does not require proof of fault, liability for negligence depends on proof that the defendant did not exercise due (reasonable) care. Usually, therefore, especially in the case of goods packaged in a sealed container by another party and resold in the same container by a retailer or middleman, any recovery for negligence is against the manufacturer or packager.

There are several advantages for a plaintiff proceeding under a negligence theory. First, no notice of the defect is required as may be required under

Sections 2–607(1)(c) and 2A–516(1)(c) of the UCC. Second, some jurisdictions do not allow a disclaimer for negligence in products cases. See Dessert Seed Co. v. Drew Farmers Supply, Inc. (1970). Third, no privity of contract is required. The plaintiff need not show that he or she purchased from the defendant or anyone else and the defendant's liability may extend to anyone who would reasonably be expected to be affected by the goods, even a bystander. Of course, a privity requirement is not necessarily involved under the UCC either. See Sections 2–318 and 2A–216.

The main difficulties to the plaintiff in proceeding in negligence are that recovery for economic loss probably is not available (see, e.g., Aloe Coal Co. v. Clark Equipment Co. (1987) and Teledyne Technologies Inc. v. Freedom Forge Corp. (2002)), and negligence on the defendant's part must be established. On the latter point, chances of recovery are much improved if the plaintiff can get the court to invoke the doctrine of res ipsa loquitur, meaning, "the thing speaks for itself." If the court holds that res ipsa loquitur is applicable, some jurisdictions treat this as creating a presumption of negligence entitling the plaintiff to a directed verdict if the defendant does not produce some evidence showing absence of negligence. Most jurisdictions treat res ipsa as only creating an inference of negligence which means that even assuming the defendant introduces no evidence it is still up to the jury whether the defendant's conduct was negligent.

The courts have generally refused to apply the doctrine of res ipsa loquitur unless the following three circumstances appear:

1. The accident is one that ordinarily would not have happened if someone had not been negligent.

2. The agency which caused the harm must have been within the exclusive control of the defendant. This means that if there is negligence, the defendant would be responsible for it.

3. There is no possibility of conduct by the plaintiff contributing to the accident. This is, of course, to eliminate the possibility that it was the plaintiff who was responsible for the accident.

Some courts have added a fourth requirement that evidence to explain the accident must be more accessible to the defendant than to the plaintiff.

Comment n to Restatement of the Law Torts: Products Liability Section 2 indicates that design and failure to warn cases under Sections 2(b) and (c) of the Restatement rest on a risk-utility assessment and that to allow two or more factually identical risk-utility claims to go to a jury under different labels, whether negligence, implied warranty, or strict liability, would create confusion, and local law should determine the stage at which plaintiff must decide which theory to pursue. On the other hand, for a claim based on a manufacturing defect under Restatement Section 2(a), negligence rests on a showing of fault leading to a product defect while strict liability (which also includes warranty) rests merely on a showing of product defect and plaintiff may assert a negligence claim in addition to a claim in strict liability.

c. Strict Liability in Tort

In the landmark case of Greenman v. Yuba Power Products, Inc. (1963), the Supreme Court of California held that a manufacturer and a retailer were both strictly liable in tort to a plaintiff who had been injured by a power lathe given to him by his wife, purchased from the retailer, and manufactured by the manufacturer. This theory is now found in Section 2 of the Restatement of the Law Torts: Products Liability. That section states in part that a product is defective when, at the time of sale or distribution it contains a manufacturing defect, is defective in design, or is defective because of inadequate instructions or warnings.

A few observations about this section follow:

(1) The liability is strict; there is no need to prove negligence. This is the same rule as in warranty.

(2) The liability applies to sellers or distributors engaged in the business of selling or otherwise distributing product components or products for use or consumption such as a manufacturer, wholesaler, retailer or other distributor. It does not apply to an occasional seller of food or other such products such as a housewife who, on one occasion, sells her neighbor a jar of jam. Sections 1 and 5 through 8, and Section 20. This is the

same rule as in the case of the implied warranty of merchantability.

(3) The liability applies when the product is defective. For a well co-ordinated body of law governing liability for harm to persons or property arising out of the sale of defective products, a consistent definition of defect is required whether the claim is under a tort label or one of implied warranty of merchantability. Official Comment 7 to UCC Section 2–314 agrees with the above Comment n to Section 2 under the Restatement. The "concept of defect in tort and the concept of merchantability in Article 2 are coextensive where personal injuries are involved, *i.e.*, if goods are merchantable under warranty law they [cannot] still be defective under tort law, and if goods are not defective under tort law they [cannot] be unmerchantable under warranty law." Thus, when "recovery is sought for injury to person or property, whether goods are merchantable is to be determined by applicable state products liability law." Comment n to Section 2 of the Restatement goes further: to allow two or more factually identical risk-utility claims to go to the jury under different labels, or a tort claim and an implied warranty of merchantability claim that rest on the same factual predicate of a manufacturing defect, should not be allowed as duplicative; if one or the other theory presents an advantage to the plaintiff, for example in connection with the statute of limitations, the plaintiff may pursue the more advantageous theory, but the trier of fact

may not consider both theories on the same facts. However, for claims based on misrepresentation, express warranty, implied warranty of fitness, or an obligation under Sections 2–313A or 2–313B, UCC Article 2 determines whether the warranty or obligation is breached.

(4) No privity of contract is required. Under the UCC, any requirement of privity may be abrogated. However, only under Alternative C is the explicit statutory rule approximately co-extensive with that of strict liability in tort. However, a similar result may be reached by case law. Morrow v. New Moon Homes, Inc. (1976).

(5) Liability under the Restatement is for "harm ... to persons or property...." Courts often have not allowed recovery in strict tort where only economic loss is involved. The recovery must be in warranty. See, e.g., Seely v. White Motor Co. (1965) and Morrow v. New Moon Homes, Inc. (1976). For example, if a truck is defective and the only losses are repair to the truck and loss of profits while the truck is idle, only economic losses are involved. On the other hand, had an accident occurred because of a defect, damaging the truck and injuring the driver, physical damage is involved. Some courts, however, have allowed recovery in strict tort where the sole loss is economic. See Santor v. A and M Karagheusian, Inc. (1965). See Section 21 of Restatement of the Law Torts: Products Liability, and see also Jimenez v. The Superior Court of San Diego County (2002) (economic loss rule does

not bar homeowner's recovery in tort for damage caused by defective window installed in home. According to a dissent, since a product malfunction almost always is due to a defective component, virtually every product failure now is a tort).

(6) No notice to the seller or lessor or supplier of the injury or defect is required. The theory of liability is tort; therefore, the provisions of the UCC, which may require notice in the case of warranties, are not applicable.

(7) Similarly, liability under the Restatement is not normally affected by a disclaimer or contractual limitation of remedy. See Section 18. This is because the liability is in tort. In some instances disclaimer clauses have been drafted very specifically to include a disclaimer of liability in strict tort. There is a division of authority as to whether such disclaimers are valid. See Vandermark v. Ford Motor Co. (1964) (invalid) and Keystone Aeronautics Corp. v. R.J. Enstrom Corp. (1974) (valid). See also the Comments to Section 18 and McNichols, Who Says That Strict Tort Disclaimers Can Never Be Effective? The Courts Cannot Agree, 28 Okla.L.Rev. 494 (1975).

(8) The UCC statute of limitations, which under Article 2, with some exceptions, begins to run when the goods are delivered in accordance with Section 2–725 (cf. Section 2A–506(b)—which includes a discovery rule), is not applicable, and the normal tort statute, which includes a discovery

rule, is. Drayton Public School District No. 19 v. W.R. Grace & Co. (1989).

The potential differences with the UCC, other than the issue of when a product is defective, raise still unresolved jurisprudential questions concerning the proper relationship between the theories. As Official Comment 7 to UCC Section 2–314 states, there is "tension between warranty law and tort law where goods cause personal injury or property damage ... the primary source of that tension arises from disagreement over whether the concept of defect in tort and the concept of merchantability in Article 2 are coextensive...." This latter cause is resolved; the other causes are yet to be definitively resolved. See Mid Continent Aircraft Corp. v. Curry County Spraying Service, Inc. (1978), Morrow v. New Moon Homes, Inc. (1976), Cline v. Prowler Industries of Maryland, Inc. (1980), and Frisch, Leary and Wladis, Uniform Commercial Code Annual Survey: General Provisions, Sales, Bulk Transfers, and Documents of Title, 42 Bus. Law. 1213, at 1219–22 (1987). The Comments to the Restatement and to Section 2–318 and the text of Section 2A–216 further address some relationship issues as previously discussed, and hopefully will be utilized by the courts to further relieve the tension which, of course, the courts themselves created.

CHAPTER 10

REPUDIATION, BREACH
AND EXCUSE

b.   Destruction of the Specific Subject Matter.
c.   Commercial Impracticability.
d.   Partial Excuse.
e.   Substituted Performance.

---

1.   INTRODUCTION

A sales contract imposes legal obligations on both parties as does a lease. The seller or a lessor is obligated to deliver the goods according to the terms of the contract while the buyer or lessee is obligated to accept and pay for the goods according to the terms of the contract. Section 2–301 and (by implication) Section 2A–103(1)(p). A failure by either party, without legal justification, to perform any of these obligations when due constitutes a breach of contract (in a lease, a "default") entitling the "aggrieved" party to one or more of the remedies discussed in the next two chapters. Sections 2–703, 2–711, 2A–508 and 2A–523. In addition, if the contract imposes other obligations and so provides, a breach or default as to those obligations may furnish a remedy to an aggrieved party. "An aggrieved party means a party entitled to resort to a remedy." Section 1–201(b)(2).

In some instances one of the parties may by word or action, and without legal cause, repudiate the contract even before the time for performance arrives. This may be treated as a breach or default. Sections 2–610 and 2A–402. Of course, anticipatory repudiation, failure to perform, or in some cases defective performance also may be legally justified, and may, therefore, not constitute a breach or default. If so, the promised performance is excused.

The purpose of this chapter is to discuss these problems, primarily to determine when one is an "aggrieved" party so as to be entitled to a remedy for breach or default.

2.   ANTICIPATORY REPUDIATION

a.   Generally

Suppose on July 1, 1975, S contracts to sell and B to buy described goods to be delivered by S to B's warehouse on July 29, 1975. According to the great weight of case authority this contract creates not only a duty on S to tender delivery of the goods on July 29 and a duty on B to accept and pay for the goods when they are tendered on that day, but also a duty on each not to repudiate their promise before July 29th. Thus repudiation without legal cause by either party before July 29th creates an immediate right to a cause of action by the other.

This common law principle is incorporated in Sections 2–610 and 2A–402 of the Code. In fact, the Code reflects sensitivity to the fact that a very high percentage of breaches or defaults result from anticipatory repudiation. See Sections 2–704, 2–708, 2–713, 2–723, 2A–524, 2A–528, 2A–519 and 2A–507.

Sections 2–610 and 2A–402 provide:

When either party repudiates the contract with respect to a performance not yet due the loss of which will substantially impair the value of the contract to the other, the aggrieved party may

(a) for a commercially reasonable time await performance by the repudiating party; or

(b) resort to any right or remedy for breach or default even though the aggrieved party has notified the repudiating party that it would await the latter's performance and has urged retraction; and

(c) in either case suspend performance or proceed in accordance with the provisions of the relevant Article on the seller's or lessor's right to identify goods to the contract notwithstanding breach or default or to salvage unfinished goods (Sections 2–704 and 2A–524).

In addition, Section 2A–402 specifically refers to any right to demand assurance of performance under Section 2A–401. No different conclusion with respect to Sections 2–609 and 2–610 should be drawn if there is a question of whether there is a repudiation, and Official Comment 1 to Section 2–610 should be interpreted in that light. See T & S Brass & Bronze Works v. Pic–Air, Inc. (1986) (communication a demand for assurance and not a repudiation) and Official Comment 5 to Section 2–610.

Repudiation may occur by either language or actions. Sections 2–610(2) and 2A–402(2). S may inform B before the date for performance that S will not or cannot perform. See Neptune Research and Development, Inc. v. Teknics Indus. Sys., Inc. (1989) (seller informed buyer goods would not be available on promised date). S may deny any contract with B. In some instances the anticipatory repudiation may result from a voluntary affirmative act by one of the parties which either renders performance impossible or demonstrates an intention not to perform, as where S contracts to sell B certain identified goods to be delivered and paid for at a future time, and before that time sells and delivers the goods to C. See BarclaysAmerican/Business Credit, Inc. v. E & E Enterprises, Inc. (1985) (closing plant and would not deliver).

Whether the language or actions constitute a repudiation is difficult to determine in some cases. If S contracts to sell goods to B at $1.00 per unit, and S calls B before the date for delivery and states: "I will not deliver unless you pay me $1.50 per unit," it seems clear that S has repudiated. On the other hand and as is more likely, suppose S calls and states: "$1.00 per unit is too low. I will lose money at that rate and deserve and would like to get $1.50. That's what others are getting." Is this repudiation? Official Comment 5 to Section 2–610 and the Official Comment to Section 2A–402 attempt to shed some light on the problem. They refer to Restatement (Second) of Contracts § 250, and state a repudiation centers upon an overt communication of intention, actions which render performance impossible, or a demonstration of a clear determination not to perform. This statement appears to reflect the common law view, but would seem of little help in deciding concrete cases. The cases heavily depend on the context of the words or action and courts no doubt will rely on pre-Code case law in dealing with the problem. See Gatoil (U.S.A.), Inc. v. Washington Metropolitan Area Transit Authority (1986) (statements that seller was having trouble obtaining fuel, would be unable to begin delivery on July 1 as agreed, and was seeking alternative sources and hoped to have a source by July 5 not a repudiation).

Most often the difficulty of determining if or when repudiation occurs impacts on the remedy, and many fact patterns are possible. See, e.g., BarclaysAmerican/Business Credit, Inc. v. E & E Enterprises, Inc. (1985) (whether repudiation occurred on certain date before notice of assignment determined whether set-off was available). Courses of action available for repudiation are discussed below.

The repudiation must be of a performance not yet due the loss of which will "substantially impair" the value of the contract to the other party. The test whether the repudiation substantially impairs the value of the contract is to be determined by the same criteria as that in installment contracts. That criteria is discussed later in this chapter. Assuming the repudiation does substantially impair the value of the contract, the aggrieved party has a choice of several courses of action.

b. Immediate Right to Any Remedy for Breach or Default

The aggrieved party is free to pursue immediately any of the relevant remedies discussed in the next two chapters. Suppose, for example, S contracts to sell B goods, but B repudiates before the date for delivery. S may immediately bring suit for damages based on the difference between the contract price and the market price of such goods prevailing at the same time S learned of the repudiation. Sections 2–708 and 2–723. For a lease, see Sections 2A–523, 2A–528 and 2A–507. Or, if the goods are identified, S could resell them and recover damages based on the difference between the contract price and the resale price. Section 2–706. For a lease, see Section 2A–527. An illustrative case is Energy Cooperative, Inc. v. SOCAP Intern., Ltd. (1987), where the trustee in bankruptcy of Energy Cooperative attempted to recover as a preference under Bankruptcy Code § 547 a payment made to SOCAP to settle a claim for Energy Cooperative's repudiation. The issue was whether the transfer was for an antecedent debt, and the court held the debt arose when SOCAP's claim arose, which on the facts was as soon as the repudiation occurred; thus there was a preference. Given the alternatives mentioned below, this conclusion seems open to question. A similar erroneous conclusion perhaps was reached in American Cyanamid Co. v. Mississippi Chemical Corp. (1987), concerning the statute of limitations. See also Cary Oil Co., Inc. v. MG Refining & Marketing, Inc. (2000). Thus to the other problems described below in awaiting performance should be added the lesson of these cases (but as to the statute of limitations, see the discussion of that matter, infra, Chapters 11 and 12).

c. Right to Await Performance

It may be that even though one party anticipatorily repudiates, the other party believes that when the time for performance actually arrives the repudiating party will perform. Or, at least, the aggrieved party does not wish to enforce the contract immediately and believes that there is a possibility the repudiating party will perform. There may be problems, however, if the aggrieved party decides to await performance by the repudiating party. A general duty is imposed on a party to a contract, upon learning of a breach or default of the other party, to take all reasonable steps to avoid any course of action which will increase the damages of the breaching or defaulting party. See Section 1–103(b). Or, stated another way, there is a general legal duty on the aggrieved party to mitigate damages. This same duty attaches when the breach or default is anticipatory; therefore, there is a possibility that if the aggrieved party awaits the repudiating party's performance additional damages will be incurred which could have been avoided if the repudiation had been treated as an immediate breach or default. To illustrate: on July 1, S contracts to sell goods to B for delivery the following September. On August 1, after S has procured the necessary goods for delivery to B, the latter repudiates the contract. At that time the market price of such goods is declining rapidly and all economic conditions indicate that the market will continue to decline. S decides, however, to hold onto the goods until September 1, with the hope that when they are tendered B will accept them. The contract price of the goods is $1 per unit; the market price at the time S learns of B's repudiation is $.70, and the market price on September 1 is $.40. It seems that S should not be allowed to base damages on the September 1 market price, for if the goods had been disposed of sooner a price higher than $.40 per unit would have been received. Under the Code, S is allowed to await the repudiating party's performance for only a "commercially reasonable" time. If S awaits performance beyond such time S will not be allowed to recover damages which could have been avoided. Official Comment 1 to Section 2–610. The Code gives no specific criteria for determining what is a commercially reasonable time. What is a reasonable time for taking any action depends on the nature, purpose, and circumstances of such action. Section 1–205(a). The nature of the goods, market conditions, usage of trade, and previous course of dealing between the parties are factors which might be relevant in making such a determination. In doubtful cases the question should be left to the trier of fact. It would seem in the above example that if S awaited B's performance until September, S awaited performance beyond a commercially reasonable time in view of the declining market.

d.   Right to Suspend Performance

Whether S chooses to await B's performance or chooses to treat B's repudiation as a breach, S may suspend its own performance. For example, if S is in the process of manufacturing goods to be delivered to B pursuant to a contract for sale or lease between the two and B anticipatorily repudiates, S in the exercise of reasonable commercial judgment may complete manufacture and identify the goods to the contract for the purpose of providing a remedy, but also may cease manufacture immediately and sell or lease the unfinished goods for scrap or salvage. Sections 2–704 and 2A–524.

e.   Right to Retract

Sections 2–611 and 2A–403 recognize the right of a repudiating party in some instances to retract the repudiation if the party does so before the next performance is due. Retraction is allowed unless the other party has done any one of the following after the repudiation:

(1) canceled the contract,

(2) materially changed position,

(3) otherwise indicated that the repudiation is considered as final.

By canceling, the aggrieved party puts an end to the contract but does not lose rights for breach of contract or default against the other party. Sections 2–106(4), 2A–103(1)(a) and 2A–505(1). Normally the aggrieved party "cancels" by simply notifying the repudiating party that the contract is "canceled," "terminated," "ended," or words to that effect. Thereafter, the repudiating party's rights under the contract cannot be reinstated without the consent of the aggrieved party. Even though the aggrieved party does not cancel the contract, that party may materially change position after the repudiation. This would create an estoppel situation thereby barring the repudiating party from retracting. For example, suppose S contracts to lease goods to B for future delivery and S anticipatorily repudiates. B then contracts to lease similar goods from C. S would then be precluded (estopped) from retracting the repudiation.

Assuming the repudiating party has a right to retract, that party may do so "by any method which clearly indicates to the aggrieved party that the repudiating party intends to perform." Sections 2–611(2) and 2A–403(2). The repudiation, however, would give the aggrieved party sufficient grounds for demanding adequate assurance of performance under Sections 2–609 and 2A–401, which are discussed below. This means, therefore, that even though the repudiating party has not lost the right of retraction by the occurrence of any one of the three things listed above, the repudiating party must provide adequate assurance of performance in order to retract if such assurance is demanded by the other party. Sections 2–611(2) and 2A–403(2). See also Official Comment 2 to Section 2–611.

Effective retraction reinstates the rights of the repudiating party under the contract "with due excuse and allowance to the aggrieved party for any delay occasioned by the repudiation." Sections 2–611(3) and 2A–403(3). The rights and obligations as to future performances of the repudiating party, therefore, are the same as if that party had never repudiated.

To illustrate how Sections 2–611 and 2A–403 might be applied, suppose S contracts to sell or lease goods to B to be delivered in five equal monthly installments, beginning on July 1, 1976. S, without legal excuse, refuses to deliver the first installment and notifies B there will be no future deliveries. In the middle of July S notifies B that indeed there will be future deliveries. B has not changed position in any way. S's failure to make the July delivery was a breach of contract for which there is liability to B for damages. Moreover, S's notice to B that there would be no future deliveries was a repudiation which gave B a right to cancel the contract and to pursue any available remedy against S both as to the July delivery and as to the future deliveries. However, S's notice to B of the intention to make future deliveries was an effective retraction of the repudiation, subject to B's right to demand assurance of performance under Section 2–609 or Section 2A–401, as applicable.

3.   ADEQUATE ASSURANCE OF PERFORMANCE

a.   Generally

When two parties make a contract, they are contracting for performances which are considered mutually beneficial, not primarily for the right to sue the other if there is a breach or default. Many times, however, after the contract is made it will appear obvious or probable that one of the parties will be unwilling or unable to give the promised performance although there is no repudiation under Section 2–610 or Section 2A–402 as discussed above. For example, S who has agreed to sell goods to B on credit, hears through a usually reliable source that B is insolvent, or S receives a letter from B which does not amount to a repudiation but expresses that B will not be able to pay the full contract price and requests a price reduction. See also Hess Energy, Inc. v. Lightning Oil Co., Ltd. (2002) (assignment of contract not a material breach of the parties' agreement; if there were doubts about the prospect of performance, termination was not the appropriate remedy; rather a demand for assurances and suspension of performance was appropriate). Should the other party be required to perform despite the probability that the second party will not? If so, the performing party's rights might be seriously jeopardized.

The Code recognizes that each party to a transaction undertakes an obligation that they will not impair the other's expectation of receiving due performance. Sections 2–609 and 2A–401 provide:

(1) A sale or lease contract imposes an obligation on each party that the other's expectation of receiving due performance will not be impaired. When reasonable grounds for insecurity arise with respect to the performance of either party, the other may demand in a record adequate assurance of due performance and until the party receives the assurance may, if commercially

reasonable, suspend any performance for which it has not already received the agreed return.

(2) Between merchants the reasonableness of grounds for insecurity and the adequacy of any assurance offered shall be determined according to commercial standards.

(3) Acceptance of any improper delivery or payment does not prejudice the aggrieved party's right to demand adequate assurance of future performance.

(4) After receipt of a justified demand, failure to provide within a reasonable time not exceeding thirty days such assurance of due performance as is adequate under the circumstances of the particular case is a repudiation of the contract.

According to the Official Comments to Section 2–609, these provisions would work as follows: If a party to a contract for the sale or lease of goods has reasonable grounds for believing that the other party's performance has become uncertain, the insecure party may (1) suspend performance, (2) ask the other party for adequate assurance that the agreed performance will be rendered, and (3) treat the contract as breached if such assurance is not given within a reasonable time. Moreover, in Central Oil Co. v. M/V Lamma–Forest (1987), even though the seller already had performed, the seller was able to use Section 2–609 to establish a breach which enabled it to obtain a timely and effective remedy.

b. Reasonable Grounds for Insecurity and Demand

What are reasonable grounds for insecurity? No specific standards are articulated except that Official Comment 2 to Section 2–611 states that repudiation of itself provides reasonable grounds for insecurity. See also Section 2A–402(b). Therefore, if a party seeks to retract a repudiation, the other party may demand assurance of performance "as an essential condition of the retraction." Sections 2–611(2) and 2A–403(2).

Reasonableness of grounds for insecurity between merchants is to be judged by commercial rather than legal standards. Sections 2–609(2) and 2A–401(4). Official Comment 3 to Section 2–609 explains that under commercial standards a ground for insecurity can arise from a matter entirely divorced from the contract in question. To illustrate, suppose B and S have been dealing with each other for some time under separate and distinct contracts. B falls behind in the account for goods purchased and delivered under contract No. 1. This, according to the comment, would be reasonable grounds for insecurity under contract No. 2. Or, suppose B, who requires precision parts for immediate delivery, contracts to purchase these parts from S. Later, before delivery of parts, B learns S is making defective deliveries of parts to buyers with similar needs. This, also would be reasonable grounds for insecurity.

The nature of the contract is relevant in determining the reasonableness of the grounds for insecurity. Official Comment 3 to Section 2–609 states that normally a report from a trustworthy source that a seller had shipped or was planning to ship defective goods would give the buyer reasonable grounds for insecurity. However, if the buyer is required by the terms of the contract to pay for the goods before inspecting them, as in a C.I.F. contract, such a risk cannot be avoided by a demand for assurance of performance. To provide a ground for insecurity under this circumstance the report would have to go to a ground which would excuse payment. For a case that demonstrates many of the possible pitfalls in using these provisions, see Scott v. Crown (1988) (reliable information provided insecurity for seller, but first demand was oral and ambiguous, and later demand was for unwarranted assurance; as a result, seller repudiated).

c.   Adequate Assurance

Assuming there are reasonable grounds for insecurity and the aggrieved party properly demands assurance of performance, what will constitute "adequate" (and proper) assurance? As in the case of the reasonableness of the grounds for insecurity, the adequacy of the assurance must be determined from the facts of each case. Official Comment 4 to Section 2–609. The reputation of the party from whom assurance is demanded is a relevant fact to be considered. A mere promise from a party of good repute giving assurance that performance will occur as agreed would usually be sufficient, whereas the same statement, with nothing more, from a "known cornercutter" might be insufficient.

The adequacy of the assurance does not rest within the sole judgment of the aggrieved party. Instead, the Code seeks to establish an objective standard by requiring that the aggrieved party act in good faith and observe commercial standards; the aggrieved party must act without arbitrariness or capriciousness.

Official Comment 4 to Section 2–609 cites the case of Corn Products Refining Co. v. Fasola (1920), as illustrative of both reasonable grounds for insecurity and "inadequate" assurance. In that case S agreed by written contract to sell B 500 cases of No. 5 Mazola, delivery to be made within sixty days after delivery order. Thirty days credit was given, but two percent discount was given if payment was made within ten days from invoice. These terms were subject to the following clause in the contract: "If at any time before shipment the financial responsibility of the buyer becomes impaired or unsatisfactory to seller, cash payment or satisfactory security may be required by the seller before shipment."

Pursuant to this agreement, S shipped some of the goods to B and dated the invoice November 12, 1918, so that payment would not become due until December 12, 1918. On November 26 B requested shipment of the balance of the cases contracted for.

S refused to make further shipments except upon payment or security, for the following reasons: (1) it had been the practice of B in prior dealings with S to pay his bills within ten days to obtain the discount at least seventy-five percent of the time, and this had not been done in the present case, and (2) S heard rumors (in fact false) that B was in "shaky" financial condition. B then sent a good credit report from his banker and assured S that payment would be made when due pursuant to the terms of the contract. Nevertheless, S refused to deliver the remaining goods. B refused to pay for the goods delivered, claiming breach of contract. S then brought suit for the price of the goods delivered and B counterclaimed. The court allowed S to recover, saying that his refusal to deliver the rest of the goods was legally justified.

The same result might be reached on these facts under Section 2–609 (or Section 2A–401 for a lease) even though the clause quoted above is not in the contract. Either the failure of B to take the cash discount or the rumors would be sufficient grounds for insecurity. If the only basis for S's demand for assurance of performance had been the rumors, the banker's report would have been sufficient assurance; however, the sudden full use of the credit term by B called for something more, either a satisfactory explanation or security. Nonetheless, there is a close question here; for example, in Scott v. Crown (1988), where the seller demanded early payment as "adequate assurance," the court held the seller had no right to force a modification of the contract as assurance. A close reading of these provisions would not seem to support that view; see Official Comment 6 to Section 2–609 in particular.

The object of these sections is praiseworthy, for in theory they prevent litigation. There might be some abuse by a timorous party who constantly demands assurance, but there are some safeguards against this possibility. The Code makes it clear that repeated claims for assurance must have an "increasingly obvious" basis. Official Comment 4 to Section 2–609. Further, both reasonable grounds and adequate assurance are governed by the obligation of good faith. Perhaps most importantly, if a party suspends performance and demands assurance without reasonable grounds, that party may be liable for breach of contract.

4. THE PERFECT TENDER RULE

Sections 2–601 and 2A–509 ostensibly adopt a perfect tender rule by stating that the buyer or lessee may reject the goods if "the goods or the tender of delivery fail *in any respect* to conform to the contract." The buyer or lessee also may accept the goods, or accept any commercial unit or units and reject the rest.

This language thus allows a buyer or lessee to reject goods even for the most trivial deviation from the promised performance. However, other sections of the Code substantially qualify the perfect tender rule. For example, in shipment contracts if the seller fails to make a proper contract for transportation of the goods or to notify the buyer of the shipment, the buyer may reject the goods only if *material* delay or loss ensues. Section 2–504. Sections 2–614 and 2A–404 (discussed later in this chapter) allow a seller or lessor to make substituted performance under certain conditions. The consequences of the perfect tender rule may be modified by agreement. Sections 2–718, 2–719, 2A–503 and 2A–504. Moreover, two of the most important qualifications of the perfect tender rule are in the case of installment contracts and the right to cure.

5.   BREACH OF INSTALLMENT CONTRACTS

a.   Generally

It is quite common for sales contracts to call for the delivery of goods in installments. A lease also may involve this situation. Section 2–612(1) defines an installment sale contract as one "which requires or authorizes the delivery of goods in separate lots to be separately accepted, even though the contract contains a clause 'each delivery is a separate contract' or its equivalent." Section 2A–103(1)(*o*) is essentially the same for a lease. Difficult problems arise in the performance of these contracts when one of the parties defaults in the performance of one or more installments. It is clear that any default of this sort gives the aggrieved party a cause of action for damages; however, the chief problems lie in determining whether (1) a buyer or lessee to whom the tender of a nonconforming installment is made must nevertheless accept the installment, and whether (2) nonconformity or default with respect to one or more installments justifies the aggrieved party in canceling the unperformed portion of the contract.

The Code deals with these problems in Sections 2–612 and 2A–510, which provide:

The buyer or lessee may reject any installment or delivery which is nonconforming if the nonconformity substantially impairs the value of that installment delivery to the buyer or lessee, or if the nonconformity is a defect in the required documents; but if the nonconformity does not fall within subsection (3) (subsection (2) in the case of a lease) and the seller or lessor or supplier gives adequate assurance of its cure, the buyer or lessee must accept that installment or delivery.

Whenever nonconformity or default with respect to one or more installments or deliveries substantially impairs the value of the whole contract, there is a breach or default of the whole. But the aggrieved party reinstates the contract if that party accepts a nonconforming installment or delivery without seasonably notifying of cancellation, or brings an action with respect only to past installments or deliveries, or demands performance as to future installments or deliveries.

b. Buyer's or Lessee's Right to Reject a Non–Conforming Installment or Delivery

The provisions which deal with the problem which is the subject of this part of the discussion recognize two possible kinds of defective performances: (1) that in which there is a defect in required documents, and (2) all other defective performances.

A defect in required documents is typified by situations where S is to ship goods to B under a C.I.F. contract and the documents tendered do not include the required insurance policy, or the bill of lading fails "to show shipment within the contract period or to the contract destination." Official Comment 4 to Section 2–612. A defect in a required document is of itself sufficient to justify the buyer or lessee in rejecting the installment covered by the document. The right to reject, however, is subject to the right of the seller or lessor to cure as discussed below. Official Comment 4 to Section 2–612.

In the case of any other defective performance, the buyer or lessee has a right to reject that delivery only if the nonconformity "substantially impairs the value of that installment or delivery." The right to reject on the basis of "substantial impairment" also is subject to an adequate assurance of cure by the seller or lessor. What constitutes "substantial impairment" is ordinarily a question of fact in each case. Such factors as the quality, quantity, or assortment of the goods, as well as time for performance would be relevant in making this determination. In addition, the normal requirements of the aggrieved party would be relevant, as well as any specific requirements of which the other party has knowledge. The standard for rejection is the same standard as that for revoking acceptance. Official Comments 4 and 8 to Section 2–612 and Official Comment to Section 2A–510. What constitutes "adequate assurance of cure" is measured by the same standards as in the case of adequate assurance of performance. Official Comment 5 to Section 2–612.

Suppose a contract calls for the delivery of a total of 5000 units of a certain good to be delivered in equal quantities on the first day of five consecutive months. On the first day of the second month S tenders only 600 units of the required goods. Probably such a disparity in quantity would "substantially impair" the value of the installment, whereas tender of 950 units might not. On the other hand, if S knew that B's specific requirements could be met only by delivery of all 1000 units, a deficiency of only 50 units probably would substantially impair the value of the installment. Official Comment 5 to Section 2–612 discusses what may constitute cure. As relevant to the above example, it might involve an allowance against the price or a further delivery.

Official Comment 4 to Section 2–612 explains that the parties may by agreement require "accurate conformity in quality as a condition to acceptance." If this were done, the right of the buyer or lessee to reject would not be determined by the standard of substantial impairment, but instead by the stricter standard set in the agreement. A clause requiring accurate compliance must itself meet certain standards in order to be enforceable. It must "have some basis in reason, must avoid imposing hardship by surprise and is subject to waiver or to displacement by practical construction."

c.   Right of Aggrieved Party to Cancel Whole Contract

A nonconforming installment or delivery may not only substantially impair the value of that installment or delivery so as to justify its rejection (as explained above), but it may also substantially impair the value of the whole contract so as to allow the aggrieved party to treat the entire contract as breached. This means that the aggrieved party may cancel the contract, refuse to take any future deliveries, and pursue any of the relevant remedies, including remedies for breach of the unperformed balance. If, on the other hand, the nonconformity does not substantially impair the value of the whole contract, the aggrieved party would not be entitled to treat the breach as one of the whole contract. In short, the aggrieved party would not be an aggrieved party with reference to the unperformed balance, and any attempt to cancel the contract would place the aggrieved party itself in breach. See Holiday Mfg. Co. v. B.A.S.F. Systems, Inc. (1974).

The question whether a nonconformity substantially impairs the value of the whole contract is one of fact to be determined by the circumstances of the particular case. As in the case of a nonconforming installment or delivery, the standard is the same as the standard for revoking acceptance. The mere fact that a nonconformity indicates a likelihood that future deliveries will also be nonconforming will not of itself make a nonconforming tender one which substantially impairs the value of the whole contract. Official Comment 6 to Section 2–612 and Bodine Sewer, Inc. v. Eastern Illinois Precast, Inc. (1986) (failure of pipe to meet specifications together with prior defective deliveries promptly cured with fully complying pipe did not warrant cancellation of entire contract). In such a case the proper procedure would be to demand adequate assurance of performance regarding future performance. Official Comment 6 makes it clear, however, that nonconforming performances in prior installments are cumulative and that when coupled with a present nonconforming tender could constitute substantial impairment of the value of the whole contract.

At common law and under the Sales Act (Section 45) the terminology was that of "material breach" instead of "substantial impairment." Under pre-Code law it was only when the nonconformity or default constituted a "material breach" of the whole contract that the aggrieved party was entitled to cancel the balance of the contract. There would seem to be little, if any, difference in results in actual cases when "substantial impairment" is substituted for "material breach." Accordingly, the two pre-Code cases discussed below should be helpful in understanding the general problem.

In Midwest Color Offset Co. v. Thermal Electric
Corp. (1927), S contracted to print and deliver
20,000 advertising folders to B at specified intervals
within three weeks. The first shipment was due
about the 19th of November, but no folders were
shipped until November 29th when 1,600 were sent
to B. On November 24th S had written to B apolo-
gizing for the delay and promising to ship 2000 to
5000 folders that week and the balance a few days
later. B did not reply and attempted to rescind
when the balance of the folders were tendered on or
about December 7th. The seller brought suit
against the buyer for breach of contract. The court
allowed S to recover on the theory that S's breach
did not materially impair the value of the contract
to B. The court stated:

Had the Corporation (B) established that its purpose in this contract was to have these folders for
use at the electrical show in New York City, and
that the Company (S) had knowledge of such purpose, and the terms of the contract had required the
delivery of the goods at a time which would have
enabled it to use them for that purpose, then time
would have been of the essence of the contract and
delivery at a time which would have permitted such
use would have been a condition precedent to a
right to recover by the seller. But since this folder
was a general advertisement of the Corporation's
products, which could be used, and would be useful,
at any time, and since the Corporation wholly failed
to show that it desired the folders for any particular
purpose, or that they were not as useful at the date

of delivery as they would have been ten days earlier, there was not only no circumstance tending to require a construction of the contract that the time of delivery was the essence thereof, but, on the contrary, the circumstances warranted the construction that it was not. The rights of the Corporation were not to rescind, but to counterclaim for such damages, if any, as it may have sustained.

For a case decided under the Code involving similar but more favorable facts for the buyer (deliveries of special food to a pavilion at the World Fair) where buyer prevailed, see Graulich Caterer Inc. v. Hans Holterbosch, Inc. (1968).

It was generally held under pre-Code law that failure or refusal by the seller to make any tender of an installment constituted a material breach, justifying the buyer in repudiating the balance of the contract. Similarly, in most pre-Code cases failure of the buyer to pay for an installment was held to constitute a material breach. The court in one of the leading pre-Code cases held otherwise only because of the special circumstances. In Plotnick v. Pennsylvania Smelting and Refining Co. (1952), S contracted to sell and deliver a quantity of lead to B in installments. Payment for the third shipment was not made, and S refused to make further deliveries unless B made the overdue payment immediately and established a letter of credit to cover future shipments. B, fearful that S would not make future deliveries in view of a rising market, countered with an offer to place the overdue payment in escrow and to pay for future deliveries by sight draft against a bill of lading. S rejected the proposal. The court in affirming a judgment by the trial court for S on the overdue payment but also for B on a counterclaim for damages for S's failure to make further deliveries stated:

Yet, the commercial sense of the statute [Section 45 of the Sales Act] yields two guiding considerations. First, nonpayment for a delivered shipment may make it impossible or unreasonably burdensome from a financial point of view for the seller to supply future installments as promised. Second, buyer's breach of his promise to pay for one installment may create such reasonable apprehension in the seller's mind concerning payment for future installments that the seller should not be required to take the risk involved in continuing deliveries.

However, the court observed that neither of these two considerations existed in this case to justify S's refusal to make complete performance. First, throughout the time for performance S had sufficient lead on hand for full performance. Second, it would be incredible if B refused to honor sight drafts for future deliveries at a time when the market price of lead was substantially higher than the contract price.

Several courts have dealt with the question of whether a default substantially impaired the value of the whole contract under Section 2–612(3). To illustrate, in Continental Forest Products, Inc. v. White Lumber Sales, Inc. (1970), S agreed to sell and deliver twenty carloads of plywood to B. Nine percent of the plywood in the first carload failed to conform to the thickness specifications. Trade code standards allowed a five percent deviation. B accepted and paid for the first carload but attempted to cancel the remaining shipments. Two more carloads which were within the five percent tolerance arrived thereafter, but B refused to accept them. In an action by S against B the court held that the nonconformity in the first installment was minor and did not substantially impair the value of the whole contract; further, the nonconformity was easily curable by an allowance against the price for the quantity of plywood not meeting specifications. See also Holiday Mfg. Co. v. B.A.S.F. Systems, Inc. and Graulich Caterer Inc. v. Hans Holterbosch, Inc., cited above.

Should a party accept a nonconforming installment which substantially impairs the value of the whole contract, that party must seasonably notify the other party if that party wishes to cancel the whole contract. Failure to give such notice "reinstates" the contract, *meaning that the aggrieved party* loses the right to cancel on the basis of that nonconforming installment. Sections 2–612(3) and 2A–510(2). In determining whether a notice has been given seasonably, it should be expected that a buyer or lessee, before deciding to cancel, might await further action from a seller or lessor or supplier who has promised to cure or adjust a nonconforming tender. Reasonable time for notice should also be extended to include reasonable attempts to negotiate the differences between the parties. Official Comment 7 to Section 2–612. Bringing suit with respect to only past installments or deliveries or making a demand for future performance also "reinstates" the contract.

6. SELLER'S OR LESSOR'S RIGHT TO CURE

The right of the seller, lessor, or supplier in a finance lease, to cure an improper tender is not restricted to installment contracts, but is a right which the seller, lessor or supplier may have in the performance of every sale or lease contract. The cure provisions of the Code are found in Sections 2–508 and 2A–513 which provide:

(1) Where the buyer or lessee rejects goods or a tender of delivery or, except in a consumer contract, justifiably revokes acceptance and the agreed time for performance has not expired, the seller, lessor or supplier that has performed in good faith, upon seasonable notice to the buyer or lessee, and at their own expense, may cure the breach of, or default in the contract by making a conforming tender of delivery within the agreed time, and must compensate the buyer or lessee for all reasonable expenses caused by the breach or default and subsequent cure.

(2) Where the buyer or lessee rejects goods or a tender of delivery or, except in a consumer contract justifiably revokes acceptance and the agreed time for performance has expired, a seller, lessor or supplier that has performed in good

faith, upon reasonable notice to the buyer or lessee, and at their own expense, may cure the breach of, or default in, the contract, if the cure is appropriate and timely under the circumstances, by making a tender of conforming goods, and must compensate the buyer or lessee for all reasonable expenses caused by the breach or default and subsequent cure.

These provisions recognize two situations when the seller or lessor or supplier may correct a nonconforming tender. The first is allowed when the contract time for performance has not expired. The second is allowed after the contract time for performance has expired, but is more limited in scope.

The first situation can be illustrated by a simple example. S is obligated to deliver 100 bushels of grain to B's warehouse no later than June 29. S tenders 100 bushels of grain, but B's inspection reveals that it contains many insects and is of an inferior grade. On the same day B notifies S of these facts and that B is rejecting the grain. S assures B that S will deliver another 100 bushels of the proper grade within the contract time. S, if the initial delivery was made in good faith (see Official Comment 3 to Section 2–508), would then have until the close of business on June 29 to tender delivery of another 100 bushels of grain at seller's own expense, and seller also would have to compensate the buyer for any expenses caused by the seller's breach and cure. As to contractual limitations in relation to those expenses, see Official Comment 5 to Section 2–508. If S does so and the grain is conforming, there has been a proper tender which B is obligated to accept.

The right to cure before performance is due for logical reasons extends to the case where the buyer or lessee is entitled to revoke acceptance due to a latent defect or the failure of assurances, except in a consumer contract.

Notice of an intention to cure is vital. See T & S Brass & Bronze Works, Inc. v. Pic–Air, Inc. (1986) (failure to acknowledge need to cure until past time for performance lost seller the right to cure and, on the facts, also rendered seller liable for conversion of materials supplied by buyer). Such notice must be given "seasonably" which means "within the time agreed or, if no time is agreed, at or within a reasonable time." Section 1–205(b). Failure to give notice might lead the buyer or lessee to the reasonable conclusion that a conforming tender is not to be expected, and the required goods should be purchased elsewhere. Official Comment 1 to Section 2–508 explains that the closer the nonconforming tender is to the contract delivery date "the greater is the necessity for extreme promptness ... in notifying of ... intention to cure." Failure to give seasonable notice defeats the right to cure. On the other hand, the failure of the buyer or lessee to enumerate the defects complained about, or to let the seller, lessor or supplier inspect the goods, may undo rejection and excuse any resulting need to cure. Sections 2–605 and 2A–514 and A.F.L. Falck, S.p.A. v. E.A. Karay Co. (1986).

The second situation in which cure is allowed is after the contract time for performance has expired. Here the right to cure is more limited and is allowed only if the conditions to cure above are met as to good faith, notice and payment of and compensation for expenses, and if the proposed cure is appropriate and timely under the circumstances.

The chief difficulty appears to lie in determining when the latter condition is met. In Wilson v. Scampoli (1967) under former Section 2–508 S, a retailer, delivered a crated color television set to B. When the set was uncrated and plugged in, the picture had a reddish tinge. A service representative was unable to adjust the picture in B's home and asked that he be allowed to take it to the shop for adjustment or repair. B refused and demanded return of the purchase price. In rejecting B's claim the court stated: "A retail dealer would certainly expect and have reasonable grounds to believe that merchandise like color television sets, new and delivered as crated at the factory, would be acceptable as delivered and that, if defective in some way, he would have the right to substitute a conforming tender." Another issue is whether that tender should be a new set, or the repaired or adjusted set. That may depend on the circumstances. Compare Leitchfield Dev. Corp. v. Clark (1988) (mobile home with $75 easily repairable damage is situation subject to cure) with Zabriskie Chevrolet, Inc. v. Smith (1968). In the latter case, B purchased a new automobile from S, and almost immediately experienced difficulty with the transmission. S attempted to cure by replacing the transmission with one not from the factory but taken from another vehicle on S's showroom floor. B refused to accept the automobile and then S brought suit. The court held that S's attempted cure was ineffective (nonconforming), and stated: "The 'cure' intended under the cited section of the Code does not, in the court's opinion, contemplate the tender of a new vehicle with a substituted transmission, not from the factory and of unknown lineage from another vehicle in plaintiff's (S's) possession." The court added: "For a majority of people the purchase of a new car is a major investment, rationalized by the peace of mind that flows from its dependability and safety. Once this faith is shaken, the vehicle loses not only its real value in their eyes, but becomes an instrument whose integrity is substantially impaired and whose operation is fraught with apprehension." These articulations would seem to also be viable under the new formulation in Section 2–508(2) (and 2A–513(2)). See Official Comment 4 to Section 2–508. The former issue of whether the seller, lessor or supplier must know of the nonconformity at the time of delivery is deleted, but see Official Comment 3 to Section 2–508.

A clear case for cure perhaps is represented by Bartus v. Riccardi (1967), where the seller tendered a newer and improved model of a hearing aid in lieu of an older model ordered by the buyer. The curative tender after performance is due must be "conforming." This means "conforming in all respects except time," as obviously a tender made after expiration of the contract time could not be conforming. Official Comment 4 to Section 2–508. The buyer or lessee need not agree to an extension.

Midwest Precision Services, Inc. v. PTM Industries Corp. (1989), involved an attempt to cure in the context of a finance lease. The lessee wrongfully rejected the attempt of the supplier to cure (a good tender by way of cure makes a subsequent rejection substantively wrongful even though it may be procedurally effective, see Integrated Circuits Unlimited v. E.F. Johnson Co. (1989)). The lessor, as a result, refused to pay the supplier for the goods because their contract provided payment was due only when the lessee accepted the goods. The court held the lessor was the responsible party in the contract with the supplier and therefore the wrongful act of the lessee was the lessor's responsibility. The contractual condition to the lessor's responsibility was interpreted to only protect against the supplier's non-performance. As wrongful rejection gives the lessor remedies against the lessee under Section 2A–523(1), this analysis may continue to be appropriate under Article 2A. Whether the lessor might alternatively argue that Section 2A–209 should be construed as a two way street limiting the supplier to dealing with the lessee is another question. Section 2A–209(2)(i) suggests this is not an appropriate analysis. So does Section 2A–509(2).

7.   BUYER'S OR LESSEE'S RIGHT ON IMPROPER TENDER

Even though a nonconforming tender is such as to give the buyer or lessee a right to reject all the goods, Sections 2–601 and 2A–509 provide that the buyer or lessee may instead accept all the goods or accept any commercial unit or units and reject the rest. As to what is a "commercial unit," see Sections 2–105(5) and 2A–103(1)(b) and Casazza v. Kiser (2002) (the commercial unit provision protects against return of less than a commercial unit having a severely reduced value). All these rights, however, may be subject to contrary agreement between the parties as provided in Sections 2–718 and 2–719 for sales and 2A–503 and 2A–504 for leases. Quite often such agreements are made; they are discussed in Chapter 12. Rejection and acceptance are discussed below.

a.   Rejection

Rejection, the first alternative listed above, may occur when the buyer or lessee refuses to accept the goods because of some defect or alleged defect in the tender. Once acceptance takes place the right to reject is lost. Sections 2–607(2) and 2A–516(2). However, even after acceptance it is possible for the buyer or lessee under some circumstances to return the goods pursuant to a right to "revoke acceptance." Sections 2–608 and 2A–517. This latter right generally is more limited than the right to reject, and this is particularly true in the case of a finance lease. Section 2A–517(1) and (2).

It should be kept in mind that the right to reject is subject to limitations. As pointed out earlier, the seller, lessor or supplier has a right under Sections 2–508 and 2A–513 to attempt to cure a defective tender, and in installment contracts the right to reject, except for a defect in required documents (but even here see Official Comment 4 to Section 2–612), is subject to a "substantial impairment" standard. Further, the right to reject because of a seller's failure to make a proper shipment contract under Section 2–504 exists only if "material delay or loss ensues."

If the buyer or lessee chooses to reject, they must do so within a reasonable time after the goods have been delivered or tendered and must within a reasonable time notify the seller or lessor of rejection. Failure to give the required notice makes the rejection ineffectual, and the buyer or lessee will be regarded as having accepted the goods. Sections 2–602(1) and 2A–509(2). This would not, of course, mean that the buyer or lessee would lose all remedies if the improper tender constituted a breach, but the remedies would be limited to those of an accepting buyer or lessee. On the other hand, a wrongful rejection is not ineffectual, but it does constitute a breach. Official Comment 3 to Section 2–602.

The timeliness of the required action for rejection under Sections 2–602(1) and 2A–509(2) has been the subject of considerable litigation. Code provisions provide only general outlines for determining timeliness. Section 1–205(a) says that a reasonable time for taking action "depends on the nature, purpose, and circumstances of such action." Official Comment 1 to Section 2–602 explains that the sections of Article 2 "dealing with inspection of goods must be read in connection with the buyer's reasonable time for action under this subsection." This indicates that the difficulty or ease of discovering a defect is a factor in determining timeliness.

In one of the leading cases dealing with this problem, Miron v. Yonkers Raceway (1968), the court held that an attempted rejection of a race horse with a broken splint bone 24 hours after the sale came too late. The court observed that had the bone been broken at the time of sale, an examination by a veterinarian at any time after the sale would have revealed the break. For another illustration of an untimely rejection, see Pioneer Peat, Inc. v. Quality Grassing & Services, Inc. (2002). On the other hand, there are cases in which it has been held that rejection several months after delivery is timely, especially where the buyer gave the seller almost immediate notice of the defect and received continuous assurances from the seller that repairs would be made.

As previously noted, in some instances the buyer or lessee who rejects, or who revokes acceptance, is required to particularize the defect on which the action is based. Failure to do so precludes reliance on the unstated defect to justify the action. Sections

2–605 and 2A–514 provide that if a defect is ascertainable by reasonable inspection the buyer or lessee must state (particularize) the defect (1) where the seller, lessor or supplier had a right to cure and could have cured the defect if stated seasonably, or (2) between merchants, if the seller, lessor or supplier has after rejection, or revocation, made a request in a record for a full and final statement of all defects on which the buyer or lessee proposes to rely. There is a need in any event to clearly communicate that the goods are not wanted. Thus in Oda Nursery, Inc. v. Garcia Tree and Lawn, Inc. (1985), the message the goods did not look "up to snuff" was held not to be up to snuff to put the seller on notice that the goods were being rejected.

b. Rights Regarding Goods Rejected

After rejection the buyer normally must refrain from any act in relation to the goods which constitutes exercise of ownership over them. Sections 2–602(2)(a) and 2–606(1)(c). This is because rejection, rightful or wrongful, vests title in the seller. Section 2–301(4). Any unauthorized action, such as use of the goods, would be wrongful as against the seller. Since a lessor retains title, the same approach was said to be irrelevant in the case of a lease. See former Sections 2A–512 and 2A–515 and the Official Comment to the latter section. Nonetheless, as rejection means the goods are not wanted, continued use of the goods without excuse could amount to an acceptance. Section 2A–515(1)(a). This is now explicitly stated in Section 2A–515(1)(c).

Under some circumstances, the Code allows a buyer or lessee rightfully rejecting the goods to exercise rights over them. For example, Section 2–711(3) provides:

> On rightful rejection . . . a buyer has a security interest in goods in the buyer's possession or control for any payments made on their price and any expenses reasonably incurred in their inspection, receipt, transportation, care and custody and may hold such goods and resell them in like manner as an aggrieved seller (Section 2–706).

Section 2A–508(4) affords a lessee similar rights subject to Section 2A–527(5).

If the buyer or lessee does resell the goods to enforce its security interest, the buyer may retain from the proceeds an amount necessary to reimburse the buyer for the items listed above and the lessee may retain enough to recover any rent and security paid as well as expenses; however, any surplus would have to be paid over to the seller or lessor. No deduction, for example, could be taken for an amount which might be considered adequate for damages. Official Comment 2 to Section 2–711. The exercise of the security interest, however, does not preclude an aggrieved buyer or lessee from pursuit of other relevant remedies. Official Comment 2 to Section 2–711.

A rejecting buyer or lessee who has physical possession of the goods, subject to rights under a security interest as described above, is under a duty to hold the goods with reasonable care at the seller's, lessor's or supplier's disposition for a reasonable time to permit the removal of them. Sections 2–602(2)(b) and 2A–509(3)(b). If the seller, lessor or supplier fails within a reasonable time after notice of rejection to give the buyer or lessee instructions as to what to do with the goods, the latter may pursue any of the following courses of action: (1) store the goods in the seller's, lessor's or supplier's name, (2) reship the goods to the seller, lessor or supplier, (3) dispose of the goods for the seller's, lessor's or supplier's account and, if the rejection was rightful, retain from the proceeds reasonable expenses of caring for and disposing of them, and if the expenses include no disposition commission, then to retain such commission as is usual in the trade or if there is none, a reasonable sum not exceeding ten percent of the gross proceeds. Sections 2–604, 2–603(2), 2A–512(1) and 2A–511(2).

When the rejecting buyer or lessee is a merchant, there may be added responsibilities regarding the goods. If the seller, lessor or supplier has no agent or place of business at the market of rejection, the merchant buyer or lessee is under a legal duty to follow any reasonable instructions received from the seller, lessor or supplier regarding the disposition of the goods. Even though the seller, lessor or supplier fails to give instructions, there is a duty to attempt to dispose of the goods if they threaten to decline in value speedily. Instructions are not binding in the case of a rightful rejection if upon demand by the buyer or lessee to furnish sufficient security to indemnify for expenses that may be incurred in following the instructions, indemnity is not forth-coming. The merchant buyer or lessee, following a rightful rejection, that disposes of the goods is enti-tled to reimbursement from the proceeds in the same manner as where the disposition is made under Section 2–604 or 2A–512 as discussed above. Sections 2–603(1) and (2) and 2A–511(1) and (2). If the buyer or lessee has a security interest in the goods, a deduction from the proceeds may be made for any payments made and reasonable expenses. Should the merchant buyer or lessee fail in any way to perform the required duties, they presumably would be subject to an action for damages by the aggrieved party. Official Comment 5 to Section 2–603 and the implication from Sections 2–603(3) and 2A–511(3). A good faith purchaser from a lessee is protected even if the disposition by the lessee is non-complying. Section 2A–511(4).

In summary, a rejecting buyer or lessee may, but is under no legal duty to, dispose of the goods if (1) that person has a security interest in the goods or (2) the seller, lessor or supplier fails within a rea-sonable time after notification of rejection to give the buyer or lessee instructions as to what disposi-tion to make of the goods. A merchant buyer or lessee is under a legal duty to dispose of the goods if the seller, lessor or supplier has no agent or place of business at the market of rejection or the goods threaten to decline in value speedily. The buyer or lessee must act in good faith and if they do so their conduct is neither acceptance nor conversion and is not the basis for an action for damages. However, a wrongful rejection, while effective, constitutes a breach by the buyer or the lessee and the seller or lessor then becomes an aggrieved party entitled to the remedies indicated in Section 2–703 or 2A–523. See Sections 2–602(3), 2–603(3), 2–604 and Official Comment 3 to Section 2–602; Sections 2A–509(3)(d), 2A–511 and 2A–512.

c. Acceptance

As indicated above, the buyer or lessee may, instead of rejecting the goods upon a nonconforming tender, accept the whole or any commercial unit or units. Certain legal consequences flow from an acceptance of goods. See Sections 2–607 and 2A–516. First, the buyer or lessee must pay in accordance with the contract. This obligation is subject to the buyer's or lessee's right to claim damages for breach of warranty or other nonconformity; however, these damages are measured against the obligation for the price or the rent. Second, the buyer or lessee loses the right to reject. There still may be a right to revoke acceptance, but, as already noted, this is more limited than the right to reject and that is particularly true in a finance lease. Third, acceptance triggers the buyer's or lessee's obligation to notify the seller, lessor, or supplier of any breach within a reasonable time or be barred from a remedy to the extent the seller, lessor or supplier is prejudiced. The case law has not been uniform in the application of this requirement to remote sellers and manufacturers. Compare Piercefield v. Remington Arms Co. (1965) (only duty to notify immediate seller) with Wilcox v. Hillcrest Memorial Park (1986) (buyer must notify remote manufacturer), see also Malawy v. Richards Mfg. Co. (1986). Official Comment 5 to Section 2–607 suggests the latter cases are correct, and Section 2A–516(3)(a) provides a clear rule for a finance lessee against a supplier.

The courts do not agree on what constitutes adequate notice. See Official Comments 4 and 5 to Section 2–607. As to whether bringing suit alone is adequate, compare Bednarski v. Hideout Homes & Realty, Inc. (1988) (yes) with Allen v. G.D. Searle & Co. (1989) (no); and see Board of Education of City of Chicago v. A, C & S, Inc. (1989) (it depends). Some courts as to the content of the notice use a strict standard; the notice must claim a breach. See, e.g., Roth Steel Products v. Sharon Steel Corp. (1983). Others are more liberal; it is enough to merely advise the transaction is troublesome. See, e.g., Chemtrol Adhesives, Inc. v. American Mfrs. Mutual Ins. Co. (1989). Many courts are more lenient as to this point in consumer third party beneficiary cases. See, e.g., Lariviere v. Dayton Safety Ladder Co. (1987).

Finally, some courts, probably in error, have excused notice when a seller sues the manufacturer after sustaining suit by the seller's buyer on the basis the suit is for indemnity. See Daugherty v. Farmers Cooperative Ass'n (1989). In any event, the better procedure here is to use Sections 2–607(5) and 2A–516(4), discussed infra.

The burden of proof to establish breach or default rests upon the buyer or lessee whereas, before the acceptance, the seller or lessor would bear the burden of showing that the tender was conforming. For example, in the *Miron v. Yonkers Raceway* case discussed supra, the court concluded that, as the buyer had accepted the horse, the buyer bore the burden of proving that the horse's leg was broken at the time of delivery. Section 2–607(4). Section 2A–516(2)(c) is the same. Had there been no acceptance, the burden would have been on the seller to prove that the leg was sound at the time of the delivery.

According to Section 2–606(1), acceptance occurs if the buyer does any of the following:

(a) after a reasonable opportunity to inspect the goods, signifies to the seller that the goods are conforming or that the buyer will take or retain them in spite of their nonconformity.

(b) after a reasonable opportunity to inspect the goods, fails to make an effective rejection by failing to reject the goods and adequately notify the seller within a reasonable time after their delivery or tender.

(c) does any act inconsistent with the seller's ownership, but if such act is wrongful as against the seller (see Sections 2–602(2)(a) and 2–608(4)) it is an acceptance only if ratified by him, such as by suing for the price.

Section 2A–515(1) is much the same except for recognizing that the lessor remains owner of the goods and the lessee will be in possession and use of the goods.

It is clear that acceptance occurs if after discovering a nonconformity the buyer or lessee states that they nevertheless will take or retain the goods. A more difficult problem arises when the buyer or lessee does not state an intention, but does some act which tends to signify acceptance. Suppose, for example, the buyer pays a part or all of the purchase price after tender. Official Comment 3 to Section 2–606 explains that such payment, while tending to indicate an intention to accept, is not conclusive of the issue, but is only one circumstance to be considered. See Zabriskie Chevrolet, Inc. v. Smith (1968). Similarly payment of a security deposit and an initial rent installment would not necessarily be conclusive in the case of a lease.

Suppose at the time of delivery the buyer or lessee signs the contract which contains a clause stating that the buyer or lessee has found the goods to be conforming. This constitutes acceptance only if the buyer or lessee had a reasonable opportunity to inspect the goods. In Zabriskie Chevrolet v. Smith, supra, the buyer signed such a purchase contract and took delivery of what was represented as a new automobile. On the way home and less than a mile from the dealer's showroom a serious defect in the transmission developed. In subsequent litigation, seller contended that the goods had been accepted because buyer had a reasonable opportunity to inspect by taking the car for the typical spin around the block before signing the contract. In rejecting this contention the court stated:

If by this contention the plaintiff[s] equates a spin around the block with "reasonable opportunity to inspect," the contention is illusory and unrealistic. To the layman, the complicated mechanisms of today's automobiles is a complete mystery. To have the automobile inspected by someone with sufficient expertise to disassemble the vehicle in order to discover latent defects before the contract is signed, is assuredly impossible and highly impractical.

Rozmus v. Thompson's Lincoln–Mercury Co. (1966), involved a very similar fact situation. There, however, the court concluded that the buyer had accepted the automobile by signing the purchase contract containing a clause acknowledging the automobile to be in good order and by driving it from the seller's showroom. The court did not consider the "reasonable opportunity to inspect language."

Acceptance also occurs when the buyer or lessee attempts to reject but fails to do so effectively by not taking the necessary action within a reasonable time. For example, it will be recalled that the court in the *Miron v. Yonkers Raceway* case discussed supra held that the buyer had accepted the horse by failing to reject within a reasonable time. Ineffective rejection should not be confused with wrongful rejection. Wrongful rejection occurs when the buyer or lessee does in fact effectively reject, but does so without a proper legal basis. An ineffective rejection may occur even though there is a sufficient legal basis for rejection.

Section 2–606(1)(c) recognizes that acceptance is the assertion of ownership over goods, and that it may result solely from acts by the buyer which are inconsistent with the seller's ownership. The acts, however, if wrongful (see, e.g., Sections 2–602(2)(a) and 2–608(4)), must be ratified by the seller to constitute acceptance. Section 2A–515(1)(a) embodies a similar concept in the lease context by providing that if, after reasonable opportunity to inspect the goods, the lessee acts with respect to the goods in a manner that signifies acceptance, it is acceptance even though an ownership claim is not involved. Section 2A–515(1)(c) more explicitly makes the same point; if the lessee uses the goods in a manner that is inconsistent with the lessor's or supplier's rights if the act is ratified.

Thus, use of the goods by the buyer or lessee may be an act signifying acceptance. However, if the action is consistent with an option or a duty, it will not constitute acceptance. See Sections 2–603(3), 2–604, 2A–511(3) and 2A–512(2) on a duty to preserve the goods, and Sections 2–608(4) and 2A–517(6) on right to use goods. Courts also have held that some use without knowledge of the defect and without a reasonable opportunity of discovering it does not yet constitute acceptance. This seems sound; otherwise any use of the goods would constitute acceptance, and use is necessary to discover some defects.

Suppose the buyer or lessee continues to use the goods after notice of rejection. As a general rule courts have held such use to be inconsistent with the rejection and to constitute an acceptance. See Performance Motors, Inc. v. Allen (1972) and Official Comment 4 to Section 2–606. The same analysis applies to continued use by a lessee under Section 2A–515(1)(c). However, under some circumstances continued use may not constitute acceptance. In Valley Die Cast Corp. v. A. C. W. Inc. (1970), the court held that B's continued use of a car wash system after notice of rejection was necessary to mitigate damages and was not an acceptance. See also Cates v. Morgan Portable Building Corp. (1985), involving the buyer's duty to mitigate per Section 1–305, Official Comment 1. The doctrine of mitigation likewise applies to leases. Sections 2–608(4) and 2A–517(6) now explicitly deal with a buyer or lessee's reasonable use of goods after rightful rejection or justifiable revocation of acceptance. See Official Comment 8 to Section 2–608 and Official Comment 3 to Section 2A–517.

A buyer or lessee may continue to use the goods with knowledge of the defect but before the notice of rejection has been given. This commonly occurs where the buyer or lessee has received assurance that the defect will be cured. In the *Valley Die Cast Corp.* case above, the court held that even though use continued for approximately four months before the notice of rejection was given, throughout that time the seller had attempted to correct the problem and had assured the buyer that the defect would be cured.

In some instances when a buyer or lessee accepts goods which are nonconforming, the goods may be resold to a third party, or may be used in such a way as to injure a third party. In either case if the buyer or lessee is sued by the third party the final responsibility may rest on the seller or lessor who sold or leased the nonconforming goods to the buyer or lessee in the first place. The Code provides in Section 2–607(5)(a):

Where the buyer is sued for indemnity, breach of warranty or other obligation for which another party is answerable over, the buyer may give the other party notice of the litigation in a record. If the notice states that the other party may come in and defend and that if the other party does not do so the other party will be bound in any action against the other party by the buyer by any determination of fact common to the two litigations, then unless the other party after seasonable receipt of the notice does come in and defend the other party is so bound.

Section 2A–516(4)(a) is much the same.

For example, suppose B purchases goods from S and resells them to P. Subsequently, P contends the goods are defective and sues B who gives S the notice indicated in the above subsection. S, however, does not come in and defend the suit and the court sets P's damage at $5000. In a subsequent action by B against S for damages, the court's finding in the litigation between P and B that P's damage was $5000 would be binding on S. But the first litigation must be a full dress, good faith, adversary proceeding. Moldex, Inc. v. Ogden Engineering Corp. (1987). Moreover, a right of recovery still must be established by B against S. See Oates v. Diamond Shamrock Corp. (1987).

If the claim on which the buyer or lessee is sued by a third party is based on infringement of patent, trademark or the like, the original seller, lessor or supplier or any other party that is answerable over may obtain complete control of the defendant's part of the litigation by making certain demands on the buyer or lessee. Provided these demands are received by the buyer or lessee within a reasonable time, failure of the buyer or lessee to turn control of the litigation over will bar the buyer or lessee from any subsequent remedy over. To be entitled to such control, the other party must make demand in record form that the buyer or lessee turn control of the litigation over, including the right to settle, or else be barred from any remedy over, and agree to satisfy any adverse judgment and bear all expense of defending the suit.

d. Revocation of Acceptance

Although a buyer or lessee that accepts nonconforming goods loses the right to reject the goods, under some circumstances the buyer or lessee may "revoke" acceptance. Effective revocation gives the buyer or lessee the same rights and duties with regard to the goods as if they had been rejected. Sections 2–608(3) and 2A–517(5). Section 2–608(1) provides:

(1) The buyer may revoke acceptance of a lot or commercial unit whose nonconformity substantially impairs its value to the buyer if the buyer has accepted it

(a) on the reasonable assumption that its nonconformity would be cured and it has not been seasonably cured (otherwise acceptance with knowledge of a non-conformity cannot be revoked because of it under Section 2–607(2)); or

(b) without discovery of such nonconformity if the buyer's acceptance was reasonably induced either by the difficulty of discovery before acceptance or by the seller's assurances.

Sections 2A–517 and 2A–516(2) are much the same, except because a lease may involve obligations of a lessor during the life of the lease and defaults of varying seriousness provided in the agreement, Section 2A–517(2) and (3) recognize a somewhat broader right to revoke acceptance. See Official Comments 1 and 2 to Section 2A–517. To the extent such situations may be replicated in a sale, the right would have to be reserved by agreement. By the same token, because of the nature of a finance lease (see Official Comment to that definition to Section 2A–103 and Section 2A–407), the right of a finance lessee, with some exception for a consumer lease, to revoke acceptance is severely curtailed. Official Comment 1 to Section 2A–516 and Official Comment 1 to Section 2A–407. A finance lessee, however, may have rights under Section 2A–209(1) against the supplier or manufacturer. See Cooper v. Lyon Financial Services, Inc. (2001). Compare General Electric Credit Corp. of Tennessee v. Ger–Beck Machine Co. (1986).

Revocation of acceptance is akin to rescission but, as Official Comment 1 to Section 2–608 makes clear, no election between revocation and recovery of damages is required. See Sections 2–711(2) and 2A–508(1). See also Andover Air Ltd. Partnership v. Piper Aircraft Corp. (1989).

In order for a revocation to be effective, it must occur within a reasonable time after the buyer or lessee discovers or should have discovered the ground for it and before substantial change in condition of the goods which is not caused by their own defects. In addition, the buyer or lessee must notify the seller or lessor of the revocation. Sections 2–608(2) and 2A–517(4).

Revocation of acceptance is limited to situations in which a nonconformity "substantially impairs the value" of the goods to the buyer or lessee. Official Comment 2 to Section 2–608 explains that substantial impairment must be measured by the buyer's (or lessee's) particular circumstances even though the seller (or lessor) had no advance knowledge of what they were. In Hays Merchandise, Inc. v. Dewey (1970), the buyer argued that this meant that the substantial impairment standard is a subjective one, depending on whether the buyer *be-lieves* that the value is substantially impaired. The court rejected a literal application of this argument by stating that substantial impairment to the buyer "is an objective factual determination of the buyer's particular circumstances rather than some unarticulated desire." The court in McCullough v. Bill Swad Chrysler–Plymouth, Inc. (1983) agreed when it stated that chronic steering, transmission and brake problems can hardly be deemed inconsequential but that even purely cosmetic defects, under the proper set of circumstances, can significantly affect the buyer's valuation of the goods. But whether a nonconformity substantially impairs an item's worth to the buyer must be based on objective evidence of any idiosyncratic tastes and needs of the buyer. See also Kesner v. Lancaster (1989), (allowing revocation for a tractor costing $9000 that became inoperable even though repairs would run only $720) and Rester v. Morrow (1986) (allowing revocation for a car involving numerous returns, one for 22 days, even though only minor defects remained unrepaired).

The proper standard by which to measure impairment is but one of many issues that reside in these provisions. Official Comment 4 to Section 2–608 suggests that attempts at adjustment must be taken into account in determining what is a reasonable time to revoke. See Aubrey's R.V. Center, Inc. v. Tandy Corp. (1987) (9 months a reasonable time given repeated assurances problems would be cured). A problem arises in that this period seems to conflict with the rule under Sections 2–608(2) and 2A–517(4) that revocation must occur before substantial change in condition, which in the case of goods like an automobile will occur in depreciation over time and with use. See, e.g., Stridiron v. I.C., Inc. (1984) (liberal interpretation of "own defects"). Extensive litigation also has occurred over continued use after notice of revocation as inconsistent with that notice. Some cases are strict. See, e.g., Waltz v. Chevrolet Motor Division (1973). More courts consider mitigation attempts and the needs of the parties, using a flexible rule (see the *Aubrey's* case above, CPC Intern., Inc. v. Techni–Chem. Inc. (1987), and Deere & Co. v. Johnson (2001) (use when manufacturer refused to accept return and cost of replacement high did not nullify revocation)), which rule may involve compensation to the seller (or lessor) for the use. See Johnson v. General Motors Corp. (1983). In some cases, use might be explained, however, pursuant to a duty to preserve the goods or a right such as a security interest. Cf. Cardwell v. International Housing, Inc. (1980). But post-revocation use that makes return impossible is fatal. J.L. Clark Mfg. Co. v. Gold Bond Pharmaceutical Corp. (1987). Sections 2–608(4) and 2A–517(6) now explicitly resolve these cases allowing reasonable use under the circumstances and appropriate compensation for that use. Official Comment 8 to Section 2–608 and Official Comment 3 to Section 2A–517.

Official Comment 5 to Section 2–608 indicates notice of revocation must be more than notice of breach. While the notice must advise of revocation, it is not insufficient because it does not contain an offer to return the goods. *CPC Intern., Inc.* case, supra.

Other questions worth mention include: (1) can revocation occur unless a properly executed certificate of title is tendered? See Herbert v. Harl (1988) (probably improperly denying revocation); (2) what if the delivery only is partly non-conforming and the goods are divisible? See S & R Metals, Inc. v. C. Itoh & Co. (America), Inc. (1988) (where several gauges of steel delivered in single lot, revocation extends to gauges that are conforming as well as to those that are not conforming) and Winterbotham v. Computer Corps., Inc. (1986) (where only software was defective but without it the value of the package was substantially impaired, revocation of both software and hardware allowed); (3) can revocation occur when the goods are not under the control of the revoking party? See Eaton Corp. v. Magnavox Co. (1984) (no, but court should be uncomfortable with this conclusion given Sections 2–602(2) and 2–608(3)); (4) is revocation available against a party not in privity? See Alberti v. Manufactured Homes, Inc. (1989) (applying majority rule which does not allow revocation; but see Gochey v. Bombardier, Inc. (1990), which allowed revocation when manufacturer's warranty passed on by dealer) and, by way of comparison, Sections 2–313A(5) and 2–313B(5); and (5) may cure be invoked after revocation? See Gappelberg v. Landrum (1984) (cure not mentioned in statute in relation to revocation and disallowed). Contra Fitzner Pontiac–Buick–Cadillac, Inc. v. Smith (1988). However, if easy repair or conforming goods are tendered, or the time for performance is not past, is the value of the contract substantially impaired so as to allow revocation in the first place? This question is not explicitly addressed in Sections 2–508 and 2A–513.

One concluding note: a large number of states have enacted so-called lemon laws, usually limited to vehicles and often limited to sale transactions, to eliminate some of the uncertainties in this area. See C. Reitz, Consumer Product Warranties Under Federal and State Laws, Chapter 14 (2d. ed. 1987). Often a buyer's or lessee's rights of rejection and revocation are modified by contract as well. This is discussed in Chapter 12.

e. Comparison: Rejection and Revocation of Acceptance

Rejection and revocation are methods of self help by which the buyer or lessee can throw nonconforming goods back to the seller or lessor. By doing so, the buyer or lessee avoids liability for the price or rent. Failure to do so obligates the buyer for the price and the lessee for the rent, but with the right to set-off against that liability (except in some situations in the case of a finance lease (see Section 2A–508(5)) any damages resulting in the ordinary course of events from the nonconformity. Sections 2–717 and 2A–508(5). Rejection, subject to some exceptions, is allowed for any nonconformity; however, it is subject to the very important right of the seller, lessor or supplier to cure under Sections 2–508 and 2A–513. On the other hand, revocation of acceptance is allowed only when the nonconformity substantially impairs the value of the goods to the buyer or lessee and there is a more limited right to cure. While the result in many cases would be the same whether the court follows the "rejection subject to cure route" or the "revocation upon substantial impairment route," in other cases the different route was the deciding factor.

8.   EXCUSE FOR NONPERFORMANCE

a.   Generally

The contracting process is filled with risks. When S contracts to sell or lease goods to B for future delivery both parties are assuming risks. If they have set a definite price or rent in the contract, S assumes the risk that the market price or market rent will go up before the date for delivery; B assumes the risk that the market price or market rent will decline. S assumes the risk that strike, flood, fire or some other occurrence beyond S's control will prevent delivery of the goods, or, at least, make the performance of obligations more onerous than anticipated at the time of contracting.

The general policy in Anglo–American law has been to place the risk that the performance of a contractual obligation will become more onerous because of some supervening event on the party who undertook that obligation, unless the risk of that event was placed on the other party in the contract. The courts have made some exceptions to this policy under such labels as "impossibility" and "commercial frustration." Regardless of the label or labels used to describe it, the problem is one of balancing the policy that contractual obligations must be performed with the recognition that special circumstances may require, in order for justice to be done, a departure from the usual policy.

The provisions of the Code dealing with such problems are discussed below.

b. Destruction of the Specific Subject Matter

One of the best recognized exceptions to the general policy of risk allocation described above is where the parties contract for a specific good and before the risk of loss passes to the buyer the good is destroyed by accidental fire, flood, or some other such occurrence. The seller is excused from the obligation to deliver and the buyer is excused from the obligation to pay the price. If the buyer has already paid the price or any part thereof, the buyer is entitled to restitution. To illustrate, suppose S contracts to sell B 50 identified desks then stored in S's warehouse, to be delivered to B's store two weeks later. Four days after the contract is made S's warehouse, together with the desks, is destroyed by an accidental fire. Both parties are excused from their obligations. Section 2–613. In essence the overall loss is split: S loses the value of the desks, absent insurance, and B loses the benefit of the bargain and may have to procure more expensive desks elsewhere.

The above fact situation is to be distinguished from the following one. Suppose S contracts to sell B 50 desks of a certain description; however, the desks are not identified at the time the contract is made. A short time later S selects 50 desks meeting the contract description and sets them aside in the warehouse for delivery to B. That night an accidental fire sweeps S's warehouse and the desks are destroyed. Neither party is excused from their obligations.

These general principles are recognized in Section 2–613 (emphasis added):

Where the contract *requires* for its performance goods *identified when the contract is made,* and the goods suffer casualty without fault of either party *before the risk of loss passes to the buyer,* then

(a) if the loss is total the contract is terminated; and

(b) if the loss is partial or the goods have so deteriorated as no longer to conform to the contract the buyer may nevertheless demand inspection and at its option either treat the contract as terminated or accept the goods with due allowance from the contract price for the deterioration or the deficiency in quantity but without further right against the seller.

It should be observed that several conditions must coalesce before a party can take advantage of this section. First, the contract must require delivery of goods identified at the time the contract is made. Goods identified after the contract is made will not invoke this excuse, nor will the destruction of specific goods unless the contract requires those goods in particular for performance. Second, the casualty suffered by the goods must not have been the fault of either party. Official Comment 1 to Section 2–613 explains that within that section fault includes negligence as well as willful wrong by a party. Third, risk of loss must not have passed to the buyer. If it has the section is not applicable and the buyer is responsible for the price. This means the buyer will have to pay for worthless goods, absent insurance, and pay again when substitute goods are acquired.

If the loss is total the contract is avoided and both parties are excused from performance of their obligations. On the other hand, if the loss is only partial Section 2–613(b) gives the buyer a choice. The buyer is entitled to inspect the goods and may either treat the contract as totally avoided as if the loss had been total or take the surviving goods with a price adjustment. If the buyer chooses the latter alternative the buyer has no rights for breach of contract against the seller for the deficiency in quantity.

Should the buyer elect to take the surviving goods some problems could arise in making a price adjustment. Suppose in the example above where the contract was for 50 identified desks only 10 were destroyed and the 40 remaining were undamaged. If B decided to take the 40 it would be simple to adjust the price, especially if the parties had agreed on a unit price or a total price and all units were of equal value. The problem becomes more complicated if the desks were not destroyed but suffered only water and smoke damage.

In Article 2A, Section 2A–221 provides similar rules, except to accommodate a finance lease the casualty also must not be the fault of the supplier, and since risk of loss does not pass to the lessee in many leases (Section 2A–219), delivery is added as an alternative point in time to passage of the risk of loss. The option to take damaged goods with a rent adjustment also is excluded in a finance lease that is not a consumer lease as inconsistent with the rule of Section 2A–407 (the hell or high water provision). The Official Comment to Section 2A–221 also leaves to the courts the even more difficult problem of allocation of a rent allowance.

c. Commercial Impracticability

As pointed out above, it has been common for courts to use the term "impossibility of performance" when finding circumstances sufficient to excuse a party from performance because of some supervening event such as destruction of the specific goods. The term has been used as well to describe performances which, although literally possible, have become extremely difficult or so difficult and expensive as to be deemed legally impracticable. The Restatement (Second) of Contracts defines "impossibility" in a broad way; performance may be "impracticable" not only because of strict impossibility, but because of extreme and unreasonable difficulty, expense, injury or loss to one of the parties will be involved. Comment d. to Section 261.

These general principles appear to provide the background for Section 2–615 of the Code and its similar provision in Article 2A, Section 2A–405. These sections are applicable to situations in which a performance may not be strictly impossible, but at least is impossible from a commercial or practicable standpoint. The Code has no provision on "commercial frustration," which differs from "impracticability" in that performance is possible but the purpose of it has been substantially frustrated by an event the nonoccurrence of which was a basic assumption on which the contract was made. An example of the doctrine is Krell v. Henry (1903), where a flat was hired to watch the coronation procession of Kind Edward VII, which was postponed due to the King's illness. Performance was excused. The doctrine as expressed in Restatement (Second) of Contracts Section 265 should be available in a sale or lease of goods pursuant to Section 1–103(b) as supplementary law.

Section 2–615 reads:

Except so far as a seller may have assumed a greater obligation and subject to the preceding section on substituted performance:

(a) Delay in performance or nonperformance in whole or in part by a seller that complies with paragraphs (b) and (c) is not a breach of the seller's duty under a contract for sale if performance as agreed has been made impracticable by the occurrence of a contingency the nonoccurrence of which was a basic assumption on which the contract was made or by compliance in good faith with any applicable foreign or domestic governmental regulation or order whether or not it later proves to be invalid.

(b) Where the causes mentioned in paragraph (a) affect only a part of the seller's capacity to perform, the seller must allocate production and deliveries among its customers but may at its option include regular customers not then under contract as well as its own requirements for further manufacture. The seller may so allocate in any manner which is fair and reasonable.

(c) The seller must notify the buyer seasonably that there will be delay or nondelivery and, when allocation is required under paragraph (b), of the estimated quota thus made available for the buyer.

Section 2A–405 is the same except the section includes the supplier in a finance lease arrangement and allows allocation to regular customers to whom sales as well as leases are made.

First, it should be noted that nonperformance or delay in performance is not excused if the seller or lessor or supplier has assumed a greater obligation (see Sections 2–615 and 1–302(a)), or if the provisions on substituted performance (discussed below) are available. A seller, lessor or supplier may assume the risk of the contingency in question either by the express terms of the contract or simply by implication because of circumstances existing at the time of contracting, trade usage, or the like. Official Comment 8 to Section 2–615. Consider Madeirense do Brasil S/A v. Stulman–Emrick Lumber Co. (1945), cited in Official Comment 8 to Section 2–615, as a case where, because of the circumstances, the seller assumed the risk of the supervening event. In that case S, who was in Brazil, contracted in the fall of 1940 to ship lumber to B in Brooklyn. Shipment was to be made no later than January 1941. When sued for breach of contract, S sought excuse from its failure to perform because there were no ships available at the time. The court, however, pointed out that at the time the parties contracted the war in Europe had been under way more than a year and though neither the United States nor any of the South American countries were to enter the war for another year, the possibility of a lack of ships was a foreseeable risk at the time the parties contracted. In short, because of general world conditions in the fall of 1940 the possibility that no ships would be available was one of the business risks assumed by S.

In another pre-Code case, Crown Embroidery Works v. Gordon (1920), a seller contracted to manufacture cloth for the buyer, but after the contract was made a governmental regulation was promulgated which prevented the seller from obtaining the yarn necessary to manufacture the cloth. The court held, however, that under the circumstances the seller should have anticipated the regulation and purchased a sufficient supply of yarn before the regulation took effect.

In each of these cases the supervening circumstances were thought by the court to have been within the contemplation of the parties at the time the contract was made. The question whether the contingency is of the nature which should have been within the contemplation of the parties poses the chief problem to the courts in applying this section. Official Comment 2 to Section 2–615 refrains from giving an exhaustive list of contingencies but does indicate that increase or decrease in the market price of goods is normally a risk which is inherent in a sales contract and is, therefore, one to be regarded as having been assumed by the parties. See, e.g., Northern Indiana Public Service Co. v. Carbon County Coal Co. (1986), where a utility company entered into a twenty-year contract for coal. The price and quantity both were fixed. When alternative fuel prices fell, the contract proved expensive and the utility was not allowed to continue to pass the expense on to its customers. The utility then ceased to purchase coal under the contract and the seller was able to obtain a large judgment for breach. See also United States v. Wegematic Corp. (1966). There Wegematic contracted to build and deliver a computer with certain capabilities to the Federal Reserve Board. Subsequently, Wegematic repudiated, claiming it was excused because insurmountable technological problems made performance impracticable under Section 2–615. The court rejected this argument on two grounds. First, Wegematic assumed the risk of the development of the technology necessary to manufacture the computer. The court stated: "If a manufacturer wishes to be relieved of the risk that what looks good on paper may not prove so good in hardware, the appropriate exculpatory language is well known and often used." Second, the court was not convinced that performance was truly "impracticable." Although the expenditure of $1,000,000 to $1,500,000 on redesign might be unattractive to management, it was not clearly prohibitive from the standpoint of the amount which might be grossed from the sale of some 800 computers contemplated in the program.

On the other hand, although increase in cost of performance normally is not sufficient to excuse performance, "a severe shortage of raw materials or of supplies due to a contingency such as war, embargo, local crop failure, unforeseen shutdown of major sources of supply or the like, which either causes a marked increase in cost or altogether prevents the seller from securing supplies necessary to his performance, is within the contemplation of this section." Official Comment 4 to Section 2–615. See also Official Comments 5 and 9 and Alimenta (U.S.A.), Inc. v. Gibbs Nathaniel (Canada) Ltd. (1986), where the contract was for fixed quantities of "1980 crop U.S. runner split peanuts." Extensive drought reduced the crop. The seller delivered 87% of the contract but to fulfill the remainder by purchase of peanuts would have cost $3.8 million when the anticipated profit on the contract originally was only $18,000 and the seller's net worth was only $2.4 million. The court appears to have treated the contract as one stipulating an agreed source that partially failed, and the seller's allocation was justified. See further SCA Intern., Inc. v. Garfield and Rosen, Inc. (1971). In this case, the seller also was excused from liability under Section 2–615. S had promised to manufacture and deliver a certain quantity of shoes to B. Because of unprecedented floods the factories in which the shoes were being manufactured were damaged, as well as some of the supplies of leather, linings, soles and inner soles to be used by S. Although it was not clear whether the contract specified that the shoes were to be manufactured in the factories damaged, the court found that the parties understood that they were. The court excused S for the delay in filling the orders.

These provisions do not excuse a party unless the nonoccurrence of the contingency that occurs was a "basic assumption" on which the contract was made. In some instances the parties agree that the goods are to be supplied from a specific and exclusive source or, even though not spelled out in the agreement, the circumstances show that the parties assumed or contemplated a particular source. If before the seller or lessor or supplier can perform the source fails because of fire, drought, flood, wind, or the like, the existence of this source would be a basic assumption of the parties at the time they contracted. For example, in International Paper Co. v. Rockefeller (1914), the seller agreed to sell the buyer a certain quantity of pulpwood to be cut from a specific tract of land. After the seller had delivered some of the pulpwood, fire destroyed all but a small number of the trees growing on the tract. The seller refused to make any further deliveries and in a suit by the buyer for damages the court refused to allow a recovery except with reference to the remaining trees. This same result would be reached under the Code, since it seems to have been a basic assumption of the parties that the trees on the tract would remain available. See also Selland Pontiac–GMC, Inc. v. King (1986) (seller excused from performance of contract for sale of school bus parts that seller was to obtain from specified manufacturer that subsequently went out of business) and the *Alimenta* case, supra.

In order to be entitled to relief on this basis, however, the seller or lessor or supplier must take all "due measures" to assure that the source will not fail. Official Comment 5 to Section 2–615. In Canadian Indus. Alcohol Co. v. Dunbar Molasses Co. (1932), the seller contracted to sell the buyer a quantity of molasses "of the usual run from the National Sugar Refinery." The seller had a contract with the Refinery for the purchase of a supply of molasses sufficient to meet its obligations to the buyer. The seller was unable to deliver the agreed quantity of molasses to the buyer as the Refinery did not produce enough. The buyer sued for damages and the seller sought to be excused. The court allowed the buyer to recover, evidently on the theory that the seller had failed to take any steps to require the Refinery to refrain from diminishing production so as to render its production insufficient to meet the seller's needs.

Finally, even if the seller or lessor or supplier has not assumed a greater obligation and the nonoccurrence of the contingency was a "basic assumption" of the contract, the occurrence of the contingency will provide an excuse only if it makes performance "impracticable." Official Comment 3 to Section 2–615 indicates that the test of whether a performance has been made impracticable should be determined by commercial standards. "Impossibility" of performance is not required. No other standards are articulated for determining when a performance has been rendered "commercially impracticable." In doubtful cases this would be a question of fact.

If a seller or lessor or supplier wishes to take advantage of these provisions, the seller or lessor must give the buyer or lessee, and a supplier must give both the lessor and the lessee, if known, seasonable notice that there will be delay or nondelivery of the goods and of any allocation. Sections 2–615(c) and 2A–405(c).

d. Partial Excuse

In some instances only a part of the seller's or lessor's or supplier's performance might be affected by the occurrence of a supervening event. Assuming the contingency affects only a part of the performance, the seller, lessor or supplier must fulfill the contract to the extent the supervening event allows. This means in some instances that more than one contract will be affected. If, for example, a number of buyers or lessees of the seller's or lessor's or supplier's goods exist and some contingency of the kind contemplated by these provisions disrupts only a part of production, the seller or lessor or supplier must, in a fair and reasonable manner, allocate production and deliveries among customers. A seller, lessor or supplier may include in this allocation, if desired, regular customers even though at the time of the occurrence of the supervening event there were no contracts with them, and the seller's or lessor's or supplier's own requirements for further manufacture. Section 2–615(b) and Official Comment 11, and Section 2A–405(b).

The seller or lessor must give the buyer or lessee, and a supplier must give both the lessor and the lessee, if known, seasonable notice of the inability to render the performance promised and of the estimated quota intended to be made available. Sections 2–615(c) and 2A–405(c). When the buyer or lessee receives such notice from the seller or lessor or supplier, the buyer or lessee may by notice in a record to the seller or lessor terminate the contract as to the goods involved. If the contract is for delivery in installments and the prospective deficiency substantially impairs the value of the whole contract, the unexecuted portion of the contract may be terminated. Sections 2–616(1)(a) and 2A–

406(1)(a). Instead of terminating, the buyer or lessee may, except in a finance lease that is not a consumer lease, by giving written notice to the seller or lessor agree to take the quota specified. If the buyer or lessee after receiving proper notification fails to modify the contract within a reasonable time not exceeding thirty days, the contract terminates with respect to any performance affected. Sections 2–616(2) and 2A–406(2).

e.   Substituted Performance

Suppose S contracts to sell goods to B and promises to ship the goods by rail to B's city. For some unforeseen reason rail transportation from S's city becomes unavailable after the contract is made; however, truck transportation is available and the goods in question are of the kind which can be shipped as readily and safely by truck as by rail. Or suppose S contracts to ship goods from New York, but because of an expected lack of shipping space in New York, ships the goods in question from Philadelphia.

Some courts have held that an agreed place or method of shipment is a condition precedent and, if not adhered to by the performing party, will justify the other party in refusing to perform the whole contract. Other courts have not been as rigid. For example, in Harrison v. Fortlage (1896), the seller agreed to ship the goods on a specified vessel, but at an intermediate point a part of them were transshipped on another vessel because of damage to the initial vessel. The court held that arrival of the goods on the ship specified was not a condition precedent to the buyer's duty to accept and pay for the goods.

The Code anticipates problems of this sort in Sections 2–614 and 2A–404 which provide:

(1) Where without fault of the seller, buyer, lessor, lessee or supplier, the agreed berthing, loading, or unloading facilities fail or an agreed type of carrier becomes unavailable or the agreed manner of delivery otherwise becomes commercially impracticable but a commercially reasonable substitute is available, such substitute performance must be tendered and accepted.

(2) If the agreed means or manner of payment fails because of domestic or foreign governmental regulation, the seller or lessor may withhold or stop delivery or cause the supplier to do so unless the buyer or lessee provides a means or manner of payment which is commercially a substantial equivalent. If delivery has already been taken, payment by the means or in the manner provided by the regulation discharges the buyer's or lessee's obligation unless the regulation is discriminatory, oppressive or predatory.

Note that not only is the buyer or lessee required to accept the substituted performance, but the seller or lessor is required to tender such performance. Official Comment 1 to Section 2–614 makes clear, however, that the buyer (or lessee) will not be required to accept nor will the seller (or lessor) be entitled to tender such performance unless the agreed performance becomes commercially impracticable.

In some instances the method or manner by which the buyer or lessee agrees to pay the price or rent will fail because of some domestic or foreign governmental regulation. Should this occur before the goods have been delivered, the seller or lessor is permitted to withdraw from the contract unless the buyer or lessee provides a means or manner of payment which is commercially a substantial equivalent. On the other hand, if the goods have already been delivered, the buyer or lessee may pay in accordance with the regulation and discharge the obligation for the price or rent even though this would not have been a commercial equivalent had the goods not been delivered, "unless the regulation is discriminatory, oppressive or predatory." Section 2–614(2) and Comment 3, Section 2A–404(2).

CHAPTER 11

SELLER'S AND LESSOR'S REMEDIES

---

1. INTRODUCTION

When a seller contracts to sell goods, the seller is bargaining for the price. If the buyer fails to pay the price the seller normally sustains a loss, at least to the expectancy interest (the expected profit on the contract), and if the buyer's failure is not legally justified it constitutes a breach of contract, entitling the seller to some remedy. The usual remedy is a legal action for monetary damages. These same observations are true as to a lessor and the rent to be derived from the lease contract.

The difficulty with this remedy is that there is no assurance that the judgment, once obtained, will be satisfied. While any of the buyer's or lessee's property can be levied on and sold for the satisfaction of the judgment, the buyer's or lessee's assets may be either nonexistent or insufficient, or they may be subject to the prior claims of other creditors. It is important to a seller, therefore, to have control over the goods until the price is paid. Control will provide recourse against the goods, which the seller may keep or resell in lieu of or in addition to the right to obtain a judgment for damages. The important point is that if the seller loses the right of recourse against the goods the seller's only alternative is to obtain a judgment and hope that the buyer will pay it, or if not, that the buyer will have sufficient assets upon which to levy. These observations should be kept in mind as the seller's remedies are discussed more specifically. It also should be kept in mind that, absent a security interest under Article 9 of the Code, a subject that is outside the scope of this book, and a very limited right to reclaim under Section 2–702, an unpaid seller who has relinquished control of the goods to the buyer has no right, as seller, to reobtain the goods. Rather the seller's action is for the price under Section 2–709.

A lessor, however, remains the owner of the goods and, as such, Section 2A–525(2) allows the lessor to obtain the goods by self-help without breach of the peace, or by judicial process. The learning under former Section 9–503 (now Section 9–609) in UCC Article 9 is relevant here. Because of this right, Article 2A contains no right to reclaim. See Official Comments 1 and 2 to Section 2A–525. Further protection of the lessor's residual interest is found in Sections 2A–532 and the common law. See Official Comment 3 to Section 2A–525. But getting back the goods will not necessarily make a lessor whole; the lessor may still have a need for money damages.

Both Articles 2 and 2A provide a statute of limitations within which the rights of the seller and the lessor must be exercised. The basic period is four years, which runs in a lease from the time when the act or omission on which the default or breach of warranty is based is or should have been discovered, or when the default occurs (many leases make an event a default only when so declared), whichever is later. Section 2A–506(2). Section 2A–506 specifically deals with actions for indemnity, so as to avoid cases like City of Wood River v. Geer–Melkus Construction Co. (1989), which held former Section 2–725 inapplicable to action for indemnity. But see Perry v. Pioneer Wholesale Supply Co. (1984) (indemnity action subject to Section 2–725). Section 2A–506 states a cause of action for indemnity accrues when the act or omission on which the claim is based is or should have been discovered by the indemnified party, whichever is later.

Section 2–725 is more complicated. It provides that an action for breach must be commenced within the later of four years after the right has accrued or one year after the breach was or should have been discovered, but no longer than five years after the right of action accrued, as the basic rule. The right of action accrues as a basic rule when the breach occurs even if there is not knowledge of the breach. Exception to these basic rules are:

(1) for breach by repudiation, the right of action accrues at the earlier of when the aggrieved party elects to treat the repudiation as a breach or a commercially reasonable time for performance has expired;

(2) for breach of a remedial promise (a promise by the seller to repair or replace the goods or to refund all or part of the price upon the happening of a specified event under Section 2–103(1)(n)), a right of action accrues when the promise is not performed when due;

(3) in an action against a person answerable over to a buyer for a claim against the buyer, the buyer's right of action accrues at the time the claim is asserted against the buyer;

(4) for breach of the warranty of title or against infringement, an express warranty, the warranties of merchantability and fitness, and the obligations to remote purchasers created by a record with the goods or by advertising, other than a remedial promise, a right of action for breach of warranty, other than of title or against infringement, accrues on tender of delivery to the immediate buyer and completion of installation or

assembly (but see Webco Industries, Inc. v. Thermatool Corp. (2002) (post-delivery obligations to inspect, test and provide instruction do not toll the accrual of a breach of warranty claim unless the contract specifically so provides)); for breach of obligation, when the remote purchaser receives the goods; for breach of express warranty or an obligation that explicitly extends to future performance and discovery of the breach must await the time for performance, when the immediate buyer or remote purchaser discovers or should have discovered the breach; and for breach of warranty of title or against infringement, when the aggrieved party discovers or should have discovered the breach, but for breach of the warranty against infringement, no later than six years after tender of delivery.

The four year period may be shortened by agreement, except it may not be reduced to less than one year in a consumer contract or, in a lease transaction, in reference to an indemnity. Note also that 15 U.S.C.A. § 2304(a)(2) (Magnuson–Moss Act), in the case of a "full" written warranty, does not allow any limitation on the duration of any implied warranty on the product. For a sale, the period also cannot be lengthened under Section 2–725(1). See Official Comments 1 and 2 to Section 2A–506 as to why the provision in Article 2A differs from that in Article 2.

Neither Code provision is exhaustive of the possible applicable limitations law; for example, the law of tolling continues to apply outside of the Code.

Sections 2–725(5) and 2A–506(4). See also Kociemba v. G.D. Searle & Co. (1988) (fraudulent concealment as tolling the statute).

In allowing an aggrieved seller or lessor a monetary remedy for breach of a sales contract or default in a lease, an attempt is made to place that party in as good a position monetarily as if the contract had been performed, but without assessing the buyer or lessee for losses which were not foreseen at the time the contract was made. Section 1–305(a). In some instances recovery of nothing less than the full contract price or rent will be sufficient to compensate the seller or lessor adequately. In other instances a lesser sum will suffice.

The remedies available to an aggrieved seller where the buyer has wrongfully rejected, wrongfully attempted to revoke acceptance, failed to make a payment when due, repudiated (statutory breaches); or wrongfully failed to perform a contractual obligation, are indexed in Section 2–703. The aggrieved seller may:

(a) withhold delivery;

(b) stop delivery by any bailee as provided in Section 2–705;

(c) proceed under Section 2–704 respecting goods still unidentified to the contract or unfinished;

(d) reclaim the goods under Section 2–507(2) or 2–702(2);

(e) require payment directly from the buyer under Section 2–325(c);

(f) cancel;

(g) resell and recover damages under in Section 2–706;

(h) recover damages for non-acceptance or repudiation under Section 2–708(1);

(i) recover lost profits under Section 2–708(2);

(j) recover the price under Section 2–709;

(k) obtain specific performance under Section 2–716;

(l) recover liquidated damages under Section 2–718;

(m) in other cases, recover damages in any manner that is reasonable under the circumstances.

All of these remedies with the exception of cancellation are discussed in this chapter. The right to cancel is discussed in Chapter 10. The sales contract may provide for contractual breaches, and the remedy structure for breaches may be supplied in the agreement or other law. Sections 2–703(2)(l), 2–718 and 2–719 and Official Comment 1 to Section 2–703.

A lessor has a similar set of remedies listed in 2A–523(1) which are triggered by a similar set of statutorily defined defaults by the lessee. Section 2A–523(1) and (2). Because a lease usually will provide for other lessee defaults by agreement, Section 2A–523(4) also provides a remedy structure for these defaults. It is the same structure as for statutory defaults if the default provided by agreement substantially impairs the value of the lease to the lessor, and it is the loss resulting in the ordinary course of events from the default as determined in any reasonable manner otherwise. This latter remedy also is applicable for a statutory default if the lessor elects not to pursue the remedies listed in Section 2A–523(1). Section 2A–523(3). Under Sections 2–703(3) and 2A–523(2), remedies upon the buyer's or lessee's insolvency are enumerated. It is also possible with respect to any statutory or agreed default for the parties to agree upon any remedy or reasonable damage provision. Sections 2A–523(4), 2A–503, 2A–504 and 2A–501(2).

It should be noted that Section 2A–501(5) provides an optional procedure if the leased goods, for example, become fixtures, and Section 2A–502 generally does not require a lessor to notify a lessee of the default or of enforcement. However, other rules of law may apply. See, e.g., 1974 Unif. Consumer Credit Code Sections 5.110–5.111.

The seller's or lessor's remedies are not necessarily mutually exclusive. Thus pursuit of one does not necessarily bar pursuit of another (others). Whether or not it does depends on the facts of each case and whether the seller or lessor has been put in as good a position as if the buyer or lessee had fully performed the contract; multiple remedies are barred only if the effect is to put the aggrieved party in a better position than if performance had occurred.

See Official Comment 1 to Section 2–703, Comments 1 and 3 to Section 2A–523, and Section 2A–501(4). Thus in Union Carbide Corp. v. Consumers Power Co. (1986), the buyer refused further deliveries when the market dropped sharply. The seller sought damages under Section 2–708(1), whereas the lost profit on account of the breach was much less. The court held the seller's request would constitute over compensation, and denied it. A similar case is Commonwealth Edison Co. v. Decker Coal Co. (1987), where the seller tried to use Section 2–708(2) rather than Section 2–709, which on the facts would produce the same dollar recovery, but use of the former remedy would allow keeping the goods. Again the court refused the requested remedy as over compensatory. See also Tesoro Petroleum Corp. v. Holborn Oil Co., Ltd. (1989) involving Sections 2–706 and 2–708(1). Section 2A–501(4) is much more explicit on requiring these results than is Article 2 but both Articles are subject to the same principle as stated in Section 1–305(a).

In most instances, however, the seller or lessor will have a choice of remedies. Which one(s) should be pursued must depend on the circumstances. The state of performance at the time of the breach or default and the nature of the breach or default are two important factors to be considered in making that determination. The breach or default may occur before or after delivery or before or after the goods have been identified. The breach or default may result from repudiation, wrongful rejection, wrongful attempt at revocation of acceptance, or failure to make a payment due, as well as from some other failure to perform, such as a failure to keep the goods well maintained.

For the purposes of discussion, it is assumed a statutorily defined breach or default has occurred. The remedies listed in Sections 2–703(2) and 2A–523(1) for such a breach or default basically are divided into two categories: (1) monetary and (2) non-monetary. If a buyer or lessee becomes insolvent, see Sections 2–703(3) and 2A–523(2), and if a lessor does not elect to exercise one of these remedies, or the default is one only defined by agreement, see Section 2A–523(3) and (4). The latter matters are in part left to agreement in Article 2.

2.   MONETARY REMEDIES

a.   Generally

A number of specific rules have been formulated as guides to what measure of damages should be used under the circumstances. Bear in mind, however, that these specific rules are mere corollaries of the general principles of attempting to give the seller or lessor, as far as possible, the benefit of the contract, and therefore must be applied with considerable flexibility to the facts of each case. To the extent that a specific rule does not realize the general objective it should not be applied; a court should never allow a specific rule to override and defeat this general objective.

The Code provides four specific rules for determining the seller's or lessor's measure of damages when the buyer or lessee statutorily breaches or defaults on the contract.

b.   Resale or Re-lease Standard

If the buyer or lessee wrongfully rejects, wrongfully attempts to revoke acceptance, refuses to pay, repudiates, or wrongfully fails to perform a contractual obligation in a contract for sale, one of the most satisfactory ways for the seller or lessor to establish the amount of damages is to dispose of the goods and set damages by any loss. See Diebold Inc. v. Positran Manufacturing, Inc. (2002). In a sale, that is the difference in the prices, plus any incidental and consequential damages and less expenses saved. Section 2–706. The seller is not accountable to the buyer if a profit is made. See Rogerson Aircraft Corp. v. Fairchild Industries, Inc. (1986) (profits seller would have earned on prospective parts supply contracts recovered under Section 2–708(2)) and Bulk Oil (U.S.A.), Inc. v. Sun Oil Trading Co. (1983) (interest on borrowed money as "incidental" damages). But see Stokes v. Roberts (1986), for a denial of interest as incidental damages.

In a lease, the comparable recovery is accrued and unpaid rent under the original lease up to the date the new lease begins, the present value as of that date of the rent for the then remaining term of the original lease minus the present value as of the same date of the rent under the new lease applicable to the period of the new lease comparable to the then remaining term of the original lease, and any incidental and consequential damages but less expenses saved. The lessor also is not accountable for any profit made. Section 2A–527.

Of course, as a general matter to dispose of the goods the seller or lessor must have possession or control of them. But see Section 2A–525(2). In this connection Section 2–706(1) states:

(1) In an appropriate case involving breach by the buyer the seller may resell the goods concerned or the undelivered balance thereof. Where the resale is made in good faith and in a commercially reasonable manner the seller may recover the difference between the contract price and the resale price together with any incidental or consequential damages allowed under the provisions of this Article (Section 2–710), but less expenses saved in consequence of the buyer's breach.

Section 2A–527(1) and (2) are substantially similar except if the disposition will be used to set damages, it must be by a lease that is substantially similar to the original lease. If it is by a lease that does not qualify, or is by sale or otherwise, damages cannot be measured by the disposition. Section 2A–527(3).

The factors to be used in determining whether the new lease is substantially similar are explained in Official Comments 4 and 5 to Section 2A–527. Even if there is dissimilarity, if it can be valued monetarily the court can adjust the difference in rent to take account of the difference and award damages under this section. For example, if the new lease requires the lessor to insure the goods while the original lease required the lessee to insure, the usual cost of that insurance could be deducted from the rent due under the new lease before the difference in rental between the two leases is determined. But see Official Comment 6 to Section 2A–527 and, as to how to handle differences in the terms of the original and new leases, Official Comment 7.

To be a basis to measure damages, the new lease also must be made in good faith and in a commercially reasonable manner. The discussion below of resale may be used to shed light on these requirements.

In the case of a resale, when the goods are identified the resale may be either by public or private sale, unless the parties have agreed otherwise. Section 2–706(2). Official Comment 5 to Section 2–706 explains that a "public sale" usually means a sale by auction. If the goods are not identified, the resale must be at a private sale "unless there is a recognized market for a public sale of futures in goods of the kind" (such as cotton). Section 2–706(4)(a). This restriction on the public sale of unidentified goods is not as encompassing as it seems in light of Section 2–704. That section allows the seller to (1) identify to the contract conforming goods in the seller's possession or control at the time the seller learned of the breach, (2) resell unfinished goods "which have been demonstrably intended for the particular contract," and (3) complete the manufacture of goods which were unfinished at the time of breach and identify them to the contract if reasonable commercial judgment is exercised in doing so. Section 2A–524 is a similar provision for leases. This means it is possible for the seller to identify goods after the breach and resell them as identified goods under Section 2–706.

In order for a resale to be valid it must conform to certain standards. In general it must be made in good faith and in a commercially reasonable manner. In determining the "commercial reasonableness" of a resale, time and place of sale are of prime importance. The sale must be made within a reasonable time after the buyer's breach. What is a reasonable time in doubtful cases is a question of fact. The nature of the goods and the condition of the market are important facts to be considered. Resale one week after breach if the goods were shoes might be perfectly reasonable, whereas it would probably be unreasonable if the goods were tomatoes already identified to the contract at the time of breach. In a rapidly falling market, one week might be too long even if the goods were shoes. Resale in a wholesale market may be unreasonable if the original sale was at retail. See Official Comments 5 and 8 to Section 2–703 and California Airmotive Corp. v. Jones (1969).

There is some case law to the effect that in order for damages to be based on a resale, the seller must resell at the place where the goods were to be delivered to the buyer unless the circumstances are unusual. Official Comment 5 explains that Section 2–706 rejects this theory, the sole test being whether the place chosen was a commercially reasonable choice. Even though the place (city, town, etc.) chosen is reasonable, if the resale is public it must be held "at a usual place or market for public sale if one is reasonably available." Section 2–706(4)(b). This is where prospective bidders are more likely to attend. If no such market is available the seller might be required to hold the resale in a different city or town where such a market is available. See Official Comment 8 to Section 2–703.

Some of the other duties in making a resale may be summarized as follows:

(1) If the resale is to be private, the seller must give the buyer reasonable notice of the intention to resell but is not required to give notification of the time and place of resale. Section 2–706(3).

(2) If the resale is to be public, the seller must give the buyer both notice of the fact that the goods are going to be offered for resale and notice of the time and place of resale. If, however, the goods are perishable or threaten to decline in value speedily no notice is required. Section 2–706(4)(b).

(3) When the resale is to be public and the goods will not be within the view of those attending the sale the notification of sale must state where the goods are located and provide for reasonable opportunity for prospective purchasers to inspect them. Section 2–706(4)(c).

(4) If the resale is public, the seller may buy the goods. Section 2–706(4)(d).

In order to recover damages from the buyer or lessee on the basis of the disposition, the seller or lessor must comply with the prescribed rules. If they do not, they must rely on one of the other standards for proving damages. Section 2–706(7) and Section 2A–527(3). See also Sprague v. Sumitomo Forestry Co., Ltd. (1985) (failure to give statutory notice; resale price nonetheless sufficed as proof of market price) and Apex Oil Co. v. Belcher Co. of New York, Inc. (1988) (seller may designate which sale is controlling for purpose of Section 2–706 but volatility of market made second sale too late as a matter of law).

Suppose, however, a disposition is not properly held and the interest of the purchaser at the disposition is contested on the theory that the purchaser could derive an interest only through a valid disposition. The Code protects the innocent purchaser by providing in Sections 2–706(5) and 2A–527(4):

A purchaser that purchases in good faith (and for value) at a disposition takes the goods free of any rights of the original buyer or lessee even though the seller or lessor fails to comply with one or more of the requirements.

Normally if the seller or lessor bases damages on a disposition, the property has been disposed of for less than the original contract and the seller or lessor is suing for the difference. Suppose the seller or lessor makes a very favorable redisposition at which the value obtained for the goods exceeds the original contract plus other recoverable damages.

Does the seller or lessor have to account for the profit? The Code provides a negative answer. Sections 2–706(6) and 2A–527(5). May the seller or lessor in this case alternatively use the market value standard to set damages? As discussed, Section 2A–501(4) and Official Comments 1 and 3 to Section 2A–523 state no, and Official Comment 1 to Section 2–703 suggests that and most cases under Article 2 agree. Otherwise, the market standard is available if there is no disposition or there is one that fails to comply. However, because the market standard may set damages before the seller or lessor can dispose of the goods in a falling market, which is most often when a buyer or lessee will breach, it often is not an attractive alternative.

c. Market Value Standard

An alternative measure of damage to any loss or resale or re-lease, which can be viewed as a statutory liquidated damage clause, can be used when the buyer or lessee breaches or defaults; it is the difference between the contract price or rent and the market price or rent. Section 2–708(1) provides:

(1) Subject to subsection (2) and the provisions of this Article with respect to proof of market price (Section 2–723), (a) the measure of damages for non-acceptance by the buyer is the difference between the contract price and the market price at the time and place for tender together with any incidental or consequential damages provided in this Article (Section 2–710), but less expenses saved in consequence of the buyer's breach.

Section 2A–528(1) is basically the same except, if the lessee has never taken possession, the date of default is used; if the lessor has repossessed, that date is used; and if the lessee has tendered back the goods, that date is used.

The market price or rent is that prevailing at the relevant time and at the place for tender or, in a lease, where the goods are located. Thus, if the agreement calls for the buyer or lessee to pick up the goods at the seller's or lessor's place of business in Philadelphia, the market price or rent is that prevailing in Philadelphia when the goods were to have been picked up. A sale agreement calling for delivery at destination would require determining the market price at time of tender at the destination point. For example, if S contracts to sell B 100 bushels of a certain grade of wheat at $2 per bushel to be delivered by S to B's warehouse in Pittsburgh on June 1, 2003, B wrongfully refuses delivery and the market price of that grade of wheat in Pittsburgh on June 1, 2003 is $1.50 a bushel, S's damage using the market standard would be $.50 per bushel or a total of $50.

As pointed out, use of market value at a fixed place and time may lead to some arbitrary results. Suppose in the case above S, whose granary is in Chicago, contracts to sell the wheat F.O.B. Chicago. Wheat is selling for $1.75 per bushel in Chicago when S delivers the wheat to the carrier. B rejects the wheat only after it arrives in Pittsburgh. The market price there is $1.50 per bushel. S's damages under Section 2–708(1)(a) would be $.25 per bushel even though the commercially reasonable procedure would be to resell the wheat in Pittsburgh (and, if that is properly done, Section 2–706 will permit the better measure). Or suppose by the time the wheat arrives back in Chicago the price in Chicago has also declined to $1.50. Again, damages based on Section 2–708(1)(a) would be limited to $.25 per bushel and again the seller could avoid this problem by reselling the wheat and basing damages on Section 2–706. Also as pointed out, these alternatives are designed to make S whole, and not to provide a windfall. Thus, suppose in the above example the terms are F.O.B. Chicago and at the time the goods are delivered to the carrier the market price in Chicago is $1.50 per bushel. When the goods arrive in Pittsburgh and B wrongfully rejects, the market price there is $1.75 per bushel. S resells the wheat in Pittsburgh for $1.75. May S recover damages under Section 2–708(1)(a) instead of Section 2–706 and recover $.50 per bushel when only $.25 per bushel has been lost? The provisions of Article 2 do not provide a firm answer, but the cases seem to deny this approach and Article 2A more explicitly is in accord for leases.

Section 2–708(1)(b) states the measure of damages for repudiation, which is the difference between the contract price and the market price at the place for tender at the expiration of a commercially reasonable time after the seller learned of the repudiation but no later than the time for tender. A troublesome problem particularly in the sales context has been in proving the market price of the goods in cases where the seller sues the buyer after the latter anticipatorily repudiates the contract and the action comes to trial before the time for performance. At common law damages are to be determined not as of the time of repudiation but as of the time fixed for performance, which means the seller has the burden of proving the market price as of a future time. This can be difficult. As noted, the Code eases the seller's problem in these cases by providing that damages based on market price are determined according to the market price of such goods at the expiration of a commercially reasonable time after the seller learned of the repudiation, but no later than the time for tender. Section 2–708(1)(b).

Proof of the market price or rent in some cases may be difficult. The Code includes some specific provisions regarding this problem in an attempt to give some leeway in meeting this burden. Suppose, for example, evidence of the market price at the time and place of tender is not readily available. The Code provides that "the price prevailing within any reasonable time before or after the time described or at any other place which in commercial judgment or under usage of trade would serve as a reasonable substitute for the one described may be used, making any proper allowance for the cost of transporting the goods to or from such other place." Section 2–723(1). Section 2A–507(2) is much the same.

In some instances the goods as to which the seller or lessor is attempting to establish a market price or rent may be traded in an established market. The Code provides that if reports of the value of or rents for such goods are made in "official publications or trade journals or in newspapers, periodicals or other means of communication in general circulation published as the reports of such market," these reports will be admissible in evidence. Sections 2–724 and 2A–507(4). Official Comment 1 to Section 2–724 explains that in order to qualify as an "established market," the market does not have to be "closely organized in the manner of a produce exchange." The market is an established market "if transactions in the commodity are frequent and open enough to make a market established by usage in which one price can be expected to affect another and in which an informed report of the range and trend of prices can be assumed to be reasonably accurate." For a representative case illustrating some of the issues, such as applicability of the Official Comment, long term or spot market price, and so on, see Manchester Pipeline Corp. v. Peoples Natural Gas Co. (1988).

d. The Profit Standard

When a seller or lessor contracts to sell or lease goods, they do so with the hope of making a profit from the transaction, and in some instances in order to compensate the seller or lessor adequately for the buyer's or lessee's breach or default, a "profit" standard for measuring damages must be used. Generally, use of this standard will result in a larger judgment than when the market price or rent standard is used, but it also is an alternative to recovery under Section 2–706. This is recognized by the Code in Section 2–708(2):

(2) If the measure of damages provided in subsection (1) [the market standard] or in Section 2–706 is inadequate to put the seller in as good a position as performance would have done then the measure of damages is the profit (including reasonable overhead) which the seller would have made from full performance by the buyer, together with any incidental or consequential damages provided in this Article (Section 2–710).

Section 2A–528(2) essentially is the same except it requires reducing the recoverable profit to present value since the profit only would have been recovered over time as rent was paid.

Under what circumstances should the profit standard be used? See Official Comment 5 to Section 2–708. One is that in which the seller or lessor is a so-called "lost volume" person which, as the Official Comment indicates, exists in the cases of uncompleted goods, jobbers or middlemen, and other lost volume sellers. Standard priced goods often are involved. The following fact situation will illustrate based on Neri v. Retail Marine Corp. (1972). S, a retail dealer, contracted to sell B a new boat of a specified model for $12,587.40. Six days later B sent S a letter refusing the contract. The boat had already been ordered from the manufacturer and was received by S at approximately the same time as B's letter. A few months later S resold the boat to C, another customer, for the same price B agreed to pay. The court allowed S to recover the lost profit on the B sale of $2,579. This was on the theory that, had B not breached but performed, S would have had two sales instead of one. S's sales were reduced by one; therefore, S should have the profit S would have made on the contract with B. S's profit in such a case is usually determined by subtracting the cost of the boat to S from the dealer or list price, and, as Official Comment 5 to Section 2A–528 notes, any expected appreciation of the goods should be included.

The court in R.E. Davis Chemical Corp. v. Diasonics, Inc. (1987), sums the analysis up well: a lost volume dealer is one that has a predictable and finite number of customers and that has the capacity either to sell to all new buyers or to make the one additional sale represented by the resale after the breach. But the dealer should not only have the capacity to sell the additional unit, but also it should have been profitable to do so. Official Comment 5 to Section 2–708. Thus in Bill's Coal Co., Inc. v. Board of Public Utilities of Springfield, Missouri (1989), where the evidence showed seller had difficulty meeting the buyer's needs and had to purchase some coal from other suppliers because seller had to close one of two principal mines, and that the second sale was possible only because the buyer refused to accept any more coal, the use of Section 2–708(2) was refused.

Another situation for the use of Sections 2–708(2) or 2A–528(2) may arise where the seller or the lessor is either a components supplier or jobber. A components supplier is one who contracts either to manufacture the goods or to assemble them for the buyer or lessee. A jobber is a middleman who acquires goods from a manufacturer and disposes of them to other dealers. Should the components supplier learn of the breach or default before the completion of manufacture or assembly and elect not to complete the goods under Sections 2–704 or 2A–524 discussed below, that person will have lost the transaction and the anticipated profit therefrom. The same is true of the jobber who learns of the breach or default before the goods have been acquired. In both instances actions for the price or rent or for damages based on redisposition are not applicable.

Sections 2–708(2) and 2A–528(2) recognize that a seller or lessor may suffer damages in addition to lost profit. Incidental and consequential damages (Sections 2–710 and 2A–530), reasonable overhead, and cost incurred in performance up to the time of breach are also recoverable. Overhead which is recoverable would be that pro rata share of the fixed cost which the contract would have satisfied. Taxes, administrative salaries, insurance, rent, heating, and lighting would be among such fixed costs. On the other hand the buyer or lessee is entitled to a credit for the resale or salvage value of partially completed goods. See Official Comment 1e. to Section 2–708.

The right to recover reasonable overhead is based on the theory that if the buyer or lessee breaches, the fixed costs will have to be spread over one less transaction, thus increasing the cost of production and decreasing profit on the remaining transactions. Conversely, in determining the anticipated profit on the transaction in question, overhead should be included as a part of costs. In short, under the formula overhead increases damages when a pro-rata share is allocated to the contract breached, but decreases damages by the same amount when included as a part of the costs in computing profit. One writer recognizes that this approach is needlessly complicated and suggests that overhead not be considered in computing damages. See Nordstrom, Law of Sales, 536–41 (1970). Lost profit can be determined merely by subtracting variable costs from the contract price or rent.

A simple example will serve to illustrate how damages could be computed, but see Official Comment 5 to Section 2–708. S contracts to build a specially designed machine for B for a $12,000 price or aggregate rent. Construction of the machine begins almost immediately. A few weeks later and before the machine is completed, B wrongfully repudiates the contract, and S immediately stops work on the machine. Ignoring allocated overhead, assume S has expended $8,000 in variable costs at the time of the repudiation, and is able to prove that $2,000 in variable costs would be required to complete the machine. The partially completed machine has scrap or resale value of $1,500. S's loss should be $8,500. This can be computed either by determining lost profit ($2,000), adding variable expense already incurred ($8,000), and subtracting the scrap or resale value of the machine ($1,500), or by subtracting from the price or total rent ($12,000) the scrap or resale value ($1,500) and the expense saved by not completing the machine ($2,000).

e. Price or Rent Standard

Section 2–709(1) provides a fourth standard by which to determine the amount that an aggrieved seller may recover:

(1) When the buyer fails to pay the price as it becomes due the seller may recover, together with any incidental or consequential damages under the next section, the price

(a) of goods accepted or of conforming goods lost or damaged within a commercially reasonable time after risk of their loss has passed to the buyer; and

(b) of goods identified to the contract if the seller is unable after reasonable effort to resell them at a reasonable price or the circumstances reasonably indicate that such effort will be unavailing.

Section 2A–529(1) is similar as to the rent due under the lease, except that (1) the lessor cannot recover the rent due because of the acceptance of the goods under subsection (a) if the lessor repossesses the goods or if the lessee tenders the goods back, and (2) the lessor is entitled only to accrued and unpaid rent until the date of judgment and then is limited to the present value of the future rent. This is consistent with better prior law. See Fairfield Lease Corp. v. Pratt (1971) and Groendyke Transport, Inc. v. Merchant (1962).

If the lessor is able to recover the rent, the lessor must hold the goods for the remaining lease term for the lessee or until the lessee pays the judgment and thus can re-obtain the goods, unless the lessor subsequently readjusts its recovery to the measure under Section 2A–527 or Section 2A–528, in which case the lessor can dispose of the goods. If the seller sues for the price under Section 2–709(1), the seller also must hold any goods identified under the contract for the buyer if they are still under the seller's control, but if resale becomes possible, the seller may resell the goods at any time before the judgment is collected. Assuming the seller does resell all or a part of the goods under these circumstances, the net proceeds of any such resale must be credited to the buyer. As soon as the buyer pays the balance due on the judgment, the buyer is entitled to any of the goods not resold. Section 2–709(2). The seller, however, is not required to relinquish possession of any unsold goods until the judgment is paid.

The above limitation on recovery of the rent for accepted goods that are repossessed or retendered reflects a general duty of mitigation of damages pursuant to the Code (the lessor would have to dispose of its own residual interest and so it should be in the best position to also dispose of the lessee's

cannot recover consequential damages, however, from a consumer.

At common law it is possible for the parties in any type of contract to insert a clause by which they agree what the damages shall be in case of breach or default. Such clauses are policed by courts and, if found not to meet certain conditions, are declared to be penalty clauses and unenforceable.

Articles 2 and 2A recognize the right of parties to sales contracts and leases to fix damages before breach or default by agreement. Section 2–718(1) provides:

> (1) Damages for breach by either party may be liquidated in the agreement but only at an amount which is reasonable in light of the anticipated or actual harm caused by the breach and, in a consumer contract, the difficulties of proof of loss and the inconvenience or nonfeasibility of otherwise obtaining an adequate remedy. Section 2–719 determines the enforceability of a term that limits but does not liquidate damages.

Section 2–718 is not explicit as to the consequences when the amount stipulated as liquidated damages is unreasonably large or small. Official Comment 3 explains that such a clause is unenforceable if unreasonable; it also could be considered to be unconscionable under Section 2–302. If a liquidated damage clause fails, the statutory remedies become available. Official Comment 4 to Section 2–718 and Official Comment 5 to Section 2A–504. If damages are limited rather than liquidated, or the parties agree on a remedy structure different than that of the Code, Sections 2–719 and 2A–503 are applicable. These provisions are discussed in the next chapter.

In applying the provision on liquidated damages, in Article 2, the courts tend to read some of the statutory language generously, or ignore it. For example, in California and Hawaiian Sugar Co. v. Sun Ship, Inc. (1986), the liquidated damages clause provided for payment of $17,000 for each day of delay, which resulted in a four million dollar claim even though the actual net loss sustained was $368,000. Notwithstanding the statutory disjunctive ("the anticipated *or* actual harm"), the court upheld the clause.

Section 2A–504 does not contain the disjunctive clause and is generally more liberal, not including the more restrictive consumer qualification and including an allowance for loss or diminution of anticipated tax benefits as well as expectation interest. Like in Article 2, the regulation of unreasonably large or small amounts is left to the general overall standard of reasonableness. Official Comments 1 and 2, and 4, to Section 2A–504. The Article 2A rule closely approximates what the courts actually were doing in lease cases. See, e.g., Bell Atlantic Tricon Leasing Corp. v. Pacific Contracting Corp. (1989) (reasonable forecast of just compensation, but also harm must be difficult to estimate) and Skyline Steel Corp. v. A.J. Dupuis Co. (1986) (focused on reasonableness without consideration of whether damages were easily determinable).

Official Comment 3 to Section 2A–504 notes a very important point in the case of a lease: a liquidated damage clause has the potential to make a lease into a secured transaction if it by agreement puts the lessor in the position of a secured party. See In re Noack (1984) and In re Zerkle Trucking Co. (1991).

In some instances the buyer or lessee will have made a down payment or deposit before delivery. Sections 2–718(2) and 2A–504(3) provide that even though the seller or lessor rightfully withholds delivery the buyer or lessee may recover such payments to the extent that they exceed the amount stipulated as liquidated damage. If there is no liquidated damage clause, the buyer or lessee may recover any amount of payment which exceeds the seller's or lessor's damages and any value or benefits provided. In a sale, payments by a buyer in goods, such as a trade-in, are valued at their reasonable value and not the trade-in amount.

g. Seller's or Lessor's Right to Continue Performance After Breach or Default

At common law once a seller learns of the buyer's breach the seller is under a duty to do nothing to increase the buyer's damage; that is, as previously noted, the seller has a general duty of mitigation. So does a lessor. Section 1–103(b). It is commonly stated, therefore, that damages are to be determined as of the time of the breach. However, the Code contains some very interesting and commercially realistic provisions in this connection. There are similar provisions for leases.

Suppose S contracts to sell or lease a stated quantity of goods to B. The goods are not identified at the time the contract is made. A short time later B notifies S that B is going out of business and will not need the goods. At that time, while S still has not identified the goods to the contract, S has in S's warehouse a large quantity of goods meeting the description in the contract.

Section 2–704(1)(a) provides:

> An aggrieved seller ... may identify to the contract conforming goods not already identified if at the time the seller learned of the breach the goods are in the seller's possession or control.

> Section 2A–524(1)(a) is the same if the goods are in the possession or control of either the lessor or supplier.

This means that in the above case S could identify goods in the warehouse to the contract and proceed in the same manner as if the breach or default had occurred after the goods had been identified. This would allow S to dispose of or attempt to dispose of the goods and recover damages on that basis. The main significance of this provision is that it would allow S to recover the price or the rent if S cannot dispose of the goods. Sections 2–709(1)(b) and 2A–529(1)(b).

Difficult problems arise when the seller or lessor is to manufacture goods for the buyer or lessee and the latter repudiates the contract before the goods are finished. By the great weight of authority at common law the seller (or a lessor) may not increase damages by continuing to manufacture the goods after such notice. Generally, damages must be determined as of the time the repudiation was learned about. There are cases, however, which hold that if damages caused by ceasing performance would be greater than those caused by completing the goods, the seller (or a lessor) may complete manufacture and recover damages based on complete performance. See Kahn v. Carl Schoen Silk Corp. (1925). It has also been held that where the repudiation of the buyer (or a lessee) occurs when the goods are nearly completed, the seller (or a lessor) may complete the goods and recover damages based on complete performance. See Mattison Mach. Works v. Nypenn Furniture Co. (1926).

One of the leading cases dealing with this problem is Buchman v. Millville Mfg. Co. (1927). There S agreed to manufacture and deliver in installments a special type of yarn. After two installments had been delivered, B repudiated the contract. S notified of its intention to continue performance of the contract and to tender delivery of the goods as they became due under the contract. Had S stopped manufacture of the goods upon B's repudiation, costs incurred to that point plus anticipated profit (the usual measure of damages in such cases) would have totaled 70 cents per pound. The contract price was $1.15 per pound. At the time of the repudiation there was no established market value for the yarn, although the market price of similar yarn reasonably indicated that the yarn in question would be worth more than 45 cents per pound. Thus loss potentially would be less than 70 cents per pound. S completed the manufacture of the yarn but found that it had no market value. In allowing S to recover the full contract price under Section 63(3) of the Sales Act the court stated:

At least, we may say that, being then forced to a decision whether to stop or go on, the seller exercised a reasonable judgment in deciding not to stop, and that this continued to be true throughout November, when the work was done. The net value of the partially worked-up cotton was certainly speculative; the market for the yarn had suffered a sudden collapse, from which it might recover; the seller was not primarily in the business of selling cotton, but yarn. These made it, in our judgment, a reasonable choice, which is all that the defaulting buyer can demand.

Despite such decisions as in the *Buchman* case, one can imagine what might be the seller's (or a lessor's) perplexed state of mind when the buyer (or a lessee) breaches before the goods are finished. Should the aggrieved party cease performance immediately and sue for damages (usually lost profit plus expenses to that point), or should the aggrieved party complete the goods with the hope that they might be disposed of for a favorable price? If the aggrieved party decides to pursue the latter course and succeeds in reselling the goods for an amount about equal to the original contract price, the aggrieved party has been made whole, or almost so, without the necessity of litigation and all the trouble and expense attendant thereto. This would also be advantageous to the buyer or lessee, since even if the goods are resold for less than the contract price, the damages for which the buyer or lessee would be liable would usually be less, perhaps far less, than if the seller or lessor pursued the first alternative.

The difficulty which inheres in the seller's or lessor's choice of action, however, is the possibility that if the choice is to complete the goods, they may not be able to be disposed of favorably, and then the damages will have been increased. Thus the aggrieved party runs the risk that a court, not as enlightened as the court in the *Buchman* case, will not allow recovery of damages on the basis of completed performance, but will assess damages based on conditions as of the time the repudiation was learned about.

The Code contains commercially realistic provisions which attempt to deal with this problem. It gives the seller or lessor considerable choice as to what course of action to pursue. The Code provisions (Sections 2–704(2) and 2A–524(2)) state:

(2) Where the goods are unfinished an aggrieved seller, lessor or supplier may in the exercise of reasonable commercial judgment for the purposes of avoiding loss and of effective realization either complete the manufacture and wholly identify the goods to the contract or cease manufacture and dispose of the goods for scrap or

salvage value or proceed in any other reasonable manner.

The burden of proving the unreasonable nature of the seller's, lessor's or supplier's action rests on the buyer or lessee. Official Comment 2 to Section 2–704. In other words, there is a rebuttable presumption that the action in completing manufacture is commercially reasonable. If the seller, lessor or supplier does act reasonably, completes the goods and identifies them to the contract, it may proceed as if the buyer or lessee had breached after the goods had been identified to the contract.

3. NON–MONETARY REMEDIES

a. Generally

As already pointed out, it is important for a seller to retain control over the goods until the purchase price is paid. If credit is not extended, the seller is not legally obligated to give up possession until the price is tendered. If credit has been extended, the full purchase price is not due until the expiration of the credit term, and delivery of the goods is due at the time indicated by the terms of the agreement. Usually, if the goods are delivered to the buyer under a credit term the seller loses all right of direct recourse against these specific goods, unless the seller under a security agreement with the buyer has retained a security interest under Article 9 of the Code. The seller could, of course, reduce the account receivable to judgment and if the goods are still owned by the buyer, levy on them as a part of the buyer's general assets. An important exception to this general rule is the seller's right to reclaim goods on the buyer's insolvency, as discussed below.

While a lessor on default does have a right to the goods under Section 2A–525(2), unlike a seller and so no right of reclamation is necessary, it is still important for the lessor to retain control over the goods until all payments initially due are made, as retained control is easier than regaining control. Thus Section 2A–525(1) allows a lessor to refuse to deliver if the lessee is discovered to be insolvent, and Section 2A–526, much like Section 2–705 for the seller, allows a lessor to stop delivery of goods in the possession of a bailee if the lessee is discovered to be insolvent or repudiates or fails to make a payment due before delivery.

b. Right to Withhold Delivery

Suppose S contracts to sell B 1,000 bushels of wheat. The goods are to be delivered July 1, and B is to have 60 days thereafter within which to pay the price. On June 20, S learns that B is insolvent. If S delivers the wheat S will have no more than an unsecured claim against the bankrupt estate or an uncollectible judgment.

Accordingly, Section 2–702(1) provides:

(1) Where the seller discovers the buyer to be insolvent the seller may refuse delivery except for cash including payment for all goods theretofore

delivered under the contract, and stop delivery under Section 2–705.

This provision allows S to refuse to deliver the wheat to B except for cash. Should B refuse to pay cash, B is in breach but should B pay cash, B is entitled to the wheat. The theory is that when a seller agrees to sell goods to a buyer on credit, the credit term is subject to an implied condition that the buyer is solvent. In short, the credit term becomes a cash one upon the buyer's insolvency. It should also be noted that in the case of an installment contract the seller may demand cash not only for the installment in question but for all unpaid installments previously delivered under the same contract. Suppose in the above example the wheat is to be delivered in six installments. S delivers three installments and then learns that B is insolvent. B has paid for the first two installments but not the third. Section 2–702 would allow S to withhold delivery of the fourth installment unless B pays cash for both the third and fourth installments.

For leases, see Section 2A–525(1).

A seller or a lessor also has a right to withhold delivery if the buyer or lessee is in breach or default as articulated in Section 2–703(1) or Section 2A–523(1), as applicable. Section 2–703(1) and (2)(a), (Section 2A–523(1)(a) is similar) provide:

Where the buyer wrongfully rejects, wrongfully attempts to revoke acceptance of goods, in a sale wrongfully fails to perform a contractual obligation, fails to make a payment when due, or repudiates, the seller may withhold delivery of the goods.

Any of the acts referred to would constitute a breach by the buyer. So too, such acts, including a failure to perform a contractual obligation if so agreed, would constitute a default by a lessee under Section 2A–523(1). Exercise of the right to withhold delivery would not preclude the seller or lessor from pursuing any other remedy, such as an action for damages, against the buyer or lessee.

The right to withhold extends only to goods "involved" unless the breach or default is of the whole contract. This would mean in installment contracts that, for example, if the buyer or lessee breached or defaulted by wrongfully rejecting the first installment, the seller's or lessor's right to withhold delivery of the balance of installments would be determined by Section 2–612 or Section 2A–510. Under those sections the seller's or lessor's right to withhold delivery of the balance would depend on whether or not the buyer's breach or lessee's default substantially impaired the value of the whole contract. See Sections 2–612(3) and 2A–510(2). See Official Comment 2 to Section 2–703.

c. Right to Stop Delivery

In some instances the goods which the seller or lessor has contracted to sell or lease may not be in the possession of the seller or lessor but in the hands of a bailee. The two most usual examples are when the goods are in the hands of a carrier for delivery to the buyer or lessee, or when they are in the hands of a warehouseman and the seller or lessor intends to deliver without moving them, usually by delivery of a warehouse receipt to the buyer or lessee.

Section 2–705(1) provides:

(1) The seller may stop delivery of goods in the possession of a carrier or other bailee when the seller discovers the buyer to be insolvent (Section 2–702) or when the buyer repudiates or fails to make a payment due before delivery or if for any other reason the seller has a right to withhold or reclaim the goods.

Section 2A–526(1) is the same, except it substitutes reference to the right to take possession rather than the right to reclaim.

As against the buyer or lessee the seller or lessor loses the right to stop delivery upon "receipt of the goods" by the buyer or lessee. Sections 2–705(2)(a) and 2A–526(2)(a). "Receipt" of goods means taking physical possession of them. Sections 2–103(1)(*l*) and 2A–103(2). See *In re* Trico Steel Co., L.L.C. (Cargill Inc. v. Trico Steel Co., L.L.C. (2002)). The right of stoppage against the buyer is also lost upon the negotiation to the buyer of a negotiable document of title covering the goods. Section 2–705(2)(d). The basic reason for this is to promote and preserve the concept of negotiability. The same should be true in a lease situation. The mere delivery of a straight bill of lading to the buyer or lessee should not terminate the seller's or lessor's right to stop delivery, however.

The seller or lessor may also lose the right to stop delivery once any one of the following events takes place:

(1) when any bailee other than a carrier acknowledges to the buyer or lessee that the bailee holds the goods for the buyer or lessee. Sections 2–705(2)(b) and 2A–526(2)(b).

(2) when a carrier acknowledges to the buyer or lessee that it holds the goods as bailee either for further transportation (reshipment) or for storage (as warehouseman). Sections 2–705(2)(c) and 2A–526(2)(c).

In each of these instances the act of the bailee is tantamount to delivery to the buyer or lessee. The carrier or warehouseman by any one of these acts has now become the bailee of the buyer or lessee. A case which applies these principles in the context of natural gas delivered by pipeline is Matter of Pester Refining Co. (1986). There delivery would occur when a product transfer order by seller and Pester as buyer was delivered to the pipeline company. While the appellate court held Pester did not have possession until the gas actually passed through its meter at its refinery, the court also found that Section 2–705(2)(c) was not satisfied until the pipeline company had entered into a separate warehouse agreement, which on the facts did not occur.

A person in the "position of a seller" also may stop delivery under Section 2–705. Section 2–707(2).

Under Section 2–707, a "person in the position of a seller" includes, as against a principal, an agent that has paid or become responsible for the price of goods on behalf of the principal or anyone that otherwise holds a security interest or other right in goods similar to that of a seller. Section 2–707(1).

A seller's or lessor's right to stop delivery is qualified under some conditions. For example, if the goods are shipped under a non-negotiable bill of lading, the carrier is not obligated to honor a stop order from anyone except the person named as consigner. Sections 2–705(3)(d) and 2A–526(3)(c). If the seller or lessor, then, is not named as consignor, the seller or lessor does not have the right to demand that the carrier stop delivery. Similarly, if the goods have been shipped under a negotiable bill of lading, the carrier is not obligated to honor a notification to stop until surrender of possession or control of the document. Section 2–705(3)(c). Both of these provisions reflect the idea that the carrier is not under a duty to honor a notice to stop from a party who is a stranger to the contract of carriage. Although the carrier is not obligated to honor the notice under these circumstances, it may do so if it wishes. If it does and the seller or lessor had a right of stoppage, the buyer or lessee has no right to complain. The carrier would be taking a risk, however. Suppose, for example, the goods had been shipped under a negotiable bill which had been delivered by the seller to the buyer who in turn negotiated it to an innocent purchaser. The carrier by holding the goods for the seller would be liable to the innocent purchaser. The seller would then in turn be liable to the carrier for the damages it incurred to the innocent purchaser. Compare Sections 2–705(3)(b) and 2A–526(3)(b), which provide that the bailee is obligated to "hold and deliver the goods according to the directions of the seller or lessor but the seller or lessor is liable to the bailee for any ensuing charges or damages." However, if a rightful stop delivery order is ignored the bailee is liable to the seller or lessor.

d. Right to Reclaim or Repossess

As previously discussed, the seller loses all right of recourse against the goods once they have been delivered on credit to the buyer unless the seller has retained a security interest in them by complying with the provisions of Article 9 of the Code. This problem is not pertinent in a lease where the lessor retains title and thus a right to obtain possession upon default. Section 2A–525(2). Indeed, a lessor under Section 2A–525(2) has a right to dispose of the goods on the lessee's premises without removal, to render them unusable if the goods are employed in a trade or business (as opposed to consumer goods), and to have the lessee "crate and deliver" the goods if agreed.

At common law, if a buyer received goods on credit with no intention of paying for them the conduct was fraudulent and the transaction could be rescinded and the goods recovered by the seller. The difficult problem was determining the buyer's intentions at the time the buyer received the goods. Several courts grappled with the question whether or not receipt of goods on credit by a buyer who knew itself to be insolvent and who also knew that the seller was ignorant of this fact indicated an intention by the buyer not to pay for the goods. This question was not resolved uniformly by the courts. Some courts held that if the buyer knew the situation was "desperate," the conduct indicated an intention not to pay and the seller could rescind on the basis of fraud. Other courts held that mere failure of the buyer to disclose a "technically" insolvent condition did not of itself constitute fraud.

Section 2–702(2) provides:

(2) Where the seller discovers that the buyer has received goods on credit while insolvent. The seller may reclaim the goods upon demand made within a reasonable time after the buyer's receipt of the goods. Except as provided in this subsection the seller may not base a right to reclaim goods on the buyer's fraudulent or innocent misrepresentation of solvency or of intent to pay.

A misrepresentation should include a check dishonored because drawn on insufficient funds. See In re Bar–Wood, Inc. (1974). It would seem that a letter or a financial statement misrepresenting solvency should qualify. This issue is of minor importance because the language is intended as inclusive, not exclusive. Official Comments 2 and 3 to Section 2–702. Moreover, Section 546(c) of the Bankruptcy Code only provides a 10 day period for reclamation, and most cases conclude it is conclusive of the right in the bankruptcy context. See, e.g., In re Rozel Industries, Inc. (1987). While an occasional dissent is heard (see In re Bearhouse, Inc. (1988)), any longer right also would have to survive the avoidance powers of the trustee in bankruptcy. See the discussion infra.

The right of reclamation only reaches those goods which are identifiable and in the buyer's possession when it receives the reclamation demand. The right in the Code does not extend to proceeds or products of the goods, but fungible goods may be reclaimed if the goods can be traced into an identifiable mass. In re Wheeling–Pittsburgh Steel Corp. (1987) and Official Comment 4 to Section 2–702.

When a buyer is insolvent there is a strong possibility that parties other than the seller will also claim an interest in the goods. With this in mind Section 2–702(3) provides:

(3) The seller's right to reclaim under subsection (2) is subject to the rights of a buyer in ordinary course or other good faith purchaser for value under this Article (Section 2–403). Successful reclamation of goods excludes all other remedies with respect to them.

Originally this provision also contained the words "or lien creditor." This caused difficulty. In re Kravitz (1960) involved the problem. There the buyer's creditors filed an involuntary petition in bankruptcy one day before the seller attempted to reclaim goods from the buyer. The trustee in bankruptcy, who under then Section 70(c) of the old Bankruptcy Act had the rights of a lien creditor as of the time the petition is filed, claimed priority over the seller under Section 2–702(3). The court concluded that the Code does not contain any provision defining the relative priorities of a lien creditor as against a reclaiming seller. The court, therefore, looked to Pennsylvania common law to determine the question, and found that under Pennsylvania law the rights of a trustee in bankruptcy are superior to those of the reclaiming seller. A few years later another Federal Court of Appeals dealt with the same question. Matter of Mel Golde Shoes, Inc. (1968). The court in that case also searched in vain for any provision in the Code which defines the priorities between the trustee as a lien creditor and the seller. The court then looked to Kentucky's common law for an answer, and found that under that law, contrary to Pennsylvania's common law, the reclaiming seller takes priority.

Thus, the question of priority between a lien creditor and a reclaiming seller under Section 2–702(3) is not answered by the Code, but must be answered by looking to supplementary principles of law in the jurisdiction. This may defeat the primary purpose of the provision in the most common case, bankruptcy. Accordingly, in 1966 the uniform Code was amended by deleting the words "or lien creditor" from Section 2–702(3). This should provide a uniform rule giving the reclaiming seller priority over a "lien creditor," including a trustee in bankruptcy.

The entire conflict between reclaiming sellers and trustees in bankruptcy was not resolved by this amendment. In two jurisdictions which adopted the amendment, U.S. District Courts held that Section 2–702 reclamations were statutory liens which first became effective upon the insolvency of the debtor and, therefore, were invalid under old Section 67(c)(1)(A) of the Bankruptcy Act. See In re Giltex, Inc. (1975) and In re Good Deal Supermarkets Inc. (1974). On the other hand, in Matter of Telemart Enterprises, Inc. (1975), the court reasoned that under Section 2–702 the receipt of goods on credit while insolvent is deemed a fraud on the seller, rendering the sale voidable. This means that the sale is defective from its inception. Therefore, since the bankrupt has only voidable title the trustee got only voidable title under old Section 70 of the Bankruptcy Act which vested the trustee "with the title of the bankrupt as of the date of the filing of the petition." Thus the court avoided holding that the Section 2–702 right of reclamation is a statutory lien. Moreover, it reasoned that even if the right were treated as a lien, the lien would attach at the time of the creation of the debt. Thus, creation of the lien would not be for an antecedent debt and would not be a preference as defined in old Section 60(a)(1) of the Bankruptcy Act. The Supreme Court declined to review the *Telemart* case. The analysis of the court seems sound and still may be relevant when the Code right to reclaim exists beyond the protection of Section 546(c), as noted earlier.

In the Bankruptcy Reform Act of 1978, Congress recognized a right of the seller to reclaim by providing in Section 546(c):

The rights and powers of a trustee under Sections 544(a) ("strong arm" clause), 545 (lien avoidance), 547 (preferences) and 549 (post-petition transactions) are subject to any statutory or common law right of a seller of that has sold goods to the debtor in the ordinary course of the seller's business to reclaim such goods if the debtor has received such goods while insolvent, but—

(1) such a seller may not reclaim any such goods unless such seller demands in writing (subject to federal "E-sign") reclamation of such goods (A) before ten (10) days after receipt of such goods by the debtor, or (B) if such 10 day period expires after the commencement of the case, before 20 days after the receipt of such goods by the debtor; and

(2) the court may deny reclamation to a seller with such a right of reclamation that has made such a demand, only if the court (A) grants the claim of such a seller priority as a claim of a kind specified in section 503(b) of this title (administrative expense); or (B) secures such claim by a lien.

Some differences or possible differences between the provisions of Sections 546 and 2–702 should be noted.

(1) The Bankruptcy Court may deny the seller's right to reclaim either by treating the seller's

claim as a claim for the price and giving it priority as an administrative expense (first priority under Section 507) or securing the claim by a lien. The seller's right to reclaim under Section 2–702 is not subject to these qualifications. These two alternatives to reclamation under the Bankruptcy Code will most likely be used when the market value of the goods has gone up. Payment of the contract price to the seller is all that is required to make the seller whole, and the two alternatives to reclamation are reasonably calculated to protect the seller's right to the price. The administrative expense route also has been used by some courts when, under Section 2–702(3), the seller's reclamation right is subordinate to the right of a secured party of the buyer and so the goods are not available to be reclaimed. See In re Misco Supply Co. (1986). Cf. In re Lawrence Paperboard Corp. (1985). Recognizing that the explicit right to reclaim is lost if the buyer sells the goods, the case distinguishes the situation where the secured party is involved, finding the right continues although in subordinate form. It seems clear that nothing in bankruptcy alters the Article 9 creditor's priority over the reclaiming seller that exists outside of bankruptcy even though Section 546(c) contains no language like Section 2–702(3). Lavonia Mfg. Co. v. Emery Corp. (1985).

(2) Section 546 provides that demand for reclamation must be made in writing, subject to the

federal E-sign act. Section 2–702 does not specifically require writing.

(3) Section 2–702 provides no ten day limitation and Section 546 does not contain any exception to the ten day rule. Whether a right exists beyond Section 546(c), although subject to the avoidance powers of the trustee, was noted above.

CHAPTER 12

BUYER'S OR LESSEE'S REMEDIES

---

1. INTRODUCTION

The general objective in awarding an aggrieved party a remedy for breach of contract is basically the same whether the non-breaching party is the seller or lessor, or the buyer or lessee. The objective is neither to penalize the breaching party nor to enrich the non-breaching party. Sections 1–305 and 2A–501(4). As pointed out in the previous chapter,

439

the Code attempts to place in most cases through money damages the aggrieved party in approximately the same position that party would occupy had the breaching or defaulting party performed all obligations, without assessing the latter with any loss which the breaching or defaulting party had no reason to foresee at the time the contract was made.

If a buyer or lessee is to have a judicial remedy, court action must be taken within the statutory limitations period, which basically is four years under Sections 2–725 and 2A–506; in a sale the statute allows an additional year after discovery if that period would end later, but in no event can an action be brought after five years from accrual of the right of action. In a sale the period normally begins at breach or delivery even if the buyer does not know of the breach. There is an exception where a designated warranty or obligation explicitly extends to future performance and discovery of the breach must await the time of such performance. Thus in Safeway Stores, Inc. v. Certainteed Corp. (1986), where the seller advertised a roof as "bondable up to 20 years," the roof leaked seven years after installation, and two years later suit was filed, the court remanded for a determination of whether the warranty referred to future performance. Most courts have concluded an express repair or replacement "warranty" does not extend to future performance. See, e.g., Tittle v. Steel City Oldsmobile GMC Truck, Inc. (1989). Article 2 now treats such a "warranty" as a "remedial promise" (Section 2–103(1)(n)), and begins the running of the statute when the promise is not performed when performance is due rather than at sale. Courts also have concluded that an implied warranty cannot extend to future performance. Britt v. Schindler Elevator Corp. (1986). Section 2–725(3)(c) confirms this. This can produce harsh results. For example, in Wilson v. Hammer Holdings, Inc. (1988), where a painting guaranteed to be that of a certain artist was discovered to be a fake 24 years later, the buyer was out of luck. Now see Section 2–725(3)(d), which begins the running of the statute for breach of a warranty under Section 2–312 on discovery, but with a repose period for the warranty of non-infringement of six years. Section 2A–506(2) also employs a discovery rule and less harsh results may be expected in lease cases.

Section 2–725 also contains several other more specific starting points for the statute of limitations, as follows: for a repudiation, the earlier of when the aggrieved party elects to treat it as a breach or when a commercially reasonable time for awaiting performance has expired (Section 2–725(2)(b)); for indemnity, when the claim against the person indemnified was originally asserted (Section 2–725(2)(d), compare Section 2A–506(2), which is similar); and for obligations in Sections 2–313A and 2–313B, other than remedial promises, when the remote purchaser received the goods.

Sometimes purchasers seek to avoid the statute of limitations by arguing that repair attempts toll the statute or estop a party from raising it. This argument seldom has succeeded. See Roy Stone Transfer

Corp. v. Budd Co. (1986). But see Sierra Diesel Injection Service v. Burroughs Corp. (1986) (attempted repairs tolled the statute). The remedial promise concept should alleviate the need to so argue. Generally as to "tolling," see Sections 2–725(4) and (5) and 2A–506(3) and (4).

In most instances money damages adequately compensate the buyer or lessee, but in other instances nothing but possession of the goods involved will suffice. In yet other cases both damages and possession of the goods may be necessary. The provisions of the Code relating to the buyer's and lessee's remedies reflect a thorough appraisal of all these possibilities and neatly counter-balance the remedies of the seller or lessor.

A seller's breach or lessor's default is specified by statute to include (1) a repudiation of the contract before the time for performance, (2) a wrongful failure to make delivery or to perform a contractual obligation, or (3) a failure to deliver conforming goods or performance. When the breach or default is either repudiation or failure to deliver, the goods may be identified or unidentified; when it results from a nonconforming delivery the buyer or lessee may reject, accept and then revoke acceptance, or keep the goods, as a general rule. The type of breach or default, the state of the goods (identified or unidentified), and the buyer's or lessee's own reaction to a nonconforming tender are all factors which determine what remedy or remedies the buyer or lessee may seek. As in the case of the seller's or lessor's remedies, the remedies given to the buyer or lessee are not necessarily mutually exclusive. See in particular Official Comment 2 to Section 2A–508.

A seller by reason of agreement may be in breach of the contract for reasons other than the above specified breaches. So too may a lessor. A remedy for a buyer in such a case also may arise from agreement. Sections 2–718 and 2–719. Sections 2A–508(2) and (3) and 2A–519(3) explicitly provide remedies for defaults that arise by agreement in the case of a lease, and the lease itself may provide a remedy structure. Sections 2A–508(2), 2A–501(2) and 2A–503 and 2A–504. See also Sections 2A–501(3) and (5) and 2A–508(5) and Official Comment 1 to Section 2A–508. Finally, Sections 2A–508(3) and 2A–519(4) contain an explicit damage formula for breach of warranty.

2. MONETARY REMEDIES

a. Generally

When determining the monetary remedy or remedies to which a buyer or lessee is entitled, it is important to distinguish between the situation in which the buyer or lessee elects to retain a nonconforming tender, and all other situations in which the seller or lessor breaches or defaults. The latter situations are governed generally by Sections 2–711 and 2A–508 and related sections, and the former situation by Sections 2–714 and 2A–519(4). The relevant parts of Section 2–711 provide:

(1) A breach of contract by the seller includes the seller's wrongful failure to deliver or to perform a contractual obligation, making a non-conforming tender of delivery or performance, and repudiation.

(2) If a seller is in breach of contract under subsection (1), the buyer, to the extent provided for by this Act or other law, may:

(a) in the case of rightful cancellation rightful rejection or justifiable revocation of acceptance, recover so much of the price as has been paid;

(b) . . . .

(c) cancel;

(d) cover and have damages under Section 2–712 as to all the goods affected whether or not they have been identified to the contract;

(e) recover damages for non-delivery or repudiation under Section 2–713;

(f) recover damages for breach with regard to accepted goods or breach with regard to a remedial promise under Section 2–714;

(j) in other cases, recover damages in any manner that is reasonable under the circumstances.

Section 2A–508(1) essentially is the same except for agreed defaults and breaches of warranty it cross-references Section 2A–519, and it provides for recovery of only so much of the rent paid and security as is just under the circumstances.

b. Recovery of the Price or Rent

Where the seller or lessor repudiates or fails to deliver or the buyer or lessee rightfully rejects or justifiably revokes acceptance, the buyer or lessee may recover so much of the purchase price as has been paid or so much of the rent paid and security as is just under the circumstances. On the latter, see Official Comment 2 to Section 2A–508. As discussed in connection with revocation of acceptance, courts in sales have tended to reach a similar conclusion to the Section 2A–508 limitation on recovery by awarding sellers the value of the use of the goods in appropriate cases. This is a basic right of restitution, and in no way affects the buyer's or lessee's right to damages as discussed below. Section 2–608(4). Also, as pointed out earlier, once the buyer or lessee accepts a nonconforming tender and loses or does not exercise the right to revoke acceptance, the buyer or lessee becomes liable for the price or the rent, although damages may still be had for the nonconformity.

c. Cover

Section 2–712 provides:

(1) If the seller wrongfully fails to deliver or repudiates or the buyer rightfully rejects or justifiably revokes acceptance, the buyer may "cover" by making in good faith and without unreasonable delay any reasonable purchase of or contract to purchase goods in substitution for those from the seller.

(2) The buyer may recover from the seller as damages the difference between the cost of cover and the contract price together with any incidental or consequential damages as hereinafter defined (Section 2–715), but less expenses saved in consequence of the seller's breach.

(3) Failure of the buyer to effect cover within this section does not bar the buyer from any other remedy.

Note this remedy is not available for a breach that consists of the failure to perform a contractual obligation or the making of a nonconforming performance as possibly inappropriate for a non-material breach, but can be made so by agreement. The same is true in a lease. Sections 2A–518(1), 2A–508(1) and (2).

Section 2A–518 is much the same, except for obvious reasons it is more specific as to the nature of the substitute lease that can be used to measure damages and, as in the similar case of the lessor's remedy, the lease must be substantially similar to the original lease and must be made in good faith and in a commercially reasonable manner. If so, the lessee may recover as damages the present value as of the commencement of the new lease of the rent under the new lease applicable to the period of the new lease which is comparable to the then remaining term of the original lease, less the present value as of the same date of the rent for the then remaining term of the original lease, plus any incidental or consequential damages, and less any expenses saved. Official Comments 3 through 7 to Section 2A–518 elaborate on the application of this provision.

These sections permit an aggrieved buyer or lessee when the seller or lessor has breached in any way defined by statute as a breach or default to acquire substitute goods and recover the difference between the cost of cover and the original contract cost. There was no similar provision in the Uniform Sales Act, and nothing in that statute which required a court to recognize a higher price paid by the buyer on a substitute purchase as a basis for damages. Some courts held proof of the new purchase price was insufficient proof of a basis for damages and required proof of the market price. However, some courts held that when the buyer purchased substitute goods at a price lower than the market price, that price was the maximum amount on which damages could be based. This rule was considered by many to be unduly harsh on the aggrieved party.

In order to qualify as "cover," forming a valid basis for damages, under Section 2–712 a second purchase must meet several standards:

(1) It must be made in good faith, which requires both honesty in fact and the observance of reasonable commercial standards of fair dealing. Section 2–103(1)(j). This also, as mentioned, is true for a cover lease under Sections 2A–518(2) and 2A–103(1)(m). If revised Article 1 is in effect, see Section 1–201(b)(20). As an illustration of the

good faith requirement, see International Cosmetics Exchange, Inc. v. Gapardis Health & Beauty, Inc. (2002).

(2) It must be made without unreasonable delay. This does not mean that the buyer must snap up the first offer or buy the first goods seen. The buyer may look around and decide the best way to affect cover. Official Comment 5 to Section 2–712. As noted, Section 2A–518(2) requires a cover lease to be made in a commercially reasonable manner.

(3) The goods purchased in substitution must be similar to those in the original contract. This does not require that they be identical, but only that they be commercially reasonable substitutes. Steel radial tires manufactured by company "B" might be commercially reasonable substitutes for steel radials manufactured by company "A", especially if those manufactured by A were not readily available. On the other hand, purchased goods may be so dissimilar from those due from the seller as not to be suitable as cover. One court held that a car wash pressure system which washed automobiles using high pressure jets of water was too different from a brush system which carried automobiles through the brushes by a conveyor to be a commercially reasonable substitute. Valley Die Cast Corp. v. A. C. W., Inc. (1970). See also Kanzmeier v. McCoppin (1987), where the substitute cattle were found not to be a reasonable substitute. See Official Comment 4 to Section 2–712. As noted, Section 2A–519(2) re-

quires a substantially similar cover lease which requirement should encompass this issue. Official Comment 4 to Section 2A–518.

(4) The new purchase must meet the general test of reasonableness under the circumstances but credit or delivery terms may differ from those of the original sale. Official Comment 4 to Section 2–712. As noted, Section 2A–518(2) requires a cover lease to be made in a commercially reasonable manner and to be substantially similar.

The reasonableness of the buyer's or lessee's action must not be determined by hindsight but by circumstances as of the time the action was taken. Official Comment 4 to Section 2–712. For example, if a buyer made a contract effecting cover on one day for one dollar per unit, the fact the market price took an unexpected drop to seventy-five cents per unit the next day would not make the buyer's action unreasonable.

Suppose after the seller or lessor breaches or defaults the buyer or lessee could easily effect cover but fails to do so. Does this bar any other remedy? It does not. Sections 2–712(3) and 2A–518(3) and Official Comment 6 to Section 2–712. Note, however, that there is a general legal duty on a non-breaching party to take all reasonable steps to mitigate the damages. The failure of the buyer or lessee to effect cover when it is possible will bar the buyer or lessee from recovering damages which could have been prevented if cover had been made.

d. Market Price or Rent

Cover generally will be the preferable route for a buyer or lessee to measure damages as the breach or default of the seller or lessor is likely to occur in a rising market where the market formula of damages discussed below, because it is set at a fixed time in proximity to the breach or default, may not equate to the ultimate cost of cover. Nonetheless, Sections 2–711(2)(e) and 2A–508(1)(d) recognize generally an alternative right to base damages on the difference between the contract price or rent and the market price or rent. Official Comment 6 to Section 2–712, Official Comments 2 and 7 to Section 2–713, and Official Comment 1 to Section 2A–519. This measure of damages for a sale is spelled out specifically in Section 2–713, which provides:

(1) Subject to the provisions of this Article with respect to proof of market price [Section 2–723], if the seller wrongfully fails to deliver or repudiates or the buyer rightfully rejects or justifiably revokes acceptance.

(a) the measure of damages in the case of wrongful failure to deliver by the seller or rightful rejection or justifiable revocation of acceptance by the buyer is the difference between the market price at the time for tender under the contract and the contract price together with any incidental or consequential damages provided in this Article [Section 2–715], but less expenses saved in consequence of the seller's breach; and

(b) the measure of damages for repudiation by the seller is the difference between the market price at the expiration of a commercially reasonable time after the buyer learned of the repudiation, but no later than the time stated in paragraph (a), and the contract price together with any incidental or consequential damages provided in this Article (Section 2–715), less expenses saved in consequence of the seller's breach.

(2) Market price is to be determined as of the place for tender or, in cases of rejection after arrival or revocation of acceptance, as of the place of arrival.

Section 2A–519(1) and (2) are essentially is the same.

One commentator has argued that an aggrieved buyer has a right to base damages on Section 2–713 even though the buyer has affected cover. See Peters, Remedies for Breach of Contract Relating to Sale of Goods Under the Uniform Commercial Code: Roadmap for Article Two, 73 Yale L.J. 199 (1963). This argument should be rejected. Official Comment 7 to Section 2–713 states: "A buyer that has covered under Section 2–712 may not recover the contract price market price difference under this section, but instead must base the damages on those provided in Section 2–712." "An apparent cover, which does not in fact replace the goods contracted for, should not foreclose the use of the contract price market price measure of damages. If the breaching seller cannot prove that the new purchase is in fact a replacement for the one not delivered under the contract, the 'cover' purchase should not foreclose the buyer's recovery under Section 2–713 of the market contract difference.'' In short, to allow a larger recovery based on the market price standard when the buyer actually has covered and sustained a lesser loss would be contrary to the general policy of attempting to place the aggrieved party in approximately the same position as performance, which policy is embodied in Section 1–305(a). This position is clear under Sections 2A–501(4), 2A–518(3) and 2A–519(1) as well.

How is market price or rent to be determined? Time, place and kind of market are three factors that must be taken into consideration in attempting to answer this question.

As to time, Section 2A–519(1) uses the date of default as the measuring date. As to that date, see Official Comment 2 to the section; it may be controllable to a degree by the lessee and so should afford at least as much discretion as the date for measuring damages in the sale. In a sale, Section 2–713(1)(a) provides that the market price to be used to measure sale damages other than in the case of repudiation is that existing at the time for tender, and for repudiation under subsection(1)(b), at the expiration of a commercially reasonable time after buyer learns of the seller's repudiation but no later than the time for tender. Usually the buyer will know of the seller's breach at the time of tender or shortly thereafter.

The rule in Section 2–713(1)(b) addresses the special interpretive problems that existed formerly under Article 2 when the seller anticipatorily repudiated. An anticipatory repudiation is not necessarily a breach. The buyer, for example, may elect not to treat the repudiation as a breach and await the seller's performance, but for how long? Further, the repudiating seller has a right under some circumstances to retract the repudiation and to perform as agreed. The Section 2–713(1)(b) language resolves that in anticipatory repudiation cases "learned of the repudiation" begins the clock running, but it runs out no later than when performance was due, and, if commercially reasonable, at an earlier date.

Of course, this formulation leaves open ambiguity as to the latter time, and thus some risk. But on balance, the proper time is when the buyer should treat the repudiation as a breach. As to the market price to be used, see Official Comment 4 to Section 2–713. Section 2A–519, the counterpart of Section 2–713, contains no similar provision, but given that the date in 2A–519 is that of default, which can be determined by the lessee, results under Article 2A may be the same as those under Article 2. See as to when default occurs, Official Comment 2 to Section 2A–519.

When a seller or lessor breaches or defaults before delivery the market price or rent to be used is that prevailing at the place for tender. Sections 2–713(2) and 2A–519(2). Thus in a contract calling for shipment in which the term is "F.O.B. Seller's City," the place for tender is Seller's City and the market price or rent is that prevailing there. When the goods are delivered and the buyer or lessee rejects after arrival or later revokes acceptance, the market price or rent to be used is that prevailing at the place for arrival. Thus if a contract calls for shipment "F.O.B. Seller's City" and the goods are shipped and arrive at Buyer's City and are rejected there because they are nonconforming, the market price or rent to be used in determining damages is that existing at Buyer's City. Sections 2–713(2) and 2A–519(2).

What kind of market should be used in proving damages? Is it a retail, wholesale, or some other type of market? The Code does not provide a specific answer. In general it is the current price (or rent) for goods of the same kind and in the same branch of trade (Official Comment 5 to Section 2–713), and is the same market in which the buyer (or lessee) would have obtained cover had that person sought that relief. Compare Official Comment 4 to Section 2–713. Should no market price be available, evidence of "spot sale prices" is admissible. Official Comment 5 to Section 2–713.

In some instances there may be no evidence available of market price or rent at the times or places described in Sections 2–713 and 2A–519. Sections 2–723(2) and 2A–507(2) provide that in such cases the price (or rent) prevailing within any reasonable time before or after the time described or at any other place (or for a different lease term) which in commercial judgment or under usage of trade would serve as a reasonable substitute for the one described may be used (making proper allowances). A party intending to offer such evidence must give the other party such notice as the court deems sufficient to prevent unfair surprise. Sections 2–723(3) and 2A–507(3).

e. Damages When Goods Are Retained

When the seller or lessor makes a nonconforming tender the buyer or lessee may elect or be required to retain the goods. Retention obligates the buyer or lessee for the contract price or rent despite the nonconformity; however, it does not bar any other remedy under Article 2 or Article 2A, which usually is an action for damages.

Section 2–714 states the measures of damages for breach in a sale in regard to accepted goods:

(1) Where the buyer has accepted goods and given notification (subsection (3) of Section 2–607) the buyer may recover as damages for any nonconformity of tender the loss resulting in the ordinary course of events from the seller's breach as determined in any manner which is reasonable.

(2) The measure of damages for breach of warranty is the difference at the time and place of acceptance between the value of the goods accepted and the value they would have had if they had been as warranted, unless special circumstances show proximate damages of a different amount.

(3) In a proper case any incidental and consequential damages under Section 2–715 may also be recovered.

Section 2A–519(3) and (4) are the same except the damage is the present value of the difference between the value of the use of the goods as warranted and as accepted for the lease term.

These provisions call attention to the notice requirement as a condition to recovery of damages. The notice required here should not be confused with the notice required when the buyer or lessee wishes to reject or to revoke acceptance. Under those two circumstances the notice required is more specific than that required here. Any adequate notice of rejection basically must state a particular defeat which furnishes the basis for the rejection. Notice of revocation of acceptance must state the buyer's or lessee's intention to revoke acceptance. In either case a mere statement of breach generally would not be sufficient. See Official Comment 5 to Section 2–608 and Official Comment 4 to Section 2–607.

Notice under the provisions requiring it for goods retained need not meet any special or formal requirements. It may be written or oral. It does not have to contain a clear statement of all the objections which will be relied on by the buyer or lessee. It does not have to contain a claim for damages or a threat to litigate. The notice is sufficient if it merely informs the seller or lessor that "the transaction is claimed to involve a breach." Official Comment 4 to

Section 2–607. Further discussion of the application of the notice requirement here appeared in Chapter 10 but two cases will illustrate the matter at this point. In Boeing Airplane Co. v. O'Malley (1964), the court held that failure of a helicopter to function properly in the seller's presence in addition to notice by B to S that the helicopter was being moved to another place in order to take care of its inadequacies was sufficient to satisfy then Section 2–607(3)(a). In Babcock Poultry Farm, Inc. v. Shook (1964), S warranted that experimental chickens furnished by S to B would lay as well or better than the chickens B had been using. The court held that the periodic egg production reports submitted by B to S showing that the experimental chickens were not as productive as warranted were sufficient notice of breach under then Section 2–607(3)(a).

Sections 2–714 and 2A–519 distinguish between damages for breach of warranty and damages for breaches or defaults not constituting breach of warranty. In the latter case, the measure of damage is "the loss resulting in the ordinary course of events from the seller's or lessor's breach or default." This equates with the common law rule, discussed below in connection with consequential damages. A typical example of a breach or default not constituting a breach of warranty, to which this measure of damage is applicable, would be where a seller or lessor makes a late delivery that is nevertheless accepted by the buyer or lessee.

Where the nonconformity constitutes a breach of warranty, the measure of damage is stated more specifically. Essentially it is the difference in values. Suppose a new automobile is sold or leased with a defective steering mechanism, and the buyer or lessee retains the automobile. The measure of damages in the sale is the difference between the value of the defective automobile and the value it would have had without the defect. Usually this amounts to the cost of repairing or replacing the defective mechanism. See Nelson v. Logan Motor Sales, Inc. (1988) (testimony of buyer that he did not drive the car due to its condition and that it was worthless rejected as a basis for damages; contract price less repair costs of $455.04 may be actual value of the goods accepted). But see Hartzell v. Justus Co. (1982), where the goods could only be partly repaired and the balance of loss of value was awarded.

In a lease, the measure is the present value of the difference in the use values of the goods for the lease term. Cost of repair in a short term lease then may not be a proper measure.

Usually the contract price or rent sets the value as warranted. But if the buyer or lessee has made a superior bargain, perhaps that value should control. Compare Chatlos Systems, Inc. v. National Cash Register Corp. (1982) (value greater than contract price) with Crook Motor Co. v. Goolsby (1988) (seller who paid $54,000 for stolen goods and resold for $69,000, limited to recovery of $54,000).

Should a defect result in an accident, injuring the buyer or lessee and damaging the goods, these damages also would be recoverable for breach of warranty. Sections 2–714(3), 2–715(2)(b) 2A–519(4) and 2A–520(2)(b).

The buyer or lessee may accept a nonconforming tender of goods and assert a claim for damages against the seller or lessor for various reasons. Suppose, for example, pursuant to a sales contract S tenders goods which are slightly defective. B notices the defect. But having immediate need for the goods and realizing that the defect can be quickly corrected, B may nevertheless accept the goods and give immediate notice of the defect to the seller. Now, assuming the price is $200, the sale was on open account, and the cost of having the defect corrected is $15, how may B best proceed in order to claim the $15 damages? Should B wait to be sued for the price and then counter-claim for the damages? Should B pay and then sue in small claims court for $15? Clearly neither of these routes make sense. The Code takes the position that the seller's claim for the price may be diminished by the amount of the damages. Section 2–717 provides:

The buyer on notifying the seller of an intention to do so may deduct all or any part of the damages resulting from any breach of the contract from any part of the price still due under the same contract.

Section 2A–508(5) is the same, except as limited in a finance lease in accordance with Section 2A–407.

The buyer or lessee could then tender a check in full settlement. See Article 3, Section 3–311.

It should be noted that the buyer or lessee must give notice of the intention to set-off against the price or the rent. Official Comment 1 to Section 2–717 explains that this is necessary if the buyer (or lessee) wishes to avoid giving the seller (or lessor) reasonable grounds for believing the buyer's or lessee's performance under the contract or some other contract between the parties has become uncertain under Section 2–609 or Section 2A–401. The required notice may be oral or in writing and is in addition to the notice required under Section 2–607(3)(a) to give the seller notice of the breach or the notice required under Section 2A–516(3)(a) to give notice of default.

f.   Incidental and Consequential Damages

The Code sections providing for the recovery of damages based on cover or market price or market rent and for damages for breach in regard to accepted goods, also provide for the recovery, in addition to the damages specifically indicated, of any incidental and consequential damages provided for in Sections 2–715 and 2A–520.

Incidental damages include "expenses reasonably incurred in inspection, receipt, transportation and care and custody of goods rightfully rejected (or the acceptance of which is justifiably revoked), any commercially reasonable charges, expenses or commissions in connection with effecting cover and any other reasonable expense incident to the delay or other breach." Sections 2–715(1) and 2A–520(1).

Official Comment 1 to Section 2–715 indicates that the items specifically mentioned are merely illustrative of usual kinds of incidental damages and are not intended to be exhaustive.

The seller's or lessor's incidental and consequential damages were discussed in Chapter 11. Both types of damages also are recoverable by buyers or lessees. For example, in Lewis v. Mobil Oil Corp. (1971), a certain type of oil which S had warranted as suitable for use in B's hydraulic equipment proved unsuitable. The court allowed B to recover as incidental damages the cost of excessive amounts of oil used in the system and costs incurred in the repair and replacement of mechanical parts damaged by use of the improper oil. Another court allowed a buyer who had revoked acceptance of a horse to recover the costs of its care, feeding and maintenance as incidental damages. Lanners v. Whitney (1967).

As to consequential damages, suppose S contracts to sell and deliver a large quantity of wood pulp on June 1, to B, a paper manufacturer. About a month after the contract is made and a week before the goods are to be delivered, wood pulp is selling at high prices and is hard to get. On May 30, S notifies B that S will be unable to deliver the pulp, whereupon B immediately attempts to effect cover. B finally succeeds in doing so on June 2 but can get delivery no sooner than June 15. On June 3, B is forced to close B's plant for lack of wood pulp until the goods obtained in the cover contract are delivered. Can B recover, in addition to the extra cost of cover, the losses suffered in closing the plant from June 3 until June 15? These latter losses are commonly called "consequential" damages.

The standard followed in the United States for determining whether such a loss may be recovered for breach of contract was articulated in the case of Hadley v. Baxendale (1854):

When two parties have made a contract which one of them has broken, the damages which the other party ought to receive in respect of such breach of contract should be such as may fairly and reasonably be considered as either arising naturally, i.e., according to the usual course of things, from such breach of contract itself, or such as may reasonably be supposed to have been in the contemplation of both parties, at the time they made the contract, as the probable result of the breach of it. Now, if the special circumstances under which the contract was actually made were communicated by the plaintiffs to the defendants, and thus known to both parties, the damages resulting from the breach of such a contract, which they would reasonably contemplate, would be the amount of injury which would ordinarily follow from a breach under these special circumstances so known and communicated.

The standard applied by the court in the Hadley v. Baxendale case may be summarized by stating that S is liable in the case above only for those losses which were reasonably foreseeable—those losses which a reasonably prudent person possessing the information known to S would have had reason to foresee as probable consequences if there was a breach.

In the above case S probably would not be liable for B's losses incurred in the shutdown. Normally a manufacturer such as B keeps a stock of raw materials on hand, and these materials are usually freely and quickly available on the open market. Special circumstances such as war which creates a scarcity or knowledge by S of B's special needs could alter the ordinary situation, however.

Some courts in applying the rule of the Hadley v. Baxendale case have followed the "tacit-agreement" test. This test allows the aggrieved party to recover damages arising from special circumstances only if it can be shown that the breaching party consciously (actually) assumed the risk of such damages. Most courts reject this more restrictive test and merely require that the consequential loss be one that a "reasonable person" in the position of the contracting parties should have foreseen. The Code for sales also rejects the "tacit-agreement" test and follows the objective "reasonable person" test by providing in Section 2–715(2):

(2) Consequential damages resulting from the seller's breach include

(a) any loss resulting from general or particular requirements and needs of which the seller at the time of contracting had reason to know and which could not reasonably be prevented by cover or otherwise; and

(b) injury to person or property proximately resulting from breach of warranty.

Section 2A–520(2) is the same for leases.

The *Lewis* case mentioned above also furnishes an example of a consequential loss held to be recoverable under the Code. There, in addition to incidental damages discussed above, the buyer was allowed to recover profits lost while his sawmill was shut down due to mechanical failures caused by use of improper oil warranted by the seller to be suitable. In another case decided under the Code the buyer was allowed to recover as consequential damages the cost of renovating his building to accommodate another car wash system after the one sold to him by the seller proved to be defective. Valley Die Cast Corp. v. A. C. W. Inc. (1970). Not all cases are so simple, however. For example, in Fortin v. Ox–Bow Marina, Inc. (1987), the issue was whether the buyer could recover interest on money borrowed to refinance a loan on a trade-in in order to make a new purchase when the buyer properly revoked acceptance. The court allowed the claim. But see Barnard v. Compugraphic Corp. (1983) (interest on money borrowed to make a purchase not recoverable) and Nachazel v. Miraco Mfg. (1988) (interest on purchase money loan recoverable or not depending on whether buyer did not or did keep the goods). In the *Nachazel* case, the cost of installing the defective goods (less any benefit to buyer) also was recovered, but in Navistar Intern. Corp. v. Hagie Mfg. Co. (1987), where a buyer sought to recover lost profits from anticipated resales of goods that it would have purchased from the seller but for the breach, the claim was denied.

Sections 2–715(2)(b) and 2A–520(2)(b) address specifically injury to persons or property resulting from breach of warranty. It will be noted that there is no requirement in such cases that the loss be foreseeable. The injury must, however, result "proximately" from the breach, or, as is commonly stated, the breach must be the "proximate cause" of the injury. This means that the damage must flow directly or closely from the breach. Official Comment 15 to Section 2–314 explains that "proximate cause" is a requirement in all implied warranty cases.

The task of determining if damage resulted "proximately" or is too remote is sometimes a difficult one. Specific standards are hard to formulate. Pre–Code warranty cases are relevant in dealing with the problem. Official Comment 5 to Section 2–715 and Official Comment 6 to Section 2–316 indicate that the buyer's (or lessee's) conduct may be relevant in determining "proximate cause." If a buyer (or lessee) uses goods without first inspecting them when it is not reasonable to do so, injury which results from a defect which should have been discovered had inspection occurred does not result "proximately" from the breach. Further, injury caused by a defect which was discovered before use of the goods does not result proximately from the breach.

General Instrument Corp. v. Pennsylvania Pressed Metals, Inc. (1973), illustrates a type of fact situation envisaged by Comments 5 and 6 above. There S sold bearings to B for use in manufacturing bomb fuses. The bearings were oily and not suitable for the intended use. The facts showed (1) the bearings were oily to touch, (2) the bags in which they were contained revealed an accumulation of oil, and (3) the assembly line bin containing the bearings also contained a noticeable accumulation of oil. B, nevertheless, used the bearings. The court held that damages suffered by B because of the defective bearings were not proximately caused by S's breach of warranty. The defect should have been discovered before the bearings were incorporated into bomb fuses.

At common law, there is a legal duty on the aggrieved party not to increase the amount of loss. The aggrieved party must use all reasonable efforts to keep loss resulting from the breach at a minimum. This concept of mitigation of damages is expressly imposed on the aggrieved buyer or lessee in Sections 2–715(2)(a) and 2A–520(2)(a) which provide that a loss can be recovered only if it "could not reasonably be prevented by cover or otherwise." Official Comment 2 to Section 2–715 explains that this language is intended to reject some case law which does not require the buyer (or lessee) to cover to prevent further loss. For example, suppose A contracts with B, for a price paid in advance, to deliver corn to B in Chicago for the purpose of fulfilling another contract there. This purpose is known to A when the contract is made. The corn is delayed and the resale profits are prevented. But B could have bought other corn at Chicago, and did not do so. Arguably, since B has already paid the purchase price, one should not expect B to invest additional capital in a second purchase in order to mitigate damages, and B's failure to buy corn at Chicago thus should not prevent recovery of profits. Section 2–715(2)(a) (and Section 2A–520(2)(a)) is intended to reject such a conclusion; if B could reasonably effect cover in Chicago and thereby fulfill the resale contract, the failure to pursue this course will preclude recovery of the contemplated resale profits.

In most instances, even though a seller or lessor may have knowledge of a buyer's or lessee's particular needs so as to potentially impose liability for loss resulting from such needs if there is a breach of the contract, the seller or lessor will not wish to assume the risk of such a large and uncontrollable liability. In this connection Section 2–719 provides:

(1) Subject to the provisions of subsections (2) and (3) of this section and of Section 2–718 on liquidation and limitation ("limitation" as used here can be misleading; see Section 2–718(1)) of damages,

(a) the agreement may provide for remedies in addition to or in substitution for those provided in this Article and may limit or alter the measure of damages recoverable under this Article, as by limiting the buyer's remedies to return of the goods and repayment of the price or to repair and replacement of non-conforming goods or parts; and

(b) resort to a remedy as provided is optional unless the remedy is expressly agreed to be exclusive, in which case it is the sole remedy.

(2) Where circumstances cause an exclusive or limited remedy to fail of its essential purpose, remedy may be had as provided in this Act.

(3) Consequential damages may be limited or excluded unless the limitation or exclusion is unconscionable. Limitation of consequential damages for injury to the person in the case of consumer goods is prima facie unconscionable but limitation of damages where the loss is commercial is not.

Section 2A–503, other than stating what is implicit with respect to Section 2–719 (that the concept of unconscionability applies to the entire section) and preserving remedies for collateral or ancillary obligations to the lease, is the same.

Sections 2–719(1) and (2) and 2A–503(1) and (2) permit the parties by agreement either to decrease or increase the remedies under the Code, subject to the requirement that there be a minimum adequate remedy and that an exclusive or limited remedy must not fail of its essential purpose. Official Comment 1 to Section 2–719, Section 2A–503(2) and Section 2–719(2). Should these requirements not be met, the aggrieved party may resort to the general remedy provisions of the Code. There is considerable authority also that any clause limiting remedies must be conspicuous. See Stauffer Chemical Co. v. Curry (1989). But see, as contra, Apex Supply Co., Inc. v. Benbow Industries, Inc. (1988). In order to better avoid an attack on grounds of unconscionability, the *Curry* decision would seem to be the better view.

When does an exclusive or limited remedy fail of its essential purpose? In Wilson Trading Corp. v. David Ferguson, Ltd. (1968), S sold B a quantity of yarn. The contract contained the following provision as well as promising a limited remedy for defects that, if the remedy was successful, would have provided buyer with the quality of goods bargained for:

> No claims relating to excessive moisture content, short weight, count variations, twist, quality, or shade shall be allowed if made after wearing, knitting, or processing, or more than 10 days after receipt of shipment. . . .

B claimed that sweaters knitted from the yarn were unsalable because of latent defects in the yarn which caused variations in color after the sweaters were washed, and that the variation in color could not have been discovered until after the sweaters were knitted and washed. S contended B could not rely on the defect as it did not give S notice within 10 days as provided in the contract. In reversing a summary judgment for S granted by the trial court, the New York Court of Appeals stated:

If these factual *allegations (of the buyer)* are established at trial, the limited remedy established by paragraph two has failed its "essential purpose" and the buyer is, in effect, without remedy. The time limitation clause of the contract, therefore, insofar as it applies to defects not reasonably discoverable within the time limits established by the contract, must give way to the general Code rule that buyer has a reasonable time to notify the seller of breach of contract after he discovers or should have discovered the defect.

The case also might be treated as one where no minimum adequate remedy was provided. The classic type of case in this respect is Schmaltz v. Nissen (1988), where a sale of seed carried with it only a remedy of return of the price if defective seed did not produce a crop. The court decided in the buyer's favor. Not all cases agree that the exclusion of consequentials in this context is unconscionable, however. See Hill v. BASF Wyandotte Corp. (1982). See also Lara v. Hyundai Motor America (2002) (a remedy limitation fails of its essential purpose when a seller unreasonably delays the replacement of the product, refuses to replace it at all, or is unsuccessful in correcting the defects within a reasonable time). In accord are Arabian Agriculture Services Co. v. Chief Industries, Inc. (2002) (refusal to repair) and Trinity Industries, Inc. v. McKinnon Bridge Co., Inc. (2001) (seller unwilling or unable to replace or repair in a reasonable time; but a remedy not invoked by the buyer cannot be said to fail of its essential purpose).

A common situation involving the failure of essential purpose concept arises when the seller or lessor is unable to fix the defective goods after several tries. The mere fact that operation time is lost during repair attempts does not in and of itself cause the repair or replacement remedy to fail of its essential purpose. Reigel Power Corp. v. Voith Hydro (1989). However, if ultimately the goods are not repaired, the Code remedy scheme becomes available unless an alternative limited remedy, such as return of the price, is provided. Ritchie Enterprises v. Honeywell Bull, Inc. (1990). A major issue on which opinions diverge is, assuming a limited remedy does fail of its purpose, does this also invalidate the common companion exclusion of consequential damages? Envirotech Corp. v. Halco Engineering, Inc. (1988), allowed the latter clause to stand; Fidelity & Deposit Co. of Maryland v. Krebs Engineers (1988) goes the other way. There are numerous cases on both sides that probably are not distinguishable on the basis of drafting or otherwise. A common line that emerges, however, is whether the action or inaction of the seller (or lessor) was in good faith under all the circumstances. Compare, e.g., Delmarva Power & Light Co. v. ABB Power T & D Co., Inc. (2002) (clear limitation, prior dealings, complicated product, commercial parties, good faith in performance of contract) with Pierce v. Catalina Yachts, Inc. (2000) (bad faith breach of warranty rendered it unconscionable to enforce the parties' allocation of risk).

Sections 2–719(3) and 2A–503(3) explicitly permit the limitation or exclusion of consequential damages subject to the test of conscionability. However, "limitation of consequential damages for injury to the person in the case of consumer goods is prima facie unconscionable." This means that in the case of personal injury involving consumer goods the buyer or lessee will prevail unless the seller or lessor perhaps is able to show that the buyer or lessee was aware of the exclusion and appreciated its import. See Collins v. Uniroyal, Inc. (1974). Sections 2–719(3) and 2A–503(3) must be distinguished from Sections 2–316 and 2A–214 which allow disclaimer or modification of the implied warranties of merchantability and fitness. Two simple examples will illustrate the distinction. S sells B an electrical motor. The contract contains the following clause:

It is specifically understood and agreed by the parties that the motor is in an "As Is" condition. S makes no representation or warranties expressed or implied whatsoever except warranty of title.

This clause is an attempt to exclude all warranties except that of title. If valid, it limits the circumstances under which the seller can be in breach. The validity of this clause should be determined by Section 2–316, although many authorities contend it should also be subject to the test of unconscionability under Section 2–302. The same points are true under Article 2A.

Suppose instead of the above clause the contract contains the following:

> S's liability to B whether in contract or in tort arising out of warranties, representations, instructions, or defects from any cause, shall be limited to repairs to the motor for a period of 90 days from the date of this contract. S shall not be liable for any consequential damages.

This is not an attempt to limit the circumstances under which S is in breach, but an attempt to limit the amount of damages once a breach is established. The validity of the clause should be governed by Section 2–719. The situation is the same under Article 2A.

Some courts have resorted to Section 2–719(3) to find a clause such as that in the first example unconscionable. See Ford Motor Co. v. Tritt (1968). Properly, any finding of unconscionability in such a case should be based on Section 2–302.

g. Liquidated Damages

The right of the parties to liquidate damages is discussed in Chapter 11. This may be done for the benefit of the buyer or lessee as well as for the seller or lessor. The earlier discussion is relevant when the parties have inserted a liquidated damage clause for the buyer's or lessee's benefit. Assuming the clause is enforceable, the buyer or lessee may recover the amount stipulated as damages. However, a liquidated damages clause that puts one party in a better position than it would have been in had the leases been fully performed was unenforceable under Section 2A–504. In re Montgomery Ward Holding Corp. (Montgomery Ward & Co., Inc. v. Meridian Leasing Corp.) (2001).

h.   Security Interest in the Goods

As pointed out earlier, the buyer or lessee may reject or accept a tender of nonconforming goods. If the buyer or lessee chooses to reject, damages may be recoverable based either on cover or the market value standard in the same manner as if the seller or lessor had failed to tender delivery or had repudiated the contract. Sections 2–711(1) and (2) and 2A–508(1). Should the buyer or lessee accept the goods and rightfully revoke acceptance under Sections 2–608 or 2A–517, the buyer or lessee has the same rights as if the goods were rejected. Sections 2–711(1) and (2) and 2A–508(1).

In either case, whether the goods have been rejected, or accepted and the acceptance subsequently revoked, so long as the nonconforming goods remain in the buyer's or lessee's possession or control, the buyer or lessee has a security interest in them for any amounts paid and any expenses reasonably incurred in the inspection, receipt, transportation, care, and custody of them. Sections 2–711(3) and 2A–508(4). In order to enforce this security interest, the buyer or lessee may dispose of the goods in accordance with the redisposition provisions of Sections 2–706 or 2A–527. The buyer's or lessee's security interest in this situation, however, does not extend beyond the items mentioned. Official Comment 2 to Section 2–711. Thus the buyer or lessee may not, for example, if the goods are sold, retain from the proceeds of the sale funds to cover anticipated damages for breach of the contract; any amount in excess of that necessary to cover the items mentioned above must be paid to the seller or lessor. Pursuit of the right of disposition of such goods, however, in no way impairs the buyer's or lessee's right to recover damages based on cover or nondelivery as mentioned above. Official Comment 2 to Section 2–711.

3. NON–MONETARY REMEDIES

a. Specific Performance

When a seller or lessor breaches a contract before the goods have been delivered, an award of money damages to the buyer or lessee generally is sufficient to place the aggrieved party in approximately the same position that party would have been in if the seller or lessor had performed. This is based on the theory that if the buyer or lessee needs goods of the kind contracted for they may be obtained on the open market and the award of money damages will be sufficient to take care of any difference in cost between the original contract and the cost of similar goods on the market. Suppose, however, similar goods are not available. If they are not, money damages alone cannot compensate the buyer or lessee and there will be no adequate relief unless there is a right to obtain the goods called for in the contract.

The common law actions for possession of goods, detinue and replevin, do not lie unless the goods which are the subject of the action can be specifically designated. This means that at law the buyer or lessee does not have a right to recover the goods unless they have been identified to the contract; therefore, when the breach occurs before the goods have been identified, the buyer's or lessee's only possibility of obtaining the goods is by the equitable remedy of specific performance. The UCC provides in part in Section 2–716(1): "Specific performance may be decreed where the goods are unique or in other proper circumstances." Section 2A–507A(1) is the same.

Equity recognizes the right of the buyer or lessee to specific performance if the goods are unique. In the vast majority of sales cases, the goods have been identified, usually at the time of contracting, but title has not passed to the buyer. At common law and under the Sales Act, if title had passed, the buyer, generally, was allowed to obtain possession of the goods by one of the legal possessory actions mentioned above. If title had not passed, the buyer's only hope of obtaining the goods was by getting specific performance in equity. Of course, title does not pass to the lessee in a lease. The equitable remedy, however, is only available if the buyer's or lessee's remedy at law is not adequate, which usually means that the buyer or lessee has to show that the goods are "unique." Some pre-Code courts were unwilling to treat any goods as unique except original works of art, rare manuscripts, family heirlooms, and the like. Others displayed a more liberal attitude by decreeing specific performance when goods contracted for could not be purchased on the open market.

The Uniform Sales Act, with little success, evidently sought to encourage the courts to expand the traditional circumstances under which specific performance is granted in sales transactions by providing in Section 68:

> Where the seller has broken a contract to deliver specific or ascertained goods, a court having the powers of a court of equity may, if it thinks fit, on the application of the buyer, by its judgment or decree direct that the contract shall be performed specifically, without giving the seller the option of retaining the goods on payment of damages.

Some courts, however, relied on the language "where the seller has broken a contract to deliver specific or ascertained goods" as a basis for refusing buyers a decree of specific performance. In one case, Cohen v. Rosenstock Motors (1946), the contract described the automobile as "one new car ... make Plymouth type Sedan year 1946 color open" but no automobile was identified to the contract. The court stated:

The language (Section 68) which is codification of the common law ... clearly implies that the remedy of specific performance is available to the buyer of personal property only when the goods are specific or ascertained....

Official Comment 2 to Section 2–716 indicates that the provision seeks to further a more liberal attitude than has commonly existed under prior law. The Comment clearly indicates that the intention of the section is not to limit specific performance to goods which are identified at the time of contracting, and states that the section is intended to enlarge the traditional idea as to what constitutes a "unique" good. The test is the commercial feasibility of replacement. Output and requirements contracts involving a particular or peculiarly available source or market are given as examples of typical commercial situations in which specific performance may be justified. The Comment concludes with a reminder that under the section specific performance is not limited to situations where the goods are unique but may be granted "in other proper circumstances," and inability of the buyer (or lessee) to effect cover is evidence of "other proper circumstances."

In one Code case, Kaiser Trading Co. v. Associated Metals & Minerals Corp. (1970), B sought a preliminary injunction and specific performance of a contract for the sale of a large quantity of cryolite. B was engaged in the production of aluminum and cryolite was an indispensable chemical compound used in this production. B had for many previous years contracted with S for large quantities of cryolite. The court in granting the preliminary injunction stated:

> ... [T]he Code comments, in conjunction with prior case law decisions in other jurisdictions, and the general trend toward a more liberalized availability of specific performance, persuade this court that the remedy should be available when goods cannot be covered or replaced. Accordingly, a preliminary injunction may issue if all other requirements are satisfied.

In another case decided under the Code, Duval & Co. v. Malcom (1975), B sought specific performance of a contract for the sale of cotton on the theory that, as the market price of cotton had soared from 30 to 90 cents per pound, he could not go into the market and replace the cotton due to the "uniqueness" of the market. The court concluded that a sharp rise in price was not of itself sufficient to entitle B to specific performance. The court criticized the "other proper circumstances" test of the Code as being vague and if liberally construed without proper guidelines "would seem to afford specific performance for all commercial goods and turn the courts into referees in commerce."

Sections 2–716(1) and 2A–507A(1) also allow the parties to contract for specific performance, except in a consumer contract and except if the breaching party's sole remaining obligation is the payment of money (as to that, see Sections 2–709 and 2A–529). Of course such an agreement cannot bind the court, but may influence it to grant specific performance even when specific performance would not otherwise be available. Official Comments 1 and 3 to Section 2–716 and Official Comment 2 to Section 2A–507A.

b. Replevin or Similar Remedy

Suppose the buyer or lessee needs the goods for which the buyer or lessee contracted but similar goods are not available at that time on the open market. Section 2–716(3) provides:

(3) The buyer has a right of replevin or similar remedy for goods identified to the contract if after reasonable effort the buyer is unable to effect cover for such goods or the circumstances reasonably indicate that such effort will be unavailing or if the goods have been shipped under reservation and satisfaction of the security interest in them has been made or tendered.

Section 2A–507A(3) is the same.

It should be observed that Section 2–716(3) in no way makes the buyer's right to replevy the goods dependent on whether title has passed nor does Section 2A–507A(3), of course, require that for the lessee. The basic criterion is the ability or inability to effect cover. Does this mean that the buyer or lessee has a choice of either replevin or specific performance if the goods have been identified and the buyer or lessee cannot effect cover after the seller or lessor wrongfully refuses delivery? The UCC gives no answer. However, there is a general principle that equity will not grant a remedy if an adequate legal remedy is available. In line with this principle, a number of courts under pre-UCC case law refused to grant specific performance of a contract for unique goods where the party had a right to a legal action for possession of the goods.

Sections 2–716(3) and 2A–507A(3) also provide that a buyer has a right to replevy the goods "if the goods have been shipped under reservation and satisfaction of the security interest in them has been made or tendered." A seller who has identified goods to a contract and who has not been paid all of the purchase price may reserve a security interest in the goods by shipping them under a negotiable bill of lading. The Code provides that so long as the seller retains the document the seller has a security interest in the goods regardless of whether the seller, the buyer, or some other party is named as consignee in the document. The reason for this has been explained in an earlier chapter. If the buyer performs or tenders performance of all obligations under the contract, the buyer terminates the seller's security interest and becomes entitled to possession of the bill of lading. Should the seller under these circumstances wrongfully refuse to deliver the document, the buyer may replevy it. This is tantamount to replevying the goods, for the document gives the buyer a right to possession of the goods. See Official Comment 4 to Section 2–716.

Section 2–716(4) a buyer's right of replevin may conflict with a security interest in or levy on the goods and provides a rule to determine priority. See Official Comment 5 to Section 2–716.

c. Insolvency of the Seller or Lessor

There are other situations in which a buyer or lessee may obtain possession of goods after they have been identified in the contract. Section 2–502(1) states:

(1) Subject to subsections (2) and (3) and even though the goods have not been shipped a buyer that has paid a part or all of the price of goods in which the buyer has a special property under the provisions of Section 2–501 (identification of goods to the contract) may on making and keeping good a tender of any unpaid portion of their price recover them from the seller

(a) in the case of goods bought by a consumer, the seller repudiates or fails to deliver as required by the contract,

(b) in all cases, seller becomes insolvent within ten days after receipt of the first installment on their price.

Section 2A–522 is the same.

Section 2–502 is a counter-balance to the seller's right to reclaim on the buyer's insolvency in Section 2–702(2). In contrast to that right, however, successful recovery of the goods under Section 2–502(1) does not bar the buyer from pursuing any other remedy to which the buyer may be entitled, such as an action for damages. Section 2–711(2) and Official

Comment 4 to Section 2–716. Section 2A–522 might be said to be a counter-balance to a degree to Section 2A–525(2).

The buyer but not the lessee may exercise the rights under these sections and recover the goods identified even though they do not conform to the contract. In some instances, however, the agreement between the parties envisages that the buyer instead of the seller is to identify the goods to the contract. In this case, the buyer may recover the goods only if they conform to the contract for sale. Sections 2–502(3) and 2A–522(2). These limitations are intended to prevent a possibility of the buyer's or lessee's being unjustly enriched by the identification of goods more valuable than those called for in the contract. Official Comment 4 to Section 2–502.

If the buyer or lessee were not given the right to obtain the goods under these sections, they would merely have an unsecured claim against the seller or lessor and would be forced to compete with other creditors for the seller's or lessor's assets. Under those circumstances the chances of recovering all that has been paid to the seller or lessor would be very remote. Perhaps they still are remote as the rights under these provisions are probably subject to those of the trustee in bankruptcy. Consumer buyers and lessees are given somewhat broader rights on the thought consumer goods are worth little and receipt of the balance of the price or rent normally would be preferable.

Again because the right of a buyer may conflict with a security interest in or levy on the goods, Section 2–502(2) states a rule to resolve priority. See Official Comment 3 to Section 2–502.

INDEX

485

D

E

H

I

M

N

O

P

Q

R

S

T

U

V

W

†